Women Overcoming Demons

"Michelle McCullar's new book, *Women Overcoming Demons: 9 Steps for Becoming Whole Again*, masterfully probes the trauma, abuse and neglect experienced by millions of women in silence. The author has lived it herself, and this is her credibility. In this articulate exposé of engaging her demons and retiring them into wisdom, Michelle is a beacon of hope and a guide for others in doing the same. As a male reader, I was amazed at how her book sustained my intense interest and intrigue from chapter to chapter, but that is part of its brilliance. *Women Overcoming Demons* is a must read for anyone, man or woman, looking to overcome a shadowy past that may still haunt them!

James Alvino
Award-winning Educational Journalist
and Author of *The Explorer's Guide to the Law of Attraction*

"From the very paragraph I felt the power of Michelle's journey and her message. As you read *Women Overcoming Demons*, you will quickly realize that Michelle not only understands you but she has been there. In my work with people to discover *The Business in Your Soul*, the part of the process that is paramount is your own healing. Michelle has captured a process of healing that will change countless lives. We all need someone to lead us on our journey to overcome our demons and return to wholeness. Let Michelle show you the way."

Ronda Wada
Creator of The Business in Your Soul

"*Women Overcoming Demons* is essential reading for all of us who want to understand ourselves better and live better lives. If you feel your life is out of control or you feel in any way powerless to change your life for the better, then take advantage of the rich and sage advice within. In short order you will experience more personal happiness, professional success, and life fulfillment. Never have so many needed this wisdom and guidance more than now."

Margit Macchia
Peak Potentials Coach and Author of *Herzipinki: Seven Short Stories of Living Life with Love, Laughter, and Happiness*

WOMEN OVERCOMING DEMONS

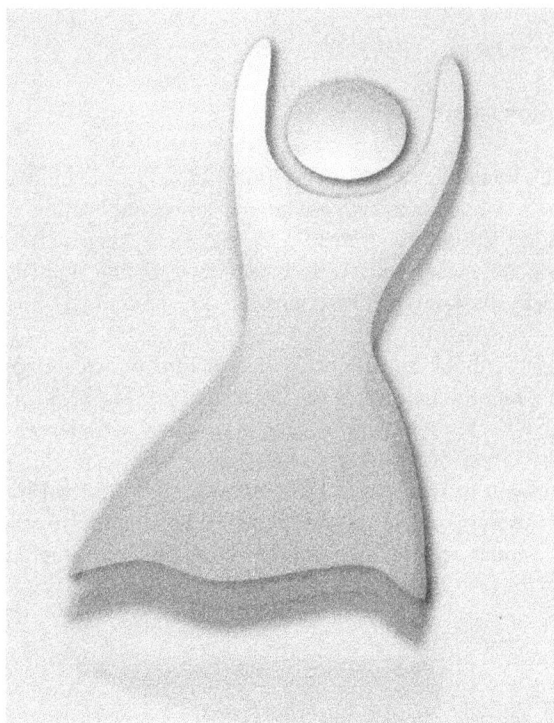

9 Steps for Becoming Whole Again

MICHELLE MCCULLAR

Women Overcoming Demons: 9 Steps for Becoming Whole Again
Michelle McCullar

Awakened Heart Press
P.O. Box 2055
Arcadia, CA 91077-2055

Because of the dynamic nature of the Internet, any web addresses or links contained in this book may have changed since publication and may no longer be valid. The views expressed in this work are solely those of the author and do not necessarily reflect the views of the publisher, and the publisher hereby disclaims any responsibility for them.

The author of this book does not dispense medical advice or prescribe the use of any technique as a form of treatment for physical, emotional, or medical problems without the advice of a physician, either directly or indirectly. The intent of the author is only to offer information of a general nature to help you in your quest for emotional and spiritual well-being. In the event you use any of the information in this book for yourself, which is your constitutional right, the author and the publisher assume no responsibility for your actions.

First Edition
Printed in the United States of America

ISBN: 978-0-9858782-0-7

Dedication

This book is dedicated to all women
courageously seeking to live their truth.
May you go forth with a bold sense of adventure,
living your life as the fullest and best expression
of the person you were born to be.

Table of Contents

Part One

THE PATH TO WHOLENESS

~~~~~

Step 4 – Challenge Your Thoughts and Beliefs: Change Your Thoughts to Improve Your Life **85**

Step 5 – Make Peace With Your Personal History: Express Gratitude to Experience Freedom From Your Demons **123**

Step 6 – Tell Your Story: Share It, Understand It, Rewrite It **143**

Part Two

BECOMING YOUR BEST SELF

~~~~~

Step 7 – Be Who You Were Born To Be: You Are Much More Than A Victim or A Survivor **167**

List of Illustrations

Foreword

People the world over dream of living a life of a life of emotional freedom – a life that is full of love, happiness, and personal fulfillment, but for whatever reason far to many believe it's just not in the cards for them.

If you're one of the many who regularly sees life as a constant and never ending struggle, full of personal pain and disappointment, you must read this book. It will provide you with the insights and tools you need to achieve the ultimate freedom: the eradication of your inner demons – those pesky inner voices who stealthy masquerade themselves as helpful thoughts and beliefs designed to keep you safe, but who are in reality are only serving to tear you down and keep you confined to living a small and unrewarding life.

Michelle McCullar is one of those rare individuals who have had the courage and tenacity to probe the depths or their heart, mind, and soul in order to heal themselves from an intensely painful past and live their truth. In doing so, she has created a simple but effective program with the power to help millions overcome their greatest barrier to living the life of their dreams – the demons in their minds.

Full of sage and timely wisdom, Michelle gives great counsel on how you can begin this very moment to quickly heal yourself from the ravages of even your most traumatic and abusive experiences. Masterfully examining the sources of pain that keeps millions trapped in silence, Michelle's book deftly leads you out of the darkness imposed by your demons and back into the light of wholeness.

Peppered with an array of arresting stories of real life women from all walks of life, and a whole host of change-your-life-in-a-heartbeat exercises, this book is designed to help you immediately begin experiencing more personal happiness, professional success, and life fulfillment. From the moment you begin reading you'll know that Michelle understands you and your situation. Having been there herself she is more than qualified to guide you on this journey. Best of all, everything in this book comes from the heart.

The great news about you having invested in this book is the freedom you seek is just a few page turns away. It's available to you right here and now. Learn from Michelle's experience. Start putting her insights and the tools she provides to use today. Then watch just how quickly your life transforms.

Living a life of self-imposed fear, pain, and dread is no way to live. In the end all you have are regrets. No matter where you are in your journey, or how big you believe your obstacles to be, you will experience great healing if you follow the guidance within this book.

Get started today. Retire your demons to wisdom to begin living the extraordinary life you were meant to live.

Raymond Aaron
NY Times Bestselling Author
www.millionairebusinessbootcamp.com

You are all things. Denying, rejecting, judging or hiding
from any aspect of your total being creates pain
and results in a lack of wholeness.
-Joy Page

Introduction

Aching For Wholeness

Do you have a sense that some part of you is missing, or that you are in some way damaged beyond repair? Do you yearn for something or someone to complete you, to make you whole? Does your life feel empty and forlorn? Maybe you feel you were born deficient, that you were never whole to begin with. Maybe you just wonder if this is all there is to life? Or possibly you question what it is you did to deserve such a miserable life, and are frequently wondering if it will ever get better?

These are all feelings I have experienced many times in my life. In fact for the better part of my life they plagued me beyond measure. If you are reading this book, it is likely you are being tormented with these and various related feelings such as loneliness, unworthiness, guilt, shame, victimization, and hopelessness. If you are like me, and many others I know, you want more than anything to have a sense of completeness or wholeness. You want the fear and pain to go away. You want to be who *you* truly are, rather than whom people want you to be or say you are. You want to be accepted. You want to be happy and enjoy life. You want to be treated appropriately, with kindness and respect. You want to be loved. And most of all you want to be free of the demons that constantly torment you and stop you from living a happy and fulfilling life.

The good news is there is hope. You *can* become whole again. I know this to be true, because I, and many others I've met on my journey, have done it. And the best part is, with wholeness everything else you desire begins to come along for the ride. When you *feel* whole, everything changes. It's as if magic happens. Come with me on a magical journey that will transform your life beyond your wildest dreams. Get ready to experience the best of you and the best that life has to offer.

Demons and Their Sources

Before we begin our journey I want to shed some light on the source of our demons and the many ways they manifest themselves. From a personal perspective there are probably as many sources as there are people on the planet. However, statistics and experience show the majority of our demons emanate from a relatively small number of factors. Some of these factors are quite easy to pinpoint, while others tend to be more elusive. And some are multifaceted, making them all the more challenging to pin down.

For most of us the sources of our demons are the result of one or more of the following factors: childhood neglect, trauma, and abuse, in any of their various forms, childhood conditioning and programming, and/or severe trauma or violence experienced as an adult. Of these, our childhood conditioning and programming typically goes unnoticed, and as we will see later it is the major source for many of the demons most all of us contend with for much if not all of our lives.

Before you get worried you'll never be able to overcome your demons and become whole again, please know you are not alone in your struggle and help is available. The truth is *we all have our demons*. We all have our private pain to deal with. We have all suffered from some injustice in our life that has had a negative impact on our well-being and given rise to the demons we now struggle with. This phenomenon affects us all to one degree or another. The only real difference from one person to the next is the severity with which they are affected by what happens and how they choose to deal with it. We'll explore this in more detail throughout the book, including what you can do to retire your demons for good, but for now I'll present a few statistical facts to provide context regarding the more obvious sources.

It's a sad fact, but the number of people suffering from demons emanating from neglect, abuse, and trauma, both literally and figuratively is staggering. Based on statistics, for childhood sexual abuse alone the number is nearly one in four for girls under aged 18, with more than one in three never reporting it to anyone. While actual statistics of the number of children abused from any one form are difficult to assess, reports of all children who were substantiated to have suffered from abuse in 2005 showed 62.8% suffered from neglect, 16.6% from physical abuse, 9.3% from emotional or psychological abuse, 2% from medical neglect, and 14.3% from other forms such as abandonment, threats of physical harm, or congenital addictions. These numbers add up to more than 100% as many children suffer from multiple types of abuse simultaneously or over the course of childhood. *[Sources: American Humane Association & Angle Roar]*

While the statistics above are only specific to abuse suffered in childhood, the numbers for adult women are equally as staggering. However, I have focused on childhood, as it is my opinion that most of our demons actually form during this period, as does our sense of brokenness and our lack of wholeness.

While abuse is traumatic in and of itself, other forms of trauma can be equally damaging to our well-being, thus providing us with a host of demons to torment us for years to come. Some example events that are often experienced traumatically include parents divorcing or leaving; the death or suicide of a close family member or friend; living with someone who is chronically or terminally ill, or who has a mental or physical infirmity; dealing with learning challenges, such as dyslexia; frequently changing schools; relocating to a very different environment from the one we are accustomed to (especially at highly influential ages); living through a natural disaster and its aftermath; being in a near fatal accident; and living in a hostile, unsanitary, or unsafe environment.

As already mentioned, for many of us the demons and lack of wholeness we experience are frequently the result of the abuses and traumas we suffered as children. However, we cannot forget the other major contributor, our childhood conditioning and programming. This factor is extremely influential in how we respond to the world and see ourselves. It is pervasive throughout our lives and precisely because it is so pervasive and commonplace it is routinely overlooked as a source of our pain.

To put this into perspective, as to why we are so unaware of it, consider the following facts. Until the age of six everything we experience and are taught is almost completely unfiltered. This is because our brain and mental capacity have yet to develop enough to allow us to make judgments and therefore filter what we believe. It isn't until after age twelve that we begin to have any significant capacity to make these judgments and therefore filter what comes in. So until age six we are basically human sponges soaking up everything we see, hear, and feel. Between ages six and twelve we begin to have limited filtering abilities. And after age twelve we finally begin to create significant enough filters to allow us to begin choosing what to believe or not about the world and ourselves. By this point much of the damage to our well-being has typically already occurred, because it is during the first twelve to fourteen years of life that much of our sense of self is formed.

Conditioning and programming is ubiquitous. It goes on all the time. It never stops. It comes from all aspects of our environment including our family and friends, educational systems, religious organizations, local and national cultures, work culture, media outlets, and political settings. It is handed down from generation to generation. It is so pervasive that we are largely unconscious of it.

In fact some 95% of the time we think and act nonconsciously, which makes it all the more challenging for us to identify, understand, and overcome what haunts us. Additionally, our demons tend to disguise themselves as behavioral and/or medical problems, which affect us in ways that often appear completely unrelated to our experiences. Regardless of their cause or how they present themselves, the underlying issue is the havoc that is wreaked upon our self-worth, self-esteem, and self-confidence. For most of us, this manifests as our having a really low or negative appraisal of our self, our abilities, and our value as a person, which correspondingly affects every aspect of our lives, from how well we do on a test or job interview, to how wonderful, or not, our relationships are.

Suffice it to say, our personal demons come in all shapes and sizes and produce a whole host of symptoms, but as we've learned, the real issue is the affect to our self-worth and self-confidence. And therein lies the solution, which we will now address.

The Journey Back To Wholeness

As we've discovered, our programming, conditioning, and life experiences can exact a huge toll on our well-being, creating a whole host of unsavory demons that wreak havoc on our self-worth, self-confidence, and overall sense of wholeness. The end result is frequently the sense that something is missing within us or fundamentally wrong with us, which leaves us feeling broken and incomplete. Added to this are the cultural mores that suggest we need someone or something outside of us to complete us. However, the reality is, there is nothing missing or wrong. Rather, our perceived lack of wholeness is most often the result of our shutting down or blocking off vital parts of our personality, feelings, and emotions in an attempt to reduce our pain. For many of us this is a way of being that we have been taught. For others, it was literally something we did as a necessity for our survival.

From this we can see that *everything about us that we consider to be missing is in reality only in hiding.* It is as if we've tucked pieces of ourselves away for safekeeping and then have either forgotten they ever existed, or we know they once existed but have misplaced where we put them. Therefore, the journey back to wholeness is an inward journey. To find what we are looking for, we must uncover what is hidden within. That is we must unblock and release what we once locked away. At times, searching outside expecting someone or something to complete us may bring temporary relief, but ultimately we are left with the feeling that what we are looking for is forever elusive or worse yet impossible to attain.

Unblocking and healing the parts of us that we have denied and hidden away is our only real salvation. Doing so returns us to our true state, to a state of wholeness, with love for ourselves and others, and a strong sense of worthiness and purpose.

To put this into perspective I'll share an example from my own life that I hope will illuminate how it is we block off aspects of ourselves and thus create our state of fragmentation replete with its chorus of tormenting demons. When I was quite young I learned it wasn't safe to show certain emotions around particular people. Showing them would frequently result in undue physical and psychological punishment, including intense beatings and all sorts of verbal admonishments that were extremely humiliating and demoralizing. In order to reduce the likelihood of exciting a rash of physical and/or psychological rage I learned to stuff my feelings and emotions. By doing so I inadvertently created a chronic succession of physical and psychological ailments for myself (demons if you will).

Here are the most common ways my demons manifested themselves: low self-worth, a feeling of intense unhappiness, and a variety of chronic physical pains, such as constant headaches, back aches, and extreme muscle spasms, as well as the adult onset of a host of unexplainable digestive disorders. Additionally, I tended to feel invisible, incomplete, and extremely alone, having the sense of a gaping hole inside of me that might never be filled. I also struggled with making myself heard and often felt as if I had a split personality that was constantly waging war within. One side of the personality was outgoing and knew I could be and do whatever I set my mind to. The other was a fraidy cat who, while very much desiring to do what the outgoing me wanted, was terrified to make a move and thus stopped me dead in my tracks, leaving me feeling bewildered and upset. While this one example is by no means the sole source of my fragmentation and resulting demons, I hope it brings clarity to the processes that bring about our sense of feeling broken and incomplete.

No matter what you have experienced, no matter how fragmented or broken you feel, and no matter how numerous your demons or disparaging they may be, this book will guide you back to wholeness. Each step provides a means for retiring your demons and unblocking the parts of yourself that you've hidden away for safekeeping. If you're reading this book then I know you believe there is light at the end of the tunnel (or at least you want to believe). Let the processes in this book be your light. Let them guide you out of the darkness. Just remember, Rome wasn't built in a day. The journey you are embarking on is not always an easy one. It takes effort and commitment, as well as a significant amount of reflection and soul searching. However, with the right attitude you will find it to be very enlightening and liberating, and most of the time you'll find it to be fun and enjoyable.

Becoming whole again is a process. Think of it as peeling an onion, layer-by-layer. With each layer you peel, you will discover a new sense of wholeness and the dissolution of more and more of those pesky demons, who, as unlikely as it may seem, are only figments of your imagination. That is, with the exception of another person who may be harming you in some way, your demons only exist in your mind. By the way, if someone else is harming you, it is in your best interest to remove yourself from the situation if at all possible, especially while going through this process.

With the awareness that most of your demons live only in your mind, I hope you can now understand why this is an inner journey. To put this into perspective, I know you've heard the saying that we are often our own worst critic or enemy. Our inner demons are a case in point. Through our thoughts and beliefs, and the stories we tell ourselves, we tend to let our imaginations run wild, and in the process we conjure up bigger and more powerful demons to battle. In the end, rather than protecting ourselves from pain, we create bigger nightmares that keep us stuck in the traumatic, abusive, and self-limiting patterns we so desperately want to escape.

While it is highly likely you will make extraordinarily quick progress as the result of applying several of the steps in this book, the effect of which at times may seem miraculous and immediate, there will also be times when you appear to have plateaued or potentially even to have taken a step backwards. This is normal. We are after all creatures of habit, and slipping into old routines is extremely easy to do. Just stay with it. If you stray or feel you've gotten off track, pick yourself up, congratulate yourself for what you've accomplished so far, and take the next step. If and when needed, repeat previously completed steps. This is part of the process. Remember you are peeling an onion, and each step or pass through a step will heal and uncover new things you were previously unaware of. Stay at it and in no time at all you will be experiencing a whole new you, complete with a whole new and wonderfully fulfilling life. And don't forget to celebrate your successes along the way. In fact, start now. Celebrate you having picked up this book and read this far.

While this is an inner journey and I personally know the processes described within this book do work, I also know you can't do it all on your own. You will need assistance at times, if for no other reason than to shine a light on the things you are blind to. A good example of this is demonstrated in the following quote, which states *"It's difficult to see the picture when you are inside the frame."* Therefore, the quicker you accept the need and acquire assistance, the more readily you will return to your natural state of wholeness.

The type of assistance required by each individual will vary, as will when a particular type is needed. Note, there are many types available and no one source is right for everyone. Some of the more common sources to consider, depending on your specific needs, include compassionate and understanding friends or partners, self-help and personal development books, seminars, and workshops, human behavioral specialists, hypnotherapists, life or personal empowerment coaches, group therapy sessions, psychologists and psychiatrists, and protective services. Feel free to explore and utilize any and all forms applicable to your particular needs and circumstances. Most importantly, find someone who has already made the type of journey you are embarking on; someone whom you feel you can trust to be your mirror and guide, for they will be able to see what you cannot see, thereby dramatically increasing the speed by which you progress.

Your goal is to return to a state of wholeness as quickly and painlessly as possible. From personal experience I know this is best accomplished when supported by a safe and encouraging environment, both mentally and physically. Without it your journey back to wholeness will likely take many years longer than necessary. So if you don't already have the support you need, please make it a priority to get it however you can. For some of you that may initially entail getting yourself to a place of safety, while for others it might be finding a coach or other specialist who can encouragingly guide you as they shine a light on your blind spots.

A Whole New Life Awaits You

Returning to a state of wholeness is an experience you can't afford to miss out on. Until you reach this state, your life pales in comparison to what it could be. Regaining a sense of wholeness changes everything. One of the best ways I know to describe it is *it feels like the weight of the world has been lifted from your shoulders.* You gain a sense of lightness and of being free, unstoppable even. Initially, if your experience is anything like mine, you will feel as if everything in your life has changed even though on the surface nothing at all may have changed. But everything has changed, because you have changed. You are no longer the same person you were before, possibly just minutes or hours before.

It still amazes me that we can melt away a lifetime of pain and anguish in almost the blink of an eye. Transformation can happen very rapidly if you truly believe in the possibility and make the effort to heal. Just as many people are curing themselves of so-called incurable or terminal diseases through the power of their mind, you can do the same with the retirement of your demons to return yourself to a state of wholeness. In fact, many chronic mental or physical ailments you may be experiencing will likely dissipate or altogether disappear in the process. As we've already discovered these ailments are often nothing more than a manifestation of our demons. More specifically, they are the aspects of true selves that we have closed off that are begging us for our love and attention. In my own case, the more whole I've become, the less I find myself to be afflicted by the mental and physical ailments I previously mentioned; some have disappeared altogether, while others are now only a minor annoyance.

To expand upon the sense of hope and belief I expect you now possess, even if it's only a small glimmer, I want you to know, when you return to and live in a state of wholeness you will feel more alive than ever before. Life becomes extremely pleasurable. Great things start happening for you, often without you doing much of anything at all. Things that once ate away at you and appeared as great obstacles become mere trifles you hardly notice, or at most minor annoyances you effectively deal with and let go of. Everything in life becomes easier when you feel whole. And most of all, you'll have a solid sense of who you truly are, including what most matters to your heart and soul. Overcoming your demons and regaining your sense of wholeness will improve the quality of your life so dramatically that the likelihood of your ever returning to a previous semblance of yourself is virtually zero, regardless of what comes your way in the future.

We are all diamonds in the rough. It's rare that one of us gets through childhood without needing to do some work to reveal the brilliant facets existing within us. With each layer we peel, we chip away at the dust and grime that has kept those facets hidden. With a little time and persistence we get to the heart of who we truly are. Having retired a good many of our demons and the mind frick that has been hiding our true nature and gifts, we can now begin polishing the beautiful jewels that we are.

Just as no two diamonds or snowflakes are ever the same, nor are any two humans. You are unique. You are also meant to live a healthy, happy, meaningful, and fulfilling life. All of this is possible the moment you begin overcoming your demons and returning to your natural state of wholeness. We each shine in our own way. Some of us shine in ways the whole world sees (as great inventors, explorers, teachers, and healers), while others of us shine quietly (as a great friend, parent, coach, or coworker). Never fear that you cannot or will not shine, as there are in all probability as many ways to shine as there are people on the planet. I look forward to seeing how you shine.

Why I Wrote This Book

For as long as I can remember I have despised seeing people struggle with what I have been referring to as demons. Additionally, it has always pained me to see people being pushed or forced to be someone or something they aren't.

In my view this pushing and forcing is actually one of the worst forms of abuse that exists. The reason I say this is because it is so pervasive and so often overlooked or ignored. Whomever the perpetrators, be they our parents, school systems, religious institutions, or any other person or organization, the end result is rarely good. These people and institutions believe they know what is best for us, yet, regardless of their intentions, the reality is we are rarely allowed to be who we are meant to be. Because of this we live lives of pain and desperation, with low self-worth and a dying soul. And until we break away, heal, discover our true self, and follow our own soul's path, we tend to live an incomplete and unsatisfying life, replete with self-doubt, low self-esteem, and frequent ailments that hinder us, or ultimately stop us in our tracks, which leaves us wondering why life feels so hard and empty.

The sad truth is far too many just give up because they don't see a way out. This is evidenced by the extreme number of criminals and homeless people throughout the world, by the number of people who have given up completely and committed suicide, and by the millions more who just go through the motions, in a day-to-day existence, repeating the same old self-sabotaging patterns until they finally pass on.

Sadly, I was once one of the people I referred to earlier as being constantly pushed to be someone or something I wasn't. In addition, I experienced and suffered from virtually every form of the abuses mentioned under the section entitled *Demons and Their Sources*. Adding to the overt abuses is a long list of traumas including deaths, suicides, and chronic family illnesses of a life threatening form, as well as moving to an isolated and academically inferior location, and for all practical purposes becoming the caretaker for my mother, my three younger brothers, and the household, at the age of seven.

While admittedly some of the responsibilities I had from a very young age did in fact allow me to develop some incredible strengths and abilities, the combined effect of the various traumas, abuses, and childhood conditioning and programming was an overwhelming blow to my confidence and self-esteem, especially with regard to building and maintaining relationships. As previously mentioned, I felt empty, invisible, and alone, with a huge gaping hole that often felt akin to a black hole sucking the life out me, to the point of its extinguishing my soul. I was also extremely unhappy and unfulfilled regardless of what I had accomplished in my life. A common feeling I had was that core parts of my being were irretrievably lost. On top of all of this I tended to be extremely hard on myself, having such high expectations for myself that I truly was my own worst enemy much of the time.

Despite it all I am one of the lucky ones. Fortunately, for some reason, no matter how tough or extreme my hardships, I have always maintained the belief that I would find a way to make my life great. And while this belief has waivered and weakened at times, I have always known in my heart that I would somehow overcome all of the obstacles thrown my way, regardless of how devastating or challenging they might be. Where I acquired this belief I cannot say. Nor can I say for sure how I managed to maintain it. What I can say is that it truly saved my life and has been my rock. It is what gave me hope and kept me persistently searching, exploring, and trying new things, until I finally hit upon the combination that unlocked it all, thereby retiring my demons and bringing myself back to a state of wholeness.

And while not so long ago I hated my job and my life, I can truly say that today I love my life. Each day it gets better and better. You might question, all retired? My truthful answer is yes. However, as with anyone, I do still harbor occasional doubts and fears and catch myself momentarily bashing myself or falling into old patterns. However, thanks to much of what you will learn in this book, I am aware of what is occurring, which allows me to recognize these thoughts and feelings for what they are, and thereby quickly return myself to a more positive and life affirming state of confidence, worthiness, and wholeness. I tell you this to empress upon you that we are all human, no matter what we know or what we have conquered.

Life is a journey of self-mastery. No matter how much we have overcome or how great our lives in turn become, we all stumble. With each level of self-mastery we attain there will always be new obstacles to navigate. This is just the way of life. So remember, overcoming your demons is a life long process. No matter who you are this will always be the case. The good news is, you have complete control over how you look at the circumstances in your life, as well as how you let them affect you. This alone makes all the difference in the world.

$$\therefore$$

It is my whole-hearted belief that we all deserve to live our lives as the whole and unique beings we are, that it is in fact our birthright. You deserve to know yourself at the deepest level, to live your life in a way that is meaningful and fulfilling to you. You deserve to live this life now, not someday or in some other life or afterlife. It is because of this belief and my own struggles to regain my own sense of wholeness that I have written this book. It is my sincerest hope that the information, stories, and practices within will provide you with the rock steady hope and belief that you *can* overcome your demons to live the extraordinary and fulfilling life your heart and soul desires, in addition to helping you shortcut your journey back to wholeness by saving you many years of heartache and many thousands of dollars. You could say this has become my life's mission.

To that end, I want to share with you the most beneficial lessons, processes, and practices I have discovered along my journey, especially those that have provided me with the most immediate and lasting results from even my most devastating of experiences. It is my sincerest desire that these processes and practices, as described in the nine steps in this book, work as well for you as they have for me and countless others. May they return you to your natural state of wholeness, whereby you live the life you were born to live. We all need a guide to help us along the way. Think of this book as one of those guides. May it provide you with a newfound lease on life.

How To Use This Book

Each chapter in this book covers one of the nine steps for becoming whole again. They are organized in the order I feel is most effective for the methodical peeling of the proverbial onion. Regardless of the order you choose to read them, it is crucial to perform the exercises, as it is in doing the exercises where you will experience the most significant and rapid results.

It is worth noting that you will want to repeat some of the steps and their exercises at various points along your journey. As you peel away the layers and heal your old wounds you will be uncovering and discovering new things about yourself that will in turn present new obstacles as you more boldly step out into the world. These obstacles will create openings for your demons to try and reestablish their hold, as they don't easily give up. However, with each layer you will more completely retire your demons, and their alter egos, for good, including those that tend to manifest themselves as mental fog or physical pain.

Finally, you will want to turn some of the practices found within these pages into lifelong habits (e.g., Step 5 – Action 1: Your Morning 10). That is, you will find them to be most effective when performed on a regular, if not daily, basis. Many of the practices in Steps Two through Five are of this nature. Others are most useful when reviewed and repeated on a more periodic basis, such as once per year, or when you have experienced a big change or transformation in your life. This will be explained in more detail within each step. Each process has merit and worth on its own, but used together they are extremely powerful and will provide you with more immediate and lasting results.

Please understand this is a life-long process. You can't expect to just read the book and be done. However, you can expect rapid results if you dedicate yourself to becoming whole again and living your life as the person you are truly meant to be. With diligence and persistence you should expect to see significant progress within a few short weeks. At times you will likely make huge leaps in a matter of hours or days. With certain steps, such as Step Five (on gratitude), you are likely to experience a dramatic and almost immediate healing unlike anything you have ever experienced.

Remember, inch-by-inch, put a little in, get a lot out. Set aside a time and place just for you. You deserve it. Make a ceremony or ritual of it, as you would in performing meditation, taking a shower, or having your morning cup of tea or coffee. Doing so makes it a pleasurable activity and increases the likelihood you'll continue with it, hopefully making it a lifelong practice. Transcend your conditioning, programming, and habits, to create the life of your dreams with relative ease.

Just keep at it, and in no time at all you'll have transformed into the being you are meant to be. And don't be surprised when you begin manifesting your dreams more quickly and easily than you've ever imagined possible. Remember, you've been doing things a particular way for a very long time, and mastery takes time and practice. It also occurs in stages. This is true regardless of what it is you are attempting to master. So when you feel like you aren't making progress, or you start being hard on yourself and feel like giving up, think about anything else you've ever learned to do, be it learning read, drive a car, or play a musical instrument or sport. I can guarantee you didn't decide to pursue the activity and wake up the next day, or even a month or year later, as a complete master. The same is true with mastering your mind. And overcoming your demons and becoming whole again is exactly that, the game of mastering your mind. This is a lifelong game, one that never ends, but with practice it becomes easier and easier, with ever more extraordinary results.

It's time to get to know the real you. So let's dive in and get you started on your path to back to wholeness, so you can experience true and lasting freedom.

While I can't promise what your exact results will be, I can promise with belief and dedication this will be one of the most liberating journeys you will ever experience, and in the end you will have overcome some of the most frightening and debilitating persecutors known to mankind, your personal demons. You *can* do this. I have complete faith in you. Always remember, with wholeness comes the courage and freedom to be and do whatever you truly desire. You were meant to shine, so let's get you shining.

∴

Throughout this book you will meet a number of inspiring women who've experienced radical transformations in their lives. Except where obviously pointed out, or in the case of my own personal stories, the names of the individuals and some of the specific details have been modified to protect the individual's privacy. May their stories open your heart, give you hope, and provide you with everlasting inspiration.

Part One

THE PATH TO WHOLENESS

~~~~~

A lot of people say they want to get out of pain, and I'm sure that's true, but they aren't willing to make healing a high priority. They aren't willing to look inside to see the source of their pain in order to deal with it.
-Lindsey Wagner

Step 1 – Decide To Heal: Healing Your Life Is A Choice

Sally's Story

Sally hated her life. It was filled with the frustration and pain from a lifetime of neglect, abuse, and many traumas. While initially the neglect and abuse were inflicted upon her, over time they were more often than not self-inflicted. Despite wanting to be free of her pain, it had become so normal to her that she didn't know any other way to live. As such, she tended to nonconsciously create painful situations in her life because they made her feel normal. These situations included repeatedly getting into unsatisfactory and unhealthy relationships, working at high-stress and unfulfilling jobs, taking care of needy friends and family, and frequently getting injured. As a result Sally almost always put her needs and desires absolutely last, if she considered them at all.

Despite Sally's nonconsciously creating situations that mimicked the feelings and circumstances she was accustomed to, she was increasingly aware of a constant nagging from an inner voice that kept telling her there is a better way to live; she can have any kind of life she desires, if she would but choose it and commit to making it her reality.

After many years of hearing this voice, saying yes she really wanted to be free, and occasionally making half-hearted attempts at changing her life, only to once again end up living an empty and unsatisfactory existence, Sally said enough is enough. I will not continue living this way. I will do whatever it takes to change my life and overcome whatever it is that keeps bringing me back to these same familiar situations, where I end up with the same painful and miserable feelings of emptiness, sadness, and loneliness. I believe it is possible. I know others have done it and so can I.

It was in that moment that everything began to change for Sally. From that point forward her life was never again the same. Did she overcome everything all at once? No. Did she ever slip back into old habits or feel those same painful feelings again? Of course she did. It took time. In fact, to this day Sally is still working on healing her old wounds, but with each passing day it becomes easier and easier for her to recognize those pesky demons and their negative voices for what they are. Today she easily puts them in their place and genuinely lives what she considers to be a happy, whole, and fulfilling life, which she says is continually getting better and better.

Your Past Is Not Your Future

Does any part of Sally's story sound familiar to you? It should, because it's a familiar story, at least up to the point of Sally having made the decision and commitment to do whatever it takes to overcome what was keeping her in the painful situations she repeatedly found herself in.

Sally's story is largely my story. And it is likely your story too. Once you make the decision and commit to becoming whole again everything can and will change for you, and it will happen so much faster than you can imagine.

Now that you've heard Sally's story and know it to be a familiar one, ask yourself the following questions: How many times in the past have you ever said you want to be rid of your demons and live in peace? How many times have you said you want to be whole again? How many times have you said you want to live a happy and fulfilling life doing something you love? And, how many times have you said you want to be in a loving and respectful relationship? You may not have used these exact words, but my guess is you've made countless statements much like these throughout your life. And in addition to making these statements, how many times did you begin doing something you thought would help, only to give up almost as soon as you started because you weren't sure how to accomplish it, you thought it required too much effort, it wasn't giving you the results you wanted, or maybe the results just weren't coming quickly enough? Or maybe it seemed an altogether impossible reality. Sound familiar?

We all go through this. We all have our demons, regardless of their cause. And as you are aware, some of those demons dig their trenches very deep, setting up a seemingly permanent base from which they continually launch an all-out assault on your very being, while others tend to be infrequent visitors, popping-up at the most unexpected of times just to mess with you. Regardless of whether your demons have a constant presence or are infrequent visitors, you now know, or at least have the general idea, that they can be dealt with. And you also know the first step is that you must choose and commit to putting them in their place. This means you have considerable control over your demons, and ultimately the circumstances of your life. This is true no matter what you have experienced, or how wretched you believe yourself or your life to be because of your experiences or your demons' relentless demoralizing assaults.

I know many of you are skeptical about whether it is really possible for you to overcome your past, and that's ok. In fact it is completely understandable, because you've likely not had or don't recall many experiences that prove otherwise. And right now, you are probably wondering whether to even go forward with the rest of this book. Let me assure you I understand your doubts, because I've had them myself. Over the years I've had numerous periods where I'd virtually given up, and for varying lengths of time floundered around while I played the pity-party song. Thankfully, I'd end up disliking myself or my life so much that I'd give myself the proverbial kick in the pants and try something new, or at least give something I had previously tried another go.

For now, suffice it to say you don't have to believe me. All you need to do is give me the benefit of the doubt. Begin telling yourself you believe you can improve your life and that you will succeed, even if only in little ways, because your past is only your future if you let it be.

So Why Are You Still Stuck In The Muck?

So you've said to yourself and others you want to improve your life; that you want to overcome the demons that hold you back and interfere with you living a comfortable, if not extraordinary, life. And you've even made changes here and there that you thought would help, but somehow you keep finding yourself essentially back where you started.

Why is this? Why are you still stuck in the muck you so desperately desire to escape? I could list many reasons, but I would venture to guess the main reason is that you have been and continue to take a limited view of your life and your potential. Most likely, the majority of your thoughts, and ultimately your decisions, have been telling you the kind of life you desire is just not possible for you, and therefore you'll just have to make the best of what you've been dealt, or worse yet continue to suffer incessantly.

While there are thousands of possibilities for the exact thoughts and decisions you've made, both consciously and nonconsciously, these are a few of the more common ones: you feel and say you aren't smart enough, you aren't pretty enough, you aren't good enough, you don't deserve better, you're too young or too old, or you just aren't brave enough to change your life and who you are being. You may have even said and decided that it isn't you who needs to change, it's those around you. But remember, wherever you go, you and your thoughts are still there. Remember too that 95% of your thoughts and the decisions you make are nonconscious and automatic; they come from your conditioning and programming. So in effect your being stuck up to this point is not your fault. Until now, you were most likely unaware of what is actually going on, or of the choices you have.

Now that we've taken a look at some of the realities for why you are still stuck in the muck, ask yourself, is any of this true for me? If yes, or even maybe, then you are most definitely taking a limited view of yourself and the possibilities for your life. And if you said no, you are probably in denial, which is a very common reaction for where you likely are at this moment. Regardless of your answer, if you are taking such a limited view then you are in effect choosing to stay where you are, no matter how you try to dress it up.

Examples Of Those Who Have Gone Before You

Before you get all distraught and think this is some impossible and hopeless task, take a deep breath and recognize that I and many others the world over, many of whom have dealt with more impossible odds than you, are living proof that you can change your life for the better – even making it extraordinary.

It doesn't matter what life has dealt you to date. It doesn't matter whether your life has demonstrated greater potential or not. And it doesn't matter whether you've been led to believe that the life you are living is just your lot, so you had better suck it up and accept it. None of this matters, because you have the choice, in each and every moment, to change your life and make it extraordinary.

If you look at the back-stories of thousands of women, and men too, who seem to have everything going for them, you will find that a large percentage of them had to overcome the most unlikely of odds and circumstances to lead their extraordinary lives. And if they and I can do it, then so can you.

To provide a few concrete examples, some of whom are very well known and others not so much, take a look at the stories of the following women, many of whom have had to overcome extreme circumstances in order to achieve their remarkable lives:

Helen Keller: Born in 1880, she became deaf and blind at the age of 19 months due to an acute illness (possibly Scarlet Fever or Meningitis). At age 6, with only 60 signs with which to communicate, her parents sought help, with the hope of teaching her to better express herself. Anne Sullivan, a visually impaired 20-year old became her instructor and shortly thereafter her governess. Within 1 year of beginning her instruction with Anne, Helen began attending The Perkins Institute for the Blind. By 1900, at the age of 20, she began attending Radcliffe College. And at age 24, she graduated from college to become the first deaf and blind person to earn a Bachelor of Arts degree. From there Miss Keller went on to become a world-famous speaker, lecturer, and author, as well as a suffragist and an advocate for people with disabilities. Through her tireless dedication to perseverance she helped found the Helen Keller International (HKI) Organization and the American Civil Liberties Union (ACLU). In the last three years of her life, she was also awarded the

Presidential Medal of Freedom and elected to the Women's Hall of Fame.

Khadijah Williams: By the time she finished high school, Khadijah had attended 12 schools in as many years. Homeless from a young age, she had rarely lived anywhere for more than a few months at a time, with a significant portion of her life being lived in shelters, parks, and motels, all while enduring the leers, jests, and taunts of pimps and drug dealers. At age 9, Khadijah learned she was a *gifted* student, and from that point forward she worked hard to maintain her top 1% standing, despite missing significant portions of the school years. In her sophomore year, with the help of teachers and counselors, she applied and was admitted to community college summer classes. To complete her high school studies in the same school she chose to endure 2 years of long bus trips, leaving at 4:00 a.m. and returning home at 11:00 p.m. After years of hiding her story, Khadijah decided to share it in her college application essay. Doing so gained her notice from numerous college admissions boards and the news media, which ultimately earned her admission to Harvard University in 2009. Today she continues her studies and uses her life lessons to inspire and help others.

Oprah Winfrey: Born into poverty to a single teenage mother on welfare in 1950's rural Mississippi, Miss Winfrey experienced considerable hardship during her childhood, including sexual abuse, teenage pregnancy, and being passed around to various family members. Despite her hardships, she became a radio host during high school and began co-anchoring a local TV news program at the age of 19. The rest as they say is history. Today Oprah Winfrey is one of the most wealthy and successful women in the world, including being the first black women billionaire in history, and as of September 2010 the richest self-made woman in America.

Aduei Riak: At age 6 Aduei was separated from her parents during the Ethiopian civil war. From then on she was on her own. As a refugee she walked over 1000 miles, along with thousands of other orphans, until reaching a refugee camp in Kenya, In 2000, at age 16, Aduei was relocated to the United States as part of a refugee resettlement program, where she lived with foster families and began attending high school, despite knowing very little English. To master the English language she studied very hard, which included watching countless hours of Sesame Street and other TV programs. Aduei quickly became a top student and in 2003 she was accepted at the very prestigious Brandeis University. In 2007, upon graduation from Brandeis, she received an award for integrating social activism with academic study. Today she is studying at The London School of Economics and Political Science, giving keynote speeches, campaigning against genocide, and starting a foundation to help Sudanese girls receive an education.

Eleanor Roosevelt: Born in 1884 to immense wealth and privilege, Eleanor was orphaned at age 10 and raised by her maternal grandmother. In adolescence, following the death of her parents and a brother, Eleanor was described as being shy, insecure, and starved for affection, while considering herself an ugly duckling. However, at age 14, she came to understand that *"no matter how plain a woman may be, if truth and loyalty are stamped upon her face all will be attracted to her"*. Around the age of 15 Eleanor was sent away to a European finishing school and at age 20 she married Franklin D. Roosevelt (a fifth cousin), to the objections of certain family members (notably Franklin's mother). Once married, Eleanor remained shy and found herself under the thumb of her domineering mother-in-law. As the years passed, she raised 5 children (a 6th died in infancy) and supported her husband's political ventures, even overcoming his infidelity (with her social secretary) and her shyness in order to make public appearances on his behalf due to his development of a paralytic condition that left his legs paralyzed. Despite her privileges, Eleanor suffered many hardships in her life (being orphaned, losing a child, infidelity, a disabled husband, and her own personal insecurities). Yet in the end, she stood up for the underprivileged. In 1933 she became First Lady of the United States, where she continued on as a spokesperson for her husband and became an advocate for Civil Rights. Following her husband's death she remained politically active, working to enhance the status of working women, and ultimately becoming a United Nations General Assembly delegate to further Human Rights the world over.

J. K. Rowling: Best known for the Harry Potter book series, Joanna Rowling has lived a true life Rags-to-Riches story. Just a few brief years following the completion of her University Education, she found herself dealing with a situation not unlike one that many women find themselves in: grieving the loss of her mother, divorced, and jobless, with a dependent child (in addition to living in a country in which she wasn't certified to teach). In Ms. Rowling's view she was, *"the biggest failure I knew"*, becoming severely depressed and even contemplating suicide. Later however, she described her failure as liberating: *"Failure meant a stripping away of the inessential. I stopped pretending to myself that I was anything other than what I was, and began to direct all my energy to finishing the only work that mattered to me. Had I really succeeded at anything else, I might never have found the determination to succeed in the one area where I truly belonged. I was set free, because my greatest fear had been realized, and I was still alive, and I still had a daughter whom I adored, and I had an old typewriter, and a big idea. And so rock bottom became a solid foundation on which I rebuilt my life."* ~ J. K. Rowling, *"The fringe benefits of failure"*, 2008.

Living on state assistance and writing in café's, while working on a teaching certificate and caring for her infant daughter, Ms. Rowling completed her manuscript (in which her characters take on much of her pain and loss). Initially rejected by 12 publishers, Bloomsbury of London finally agreed to publish it, but suggested she get a day job as it wasn't likely to sell many copies. However, as we all know, it is the best-selling book series ever, and Ms. Rowling is one of the richest and most influential women in the United Kingdom. In addition to writing, she now supports a variety of charities and foundations committed to combating poverty, social inequity, and finding a cure for Multiple Sclerosis (the cause of her mother's death).

Marjorie Elliott: Marjorie Elliott, an Orange County, California resident, is not your typical student. Taken out of school at age 14 to help support her family, whom were poor farmers struggling to make a living; she went on to raise her own family (3 daughters whom she raised on her own from a young age). Not being very well educated herself made it difficult for her to help her daughters. To ensure they received a proper education, completing high school at minimum, she made a number of sacrifices, including the postponement of her own education, to pay for tutors. In 2008, after being laid-off from her job (at the age of 73), she decided she had struggled long enough as the result of not having an education. So she made up her mind to get her high school diploma. In 2010, at the age of 75, Marjorie graduated with a 4.0 GPA. Following graduation she began looking for a job and preparing to attend University to obtain a Computer Science degree. Despite some struggles (Algebra being one) Marjorie stated for the Orange County Register, *"If I make up my mind that I'm going to do something, I don't care what it is, I'm going to dig in there and get it done. I won't say I can't, because I know I can, and I know I will."*

Maya Angelou: Ms. Angelou is one of the most renowned and influential voices of our time – a true trailblazer. She has lived and continues to live an extraordinary life. If ever there were a woman who has been and done it all, it is Maya Angelou. Born in the American South in 1928, Ms. Angelo experienced first hand the prejudices and brutality of racial discrimination, but as evidenced, she has never let that get in her way. Despite having been sexually abused and raped at age 8, becoming mute for 5 years because she thought her voice killed her perpetrator, giving birth as a single mother at age 17, and for some time thereafter living a life of poverty and crime, she has gone on to live the fullest life anyone could ever imagine. The list of her occupations includes waitress, cook, streetcar conductor, pimp, prostitute, dancer, performer/actor (night club, opera, TV variety shows...), coordinator for Martin Luther King Jr.'s S. Christian Leadership Conference, composer, author, poet, foreign journalist and teacher (Egypt, Ghana), political activist, writer, director (plays, movies, public TV), and university professor, in addition to serving on two presidential committees. She has received numerous honors and awards from universities, literary organizations, government agencies, and special interest groups for her work, including over 30 honorary degrees and a Pulitzer Prize nomination. At 85 she tirelessly continues her work, including her teaching of American Studies at Wake Forest University.

$$\therefore$$

One of the common themes you will find running among these women's stories is the great pain and adversity they've had to overcome. Each of them has overcome overwhelming odds to become whole again, and to ultimately accomplish something extraordinary, something that has fundamentally benefited countless others. Interestingly, none of these women initially set out to do what it is they ultimately accomplished. What they did do is to make a decision to stand up for themselves in order to create a better life, which in the end healed them. They accomplished this one thought, one decision, and one action at a time.

Not a single one of these women knew where their actions would lead them. What they did know was that accepting their current circumstances was no longer acceptable. They knew they must do something different, because anything less was dooming them to more of the same. This decision is admirable, especially since for many of these women the consequences could have been disastrous; that is, their decision could easily have led to their death. On the other hand staying where they were could just as likely have led to their demise. Regardless of the consequences, these women knew in their heart and soul they had to take the risk. They had to step into the unknown, because the status quo was too unbearable.

I know many of the women I have listed here are somewhat famous, if not extremely so, and that may make it appear that their lives are beyond comparison to your own. But if you take the time to know their stories and what they've had to overcome, you will see that their story is your story. They've lived with the same hardships, adversity, and personal demons as you. The big difference is that they have done what it takes to overcome their demons and become whole again, and for some, if not all of them, they have continued throughout their lives to peel away the old layers of pain, in order to become more and more whole. And this will be the same for you, because the reality is we will always have some demon or adversity that creeps into our life to trip us up. So while the list of women I shared are famous to one degree or another, for every one of them there are thousands more who aren't the least bit famous who have overcome equally as challenging of circumstances and pain to lead happy and fulfilling lives.

Healing and Becoming Whole Again Is A Choice!

As we've seen so far, none of those who have overcome their demons to become whole again, and end up leading happy and fulfilling, or even outrageously extraordinary lives, did so without first choosing to break free of the lifelong patterns to which they had been enslaved. Therefore, the first step for becoming whole again is to make the decision. But success takes more than a decision. It takes an ever-present commitment to action that must be maintained with the most powerful of resolves. That is, you must continually recommit yourself to your decision. You must begin anew as often as it takes. In the words of Maya Angelou, *"Success is not fame or fortune. It is picking up your burden and keeping on walking and not letting the pain trip you up."*

Believe There Is A Reason For Where You've Been So Far

To help you make your decision to heal and become whole again, along with the commitment you'll need to see it through, let's first give some positive perspective to your struggles. Now before you start thinking I'm crazy, that there is nothing positive about your hardships, be open-minded and pretend for a moment that I could be right.

While it's obvious your struggles are painful, there's also a bright side, because with every adversity comes opportunity. And while that opportunity may not jump out at you, I assure you it's there. Every person you can think of who has truly overcome something painful, has almost always turned that pain into something fortuitous – something that frequently benefits many others beyond themselves.

We all have struggles and we all have gifts, whether we are aware of them or not. And as history has shown us, it is often at the juncture of those gifts and struggles that people create fulfilling and extraordinary lives. Very often it is our most challenging struggles that lead us to understand and develop our gifts, gifts that otherwise lay dormant or are barely acknowledged. Therefore, as I now see it, there is a reason for our suffering, a reason for our having travelled the road we have, and a reason for our experiences, no matter how painful they may have been.

Face it, life is challenging, so why not use your challenges to create a beautiful life. And what is life anyway? Is it not a school of sorts, where we are to learn from our experiences and apply the knowledge and wisdom we've gained from those experiences to the next chapter of our lives? It's funny how if you look at life from this perspective it seems that most of us ignore the lessons. Rather than making detours or forging new paths, as some of our experiences strongly suggest we should, we hold true to the road we are on, digging an ever greater rut that makes taking alternative routes all the more difficult.

Whether the reason for this oversight is our conditioning and programming, blatant threats made to our safety, or some inherent flaw in our makeup, the reality is the vast majority of us tend to repeat our actions and mistakes over and over again, very often expecting we will get different results if we just keep giving it another go. While not a very pleasant thought, Albert Einstein referred to this pattern of doing the same thing over and over again, while expecting different results, as insanity. Now I'm not insinuating in any way that you are insane, but if this is a common pattern in your life in any way then it definitely begs attention.

To get started on a new path, just accept your life to this point for what it is. Believe the life you have lived so far is completely perfect, that everything you have experienced to date is exactly what you needed to learn in order to put you on the path you are now on, a path to freedom and fulfillment. To reinforce in your mind that you *can* succeed, I'll state it again: *Your past is not your future.* As soon as you decide and commit to overcoming your demons and becoming whole again, you will begin to see the truth in these statements. For now, just accept your past is just that, your past. You can't change it. And who you are today is because of the decisions and actions you've previously made. Yet today, and each day hereafter, is a brand new day, another chance to do something new and different, a chance for a whole new you and a whole new life. With each new decision and action you have the power to dramatically change everything in your life for the better.

One more point. Recognize that where you are now is absolutely perfect. It is the perfect place for you to begin this journey. In fact, wherever you are is always the perfect place to begin. And the fact that you are still hanging in there with me is evidence of your courage and your desire to overcome what keeps you from living the life you desire.

Are You Uncomfortable Enough To Take Action?

Before we get to the actual decision and commitment making part of this step I want to cover one more topic that is absolutely essential for your success. In truth, it's often the biggest reason most people don't take action, regardless of how frequently they say they want something different from what they are experiencing. So what is this showstopper that impedes so many? Believe it or not, it is their level of uncomfortableness. Very often the reason we don't make a decision at all, or we don't commit to the decision we do make, is that we are not yet uncomfortable enough with our present pain and circumstances to take the action that would ultimately provide us with a better life.

I'm sure you're thinking how can this be true? And you're probably saying to yourself that your life, or some aspect of it, feels mighty uncomfortable right now. If this sounds like anything you are thinking or saying, then ask yourself, why haven't I taken action? I can guarantee that whatever your answer, if you haven't yet taken action, then you haven't yet reached the point where your current level of pain or your current circumstances are uncomfortable enough. When you are uncomfortable enough, nothing will stop you, not even your absolute worst fears. When you have reached that point, you will have decided enough is enough, no more. And from that point forward you will do whatever it takes to heal and create a better life for yourself.

The reality is, we are most often *more comfortable* with where we currently are, than we are with the unknown of being whole and free from our demons and struggles. While I know this may be difficult to believe, it's entirely true. Example after example demonstrates it. Look at any aspect of your life. How often do you hear yourself talking about making a change to your life? A change you know would significantly improve your life in some way, yet you find yourself doing absolutely nothing to make it a reality, or you give up almost as soon as you start. It doesn't matter what the something is. Some common examples include losing weight, getting a new job, making a big move someplace you've always dreamed of living, taking a dream trip, or leaving an abusive or less than satisfactory relationship.

No matter how big or small your desired change, the underlying cause for you not making it is almost always the same, and that cause centers around you not being uncomfortable enough to stand up to the demons who bully you, be they fear, shame, guilt, lack of confidence, or even a lackadaisical complacency that you can do it later. And in the off chance you do make a change, it's often more of a

15

knee-jerk reaction or an act of utter desperation, than it is a contemplated and committed decision. When this is the case, it is typically because you don't really understand the true drivers behind what motivated you to act, or for that matter, who you really are and what it is you really want. So in the end, you wind up repeating the same old unhealthy patterns in a new place, a new job, or with a new person.

If you doubt this, take a look at the lives of your friends and family, your co-workers, and many of those who are celebrities. You see this trend all the time. Until push comes to shove, and a situation has become completely unbearable, the tendency is to fear the unknown and continue living with the present circumstances, even when everyone, except possibly the person in question, sees that a radical change is essential for their well-being. And when these people *do* make a change, what normally happens? In short order they are repeating their past yet again, and in some cases they end up going down an even worse rabbit hole. Only rarely do you see someone who really turns his or her life around in a significant way, and then continues on that improved path.

So if you haven't yet made the decision, and declared to yourself and the universe, that you will heal and become whole again, then take a look at how uncomfortable you really are with your present circumstances. Ask yourself the following questions. Am I so uncomfortable with the status quo that I'm willing to do whatever it takes to be free of my pain and misery forever? Am I so uncomfortable that I'm willing to try new things, even if they go counter to what seems to make sense? Am I so uncomfortable, and sick of being tired, frightened, and demoralized, that I will make healing and becoming whole again my mission? Am I so uncomfortable that I'm willing to look within and face my demons head on? Am I so uncomfortable that I will find a mentor, teacher, or other professional to guide me?

Really examine what is stopping you from making the most important decision of your life. Because that is what this is, it's the most important decision you will ever make. The level of overall life happiness and satisfaction you ultimately experience is linked 100% to the level of success you achieve in overcoming your demons and becoming whole again. While that may sound daunting, I promise you it is absolutely the most rewarding journey you will ever take, a journey that brings the ultimate form of freedom, allowing you to face anything thrown your way with an open heart, courage, and resilience.

Believe with all your heart that with each step you complete you will be living an ever more joyful and fulfilling life. Know that you will be gaining the wisdom and confidence to be your true self and live a life that truly inspires you. Get ready to feel your heart sing, because that is exactly what it will do. In no time at all you'll be looking forward to each and every day. You'll find yourself waking up and shouting at the top of your lungs *I LOVE MY LIFE*. Just imagine how great that will feel. Actually, why not start now. Shout *I LOVE MY LIFE* as loud as you can. Do this every day until it has become your reality.

It's Decision Time – So Let's Get Started

We've covered a lot so far. We've looked at a variety of reasons for why you are likely still stuck in the muck – your own personal hell if you will. We've looked at some of the instigators that propel people to take full responsibility for their lives and therefore overcome what had previously haunted or perplexed them. And we've even taken a brief look at some role models who have successfully overcome a wide range of personal demons and overwhelming odds to lead happy and fulfilling lives, some of whom have or are leading extraordinary lives.

I guarantee a better life awaits you, but only if you choose it. And while it is 100% possible for you to overcome your demons, become whole again, and live an amazing life, I can't guarantee it will always be easy. Hey, if it were, we'd all be happy and living exceptional lives.

Believe you can and will do this, because, as you've hopefully learned by now, fear and complacency will get you nowhere. In fact, fear and complacency will only give you more of the same, and then only for a while, after which everything begins going downhill from wherever you find yourself. So, as I see it, and hopefully you do too, the only real choice is to broaden your horizons and take a much more positive and grander view of your potential and the possibilities for your life.

Therefore, it's time to see beyond your past and even your current circumstances. Begin believing in the possibility of a better life. Look beyond wherever you are and whatever has happened to you. *Make the decision NOW that you will take control of your life and become whole again. Declare to yourself and the world that from this moment forward you will do whatever it takes.* This is the only way you will ever rise above your pain and overcome what it is that keeps you stuck in a dead-end life full of needless suffering and challenges.

Just to be clear, your successfully completing these 9 steps for becoming whole again doesn't mean you will never again experience any suffering or challenges. However, by completing them you will have an intimate understanding of the things causing your pain, suffering, and challenges, which will make it possible for you to more easily navigate them rather than finding yourself lost in them. Remember, you are peeling layers, and with each level of self-mastery will experience new challenges. Challenges are good. We need them to grow. Growth is the way of life. We are either growing or we are dying.

Believe you can succeed. And remember to get help when you need it. As already discussed, you can't do this totally on your own; help is readily available in many different forms. To reiterate the need for help, ask yourself if it is worth losing additional years of your life to the demons who persecute you because you were too fearful or too proud to ask for help? Please don't let your demons continue stealing precious years and happiness from you. Do anything you can to get started. Start small if need be. But please, just get started.

Two good methods to help you get started and keep moving, in addition to implementing the steps outlined in this book, are 1) to read and listen to inspirational, personal development, and self-help books and CD/DVD programs, and 2) to read or watch biographies and inspirational stories about others who have overcome great adversity. These methods are inexpensive, easy to find, and easy to fit into your schedule. No matter what form you use, make sure you employ some type of inspiration in your life each and every day. Doing so will fuel your resolve and give you the hope and confidence you need to continue on your path to wholeness and freedom.

Your Commitment To Wholeness

You've made the decision to do what it takes to become whole again, but are you truly ready to commit? And we're talking lifetime commitment here, because without a lifelong commitment your decision doesn't really mean much. Ugh. Lifelong? Yes, lifelong. I know that might sound impossible, but it's not. As with any type of significant behavioral change, it starts as a day-to-day discipline that over time only requires periodic recommitment. Just like the formation of any new habit, or the breaking of an old one, it will become second nature, so that after a while you rarely need think about it. Think of this just as you would the creation of any new habit, which in many ways is exactly what it is. Then make your commitment. To support you, place helpful reminders and implements where you will continually see them.

IT'S NOW TIME TO MAKE YOUR COMMITMENT. Remember, you're making a commitment to yourself and your life. If you're ready, print a copy of the certificate shown in Figure 1, sign and date it, and if possible have two witnesses sign it as well, that way you'll have someone to hold you accountable to your commitment. Then place it somewhere you'll be sure to see it each and every day. DO THIS NOW. Do it before reading any further.

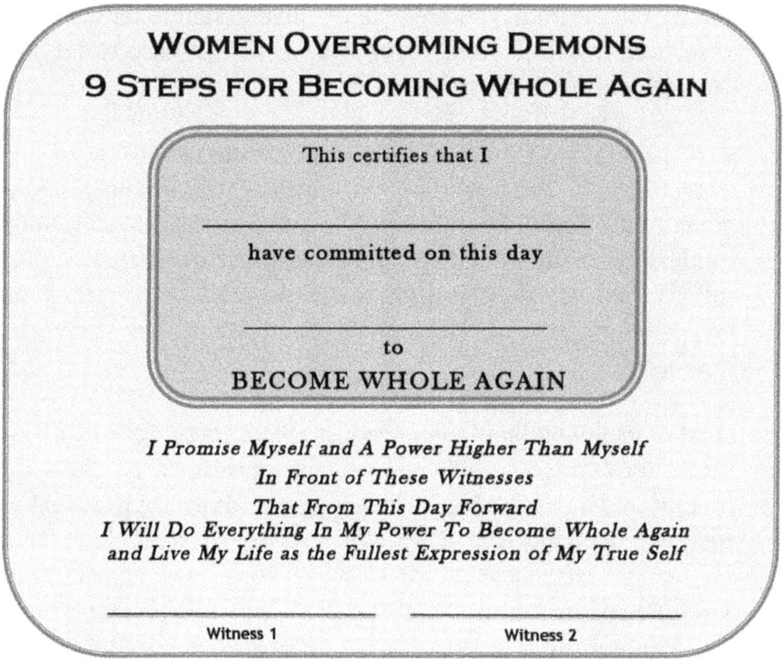

WOMEN OVERCOMING DEMONS
9 STEPS FOR BECOMING WHOLE AGAIN

This certifies that I

_____

have committed on this day

_____

to
BECOME WHOLE AGAIN

I Promise Myself and A Power Higher Than Myself
In Front of These Witnesses
That From This Day Forward
I Will Do Everything In My Power To Become Whole Again
and Live My Life as the Fullest Expression of My True Self

_____   _____
Witness 1   Witness 2

Figure 1: Becoming Whole Again Commitment Certificate

You'll find a larger version of the commitment certificate in the Appendix, as well as a downloadable version on the resources page at www.WomensWholenessConnection.com.

CONGRATULATIONS!!! You've just completed the first step of the process. You are now ready to begin the steps that will help you quickly retire your demons and thereby recover those parts of yourself you inadvertently hid away for safekeeping. In no time at all you'll be experiencing yourself and your life in a whole new and exciting way. You'll wake up with renewed energy and vigor, enthusiastic about the possibilities awaiting you.

The Importance Of Commitment

Before moving on to the next step I feel it's important to reiterate a few things.

1. Deciding to do something is always the first step. And not deciding is still a decision, whether you recognize it as such or not. By not deciding you are making the decision to let the winds of fortune take you where they will, or in this case to let your demons shape and control your life.

2. Most people don't make the effort to overcome what is causing them to suffer because they are afraid of the unknown. Even though they don't like where they are, the truth is they are more comfortable with what they know, despite how it makes them suffer. That is, they feel more comfortable where they are because they generally know how to navigate it; they know what to expect.

3. Most of us are willing to change just about anything in our lives, except for ourselves. We'll change our appearance, our jobs, our friends, and our spouses; we'll change just about anything except what will really provide us with the freedom we are looking for.

   On the surface some of these changes may appear to be solutions. However, most often they are only an escape or distraction from the pain, rather than a true solution. When changes are merely to distract us from our pain or some truth we are fearful of acknowledging, the result is always continued suffering, with a corresponding decline in well-being that is commensurate with the degree of suffering we sustain. Think of it like what happens to those who continually hide their pain in food, drink, drugs, TV, or gambling.

Sadly, this pattern generally continues until our only choice is to look within and make a drastic change, or face death. Sadly, for many it only occurs because imminent death *was* their wakeup call; that is, the prospect of death became more painful than digging within and facing their demons head on.

4. *Real and lasting change only occurs when we face the true source of our pain – our inner demons.* Until then we continue to struggle, making at best half-hearted attempts to heal, spending most of our time going through the motions, doing whatever we can to temporarily distract ourselves from the pain being caused by the war our demons are waging in our minds and bodies.

5. Nothing really changes for the better, or for long, until we make a conscious commitment to overcome our demons and become whole, which means doing something that feels not only different, but uncomfortable (i.e., stepping outside our comfort zone).

Remember, 95% of the time we are acting from nonconscious beliefs, conditioning, and programming. That means for 15.2 of 16 waking hours we are acting on autopilot (more like an automaton or zombie than a conscious, living, human being). That's only 48 minutes per day that we are thinking, acting, and responding from conscious thought or intention. This is one of key reasons for the need to make a conscious commitment.

6. Only you can make the decision and commit to it. No one else can do it for you. You must want it for yourself. No one is stopping you but you. So don't let anyone bully you into believing otherwise, not even the tricksters in your mind.

7. Regardless of what you've been through or where you are today, YOU CAN DO THIS. I HAVE COMPLETE FAITH IN YOU. I've done it, as have countless others. Use those of us who've

successfully overcome our demons as your mentors and role models.

Remember, you've been doing the same thing for a very long time, likely with little improvement to show for it. So isn't it time you tried something new. All success requires commitment, a strategic plan (which is provided in this book), and disciplined action. Therefore, unless you'd rather continue blowing in the wind, being taken wherever the tides of pain and circumstance carry you, hoping and praying your next landing spot will be free of restless and troublemaking natives that quickly stir up your pain, then why not make the commitment to a new approach that will bring you the peace and wholeness you are looking for?

Do you really want to wait until something as painful and challenging as the prospect of death forces you to decide? I hope not. Because as any good doctor, or any person who has been extremely ill, will tell you, it is more difficult to get well than it is to stay well. What this means is, the longer you wait to do something about your demons, the stronger they will become and the more difficult it may be to overcome them. Realize they are not only affecting your confidence and self-worth, they are also affecting your physical vitality. The more control they have the more mental and physical ailments you tend to experience.

So I ask again, do you really want to continue letting your demons control you so completely that they take you to death's doorstep, making you suffer and endure potentially years more of needless pain and hardship? I truly hope not, because I would hate to see you continue suffering when the solution is at hand.

You *can* overcome your pain and insecurities, and in the process create a better life. You *can* be free and whole. And you *can* be wildly successful in countless ways beyond anything you can currently imagine. Hey, until fairly recently I never imagined I'd be writing this book or speaking to large groups as a means to help as many women as possible overcome the demons holding them back from leading the whole and fulfilling lives they deserve and desire.

To make any of this happen you first have to commit to making it your reality. Therefore, if you haven't already filled out the commitment certificate, I implore you to do it now. I know it may seem a trivial thing to do, but by doing so you will have a feeling of accomplishment and truly be ready to begin the next step.

Now That You've Chosen To Become Whole Again – What's Next?

Now that you've made the decision to overcome your demons and have committed yourself to becoming whole again, it's time to put into play the steps that will bring you the greatest freedom you can ever experience, that of being whole. I say it is the greatest freedom because of what it gives you, which is the ability to be the person you are truly meant to be, living a life that fulfills your soul.

Think of this process as a rebirth, a renaissance of you, the real you, the whole you. Be prepared to let go of your illusions of who you think are and what you think you are capable of, and in short order there will be no turning back to the life you currently know.

With each step you successfully complete you'll find you are no longer willing to continue living in the dream (or nightmare) of your usual life. While most of the changes you make will be internal changes, at least initially, there may be times when you find you need to make some external changes in order to continue your progress. A couple of examples include spending less time with negative friends and family, and altering some of your habits, especially those that deplete your energy.

Additionally, be prepared for periodic surges in your confidence and energy levels. Expect some surprises, most of which you'll find pleasing or exciting. Recognize, however, that some of the surprises may at first seem like a crises or unfortunate event. This is most often the result of your stepping outside of your comfort zone, which almost always feels uncomfortable in the beginning. Please don't let this stop you. It means you are experiencing growth, which is exactly what you want.

Look at these surprises as gifts that offer valuable lessons. See them as a doorway to opportunities you were previously incapable of seeing. Be open to these surprises. Look at them from multiple perspectives, not just your perspective of habit. Remember those demons of yours are tricksters and they do *not* want to give up their control. We'll cover this in depth in the following steps, especially Steps 3 and 4.

To increase your chances of sticking with the process, the rest of this step will focus on specific actions you can take on a daily basis to reinforce your commitment.

Actions To Reconfirm Your Commitment

1. **Repeat your commitment daily. Say it out loud with feeling.**

   I, *Your Name,* promise myself and a source higher than myself (fill in with what works for you; god, the universe, great sprit...) that from this day forward I will do everything in my power to become whole again and thereby live my life as the fullest expression of my true self.

   Example: *"I, Sally Goforth, promise myself and the wisdom of the universe that from this day forward I will do everything in my power to become whole again and thereby live my life as the fullest expression of my true self."*

2. **Repeat the following declarations with feeling, at least five times each morning and evening.**

   - I choose wholeness.
   - I commit to becoming whole again.
   - I accept there is nothing missing from me, that I have only blocked it from my current awareness.
   - I allow myself to be whole and complete, just as I was when I was born.
   - I am already whole; I live a joyous and fulfilling life.
   - I LOVE MY LIFE!

3. **Create a support team.**

   The more challenging your situation, the more support you will likely need. Find someone you consider safe and encouraging to share your commitment with and hold you accountable. Have them sign your Commitment Certificate and regularly encourage you. Share with them how things are going, including what seems to be tripping you up. They will be able see your progress as well as your blind spots more readily than you will. Therefore, their feedback can dramatically increase the speed of your progress

   This is where a personal empowerment or life coach can be tremendously beneficial. Since they don't have the same type of investment in whether you heal or not as do your friends and family, they'll be honest with you and generally much more helpful. Friends and family can be well-meaning, but overcoming your demons and becoming whole again may be unsettling to them. Often they feel you will leave them behind, which can cause them to wittingly, or unwittingly, sabotage your progress.

4. **Write out why you will stay committed to becoming whole again.**
List all the benefits you expect to gain by overcoming your demons; such as all the things you will finally have the confidence to do. Review this list every day for one month, and weekly thereafter. Refine it as you recognize more benefits.

5. **If you're living in an unsafe or abusive environment, begin looking for a way to extract yourself from that environment.**
If it's unsafe for you to do the exercises in this program at home, then find somewhere you can go on a regular basis where you will feel safe and have the strength and peace of mind you need to complete the program. Remember, the more regularly you perform the exercises in the program the more mentally and physically strong you will become, which will result in you garnering the courage you need to take the necessary actions to leave or positively affect your current environment.

6. **Congratulate yourself for completing this step. Do something special just for you. You deserve it.**
Your something special doesn't have to be fancy. It doesn't even have to cost anything. It just needs to be something that makes you feel good, and allows you to celebrate you. Some simple examples are taking a nice long bubble bath, sitting somewhere quiet while sipping a cup of tea, taking a walk in a park or local gardens, or going out with a girlfriend you don't get to spend much time with. Whatever you choose, just make sure it is special to you.

∴

Regarding the use of declarations, it's best to repeat them several times a day, especially at the beginning of your day and just before bed. To make them more effective, repeat them to yourself out loud and in front of a mirror, saying them with as much feeling and belief as you can possibly muster. The more you repeat them in this manner the more quickly you'll come to accept them as your truth. I know in the beginning they'll feel awkward and as if you're lying to yourself, but this is just those pesky demons way of attempting to stay in control and prevent you from becoming whole again.

If you find your mind arguing with you and challenging the validity of your declarations you can restate them in the following manner: *"I am in the process of attracting everything I need to do, know, and have in order to _____."* By prefacing your declarations with *"I am in the process of attracting..."* your mind (those demons) won't be able to refute them. After a while, you'll find that you can easily state them without the preface.

Have fun with it. Make the declarations throughout this book your own. Sing them. Chant them. Do whatever makes them real for you. You want to feel a positive shift in your energy. You want them to inspire you to take action.

To track your progress it is recommended you begin keeping a wholeness journal. Simply record your responses to the exercises in the steps of this book, in addition to your ongoing thoughts and feelings.

Doing so will provide multiple advantages. First, you'll create awareness of things you are currently blind to. Secondly, you'll have a means for observing your patterns and habits, both the self-defeating one and the self-nourishing ones. Finally, you'll have a concrete means of observing just how quickly you are progressing.

Our stresses, anxieties, pains, and problems arise
because we do not see the world, others, or
even ourselves as worthy of love.
-Prem Prakash

Step 2 – Believe You Are Worthy: Love and Honor Yourself

Jan's Story

Jan had struggled throughout her life to feel accepted, fit in, and be taken seriously. For as long as she could remember, no matter how hard she worked she felt like she was always being passed over for someone else, often for someone who wasn't nearly as attractive, talented, giving, or dedicated as herself. This trend frustrated and baffled her. For the life of her she just couldn't figure out why it tended to be the perpetual norm in her life, be it school sports, personal relationships, or positions at work. To her mind it didn't matter what area of her life you were to look at; in all cases she was forever being overlooked, so much so it was as if she were invisible.

From Jan's point-of-view she had done everything right. She was the good girl. She was responsible. She was pleasant and unassuming. She worked hard. She helped others. And she rarely made waves about things that hurt or upset her. So why was she continually overlooked? Why was she so invisible? What was the real cause for her state of affairs? Jan decided she had to find out; she promised herself she wouldn't stop looking until she had found the answer and had turned things around.

To uncover the truth she was so desperate to discover, Jan began reflecting on her life; she also began contemplating the lives of the friends and acquaintances she considered to be more successful than her. She noted everything she could think of about her life, giving extra attention to what she had been taught. She then compared her experiences and life lessons to those of her more successful friends and acquaintances, most especially the ones who seemed to have what she wanted and for whom it seemed to come with relative ease.

After what seemed an eternity of exploration, Jan discovered a fundamental difference that made it all make sense. That difference was worthiness. She realized she had never really felt worthy of the things she desired. So as much as she really wanted love, respect, success, and other good things in life, she honestly didn't feel worthy of them. No matter how good her actual experiences, she had been conditioned to expect very little for her efforts, so she therefore received very little (hence her perpetually being overlooked). She'd also been taught (programmed if you will) to believe that life is hard; you work hard and do your best, and if you're lucky, maybe on occasion you'll catch a break. At the core of her programming was the deep-seated belief that you can't trust or rely on anyone, which adversely affected her ability to trust herself or anyone else.

Jan now understands how severely these beliefs were affecting her confidence, self-esteem, and ability to trust her instincts. With this new perspective, she could readily see how her frustrations and so-called failures were directly linked to her sense of worthiness.

Feeling hopeful and inspired, Jan began actively working to restore her intrinsic self-worth. Initially she learned we are all worthy; no one is more worthy than anyone else, of love, of opportunity, or of living a fulfilling life. She also learned that when we feel unworthy, people who are more successful in the areas we'd like to be aren't typically drawn to us, so as a result we tend to be overlooked. And if by chance we are considered, we're likely to be perceived as too much of a risk. That is, we'll take too much effort; we'll need too much handholding. In general, we just won't cut it.

Jan's discovery led her to one of life's great truths. We all deserve to live an exceptional life. It is our birthright. But to live an exceptional life we must first believe we are worthy of an exceptional life.

∴

The most expeditious method I know for restoring your innate self-worth is to love and honor yourself. By loving and honoring yourself you will in turn truly love and honor others. When you love and honor yourself life is easier and more fulfilling, people respect you, opportunities miraculously up, your relationships are more rewarding, and much of what used to frustrate you just melts away.

You Are Worthy – It's Your Birthright

Do you relate to Jan's story? While being only one example of the many ways the feeling of unworthiness can affect us, it is once again a common story. Yet it brings to light one of the keys to successfully overcoming your demons and becoming whole again; that is, you must feel worthy of being whole, having the things you truly desire, and living a fulfilling life. Until you do, you will continue to struggle and feel the emptiness that has forever haunted you, an emptiness that brings many to despair.

It's a sad reality that the feelings of unworthiness are so prevalent. Far too many truly believe they are unworthy of so many things: love, acceptance, compliments, praise, a good job, a great partner, a university education, their dreams, etc. However long your list, the reality is the feelings of unworthiness are rampant the world over. But why is this? We are each worthy of all of these things and so much more. It doesn't matter who we are or where we were born. Neither does it doesn't matter our family, race, education, religion, experiences, or anything else. By virtue of the fact we were born, we are automatically worthy. Most of all we are worthy of love.

But what is worthiness? And if we were born worthy, then how is it we come to believe we are unworthy? And if we feel unworthy, then how do we go about restoring our sense of worthiness?

Worthiness is a healthy respect and favorable opinion of yourself and your abilities. It is reflected in your confidence, your self-esteem, and your self-respect. The higher your level of *genuine* confidence, self-esteem, and self-respect, the higher your level of self-worth. The higher your self-worth, the more genuinely you will love and honor yourself and others, and the more fulfilling your life will be.

Signs Of Feeling Unworthy

How worthy you feel is directly reflected in every aspect of your life. It shows up in your thoughts, your actions, in how you present yourself, in how others perceive you, and ultimately your results in life.

One effective measure of how worthy you feel is reflected in your ability to receive compliments. If you are challenged with gracefully accepting compliments then you are most definitely experiencing diminished feelings of self-worth.

Regardless of how you personally express a diminished self-worth, the fact that you are should raise a red flag. Expressions of low self-worth mean your demons are in control; they are preventing you from living your life as the whole and amazing being you are. It also means you're missing out on a lot of great opportunities that are yours for the taking as soon as you believe in you.

The following list highlights many of the common ways we go about expressing our feelings of low self-worth:

- Not being enough (good enough, smart enough, attractive enough, old enough, young enough...)
- Hopelessness
- Suicidal thoughts
- Negative body image
- Persistent sadness
- Apathy (extreme loss of interest, feeling, or emotion)
- Persistent feelings of rejection
- Comparison to others (body, home, possessions, abilities)
- Having to do it all yourself (no one else will help)
- Overly responsible for others
- Frequent defensiveness (about performance, opinions, when complimented)
- Frequent crying
- Depression
- Withdrawal from relationships (friends, family, society)
- Use of drugs and alcohol to cope or escape
- Diminished emotional expression
- Avoiding eye contact
- Not caring for one's self (hygiene, health)
- Feeling unlovable (includes feeling totally alone)
- Poor performance or conduct (at home, in school, on the job)
- Persistent negative thoughts and outlook on life
- Frequent complaining, whining, and speaking negatively

- Needing to control others
- Constantly showing off (trying hard to look good to others)
- Talking too much, not letting others speak
- Routinely feeling criticized, blamed, or accused
- Habitually second-guessing and doubting one's abilities
- Feeling like a loser
- Feelings of being ostracized
- Routinely angry
- Habitually losing one's temper
- Extremely perfectionistic
- Frequently feeling put down or put upon
- Few personal boundaries
- Frequent self-hatred (bullying self through negative self-talk, overachieving, perfectionism)

Put a check mark beside the expressions you commonly experience. The more checkmarks you have, and the more frequently you experience the expression, the lower your overall self-worth. The lower your overall self-worth, the more important it is for you to complete this step of the process. Improving your self-worth will go a long way towards healing your wounds and restoring your sense of wholeness. It's important to understand that most everything you truly desire in life will continue to elude you or come at a much higher price than necessary until you do.

From time to time we all experience negative thoughts, angry feelings, and the occasional blues. Additionally, we all periodically complain and doubt ourselves. The problem arises when we let our negative feelings and emotions overtake us to the point where they control our lives. When this occurs, our naturally occurring thoughts, feelings, and emotions turn into our biggest and most powerful demons; little by little they strip us our confidence, self-esteem, and self-respect. Ultimately they undermine our dignity and destroy the very things that would otherwise make our lives pleasurable.

Before we move on I want to make it perfectly clear that you *are not* stuck with your current level of self-worth. I hope this is great news, because it means you have complete control over your level of self-worth. With just a little effort *you can dramatically improve it.* This is possible because for the most part your self-worth is a reflection of how you have been conditioned to see yourself and your experiences. And while you can't change your experiences, at least not your past experiences, you can change how you choose to respond to them. In effect, you can reprogram how you see and react to the events and circumstances in you life – past, present, and future.

How We Lose Our Self-Worth

The main source of our loss of self-worth is almost always our conditioning and programming; that is, it is a reflection of what we have been taught. From birth the majority of us are specifically conditioned to feel inadequate in one way or another, such that our self-worth sustains continuous blows over the course of our lives.

Secondary to our conditioning and programming are our experiences. The reason our experiences are secondary is that how we think, feel, and respond to what occurs in our life is intimately connected to, if not a direct result of, our conditioning and programming. This isn't to say that many of our more traumatic experiences don't negatively affect our self-worth. They can and they do; and for many people the more traumatic or repetitive the experience, the more negatively they are affected.

The degree to which our experiences, traumatic or otherwise, impact our self-worth is highly correlated to how we perceive ourselves. Our perceptions, of our experiences and ourselves, are highly linked to our conditioning and programming. Therefore, what you were taught, that is how you were conditioned, makes a big difference in how your life experiences, including common events like divorce, job loss, and accidents, will affect your self-worth.

To put this into perspective, let's look at the effects of the near opposite conditioning and programming experienced by Sandra and Jesse. Here we have two women who as young girls were both of average intelligence and ability. Both could have easily grown up to be and do many extraordinary things in their lives. However, as with many people the world over, Sandra, throughout childhood, was more often than not neglected and abused. Jesse on the other hand was one of the fortunate ones who were spared many of these and other such offenses.

As a child, Sandra was continually berated and threatened with bodily harm. Nothing she did was ever considered good enough. On an almost daily basis she was slapped around and told to be quiet.

Her family harshly criticized everything she did, said, and was interested in, often telling her that she, her opinions, and her interests were irrelevant. Adding injustice to injustice, Sandra was frequently told she was clumsy and worthless and would never be good at anything. In fact, she was frequently told she had better hope to find some poor fool who would be stupid enough to take care of her, because she would never be able to take care of herself. As a result, Sandra lived in constant fear with no sense of trust in herself or in anyone else. As time passed she became more and more withdrawn, wondering what there was to live for.

Jesse, in contrast, had a happy, supportive, and loving childhood. She was respected and listened to. She was taught that her opinions and feelings matter, that she mattered, and that she could do whatever she set her mind to. Jesse learned from a young age to believe in herself and her abilities. She enjoyed being challenged and trying new things. She learned to trust herself, her instincts, and others. As time passed she became more confident and self-assured; because she was valued and supported she took challenges in stride. As a result she continued to pursue her interests and develop her talents.

As can be expected, Sandra has lived a challenging life in a persistent state of depression and insecurity since early childhood. Her feelings about herself, her life, and most anything she has ever experienced have been understandably negative and self-deprecating. At every turn she has been in and out of a bad relationship, lost her job, or become ill or injured. Over time she began drinking and overeating, ultimately becoming suicidal, all because she truly believes she is worthless and really has nothing to live for.

In Sandra's eyes she is a failure at everything she does, so much so she wonders why should she continue living. She has so thoroughly embodied her conditioning and programming that everything she thinks, does, and experiences is a direct reflection of her instilled belief that she is worthless. She has become what she had been repeatedly conditioned to be.

Jesse's life, as you might imagine, has turned out quite differently from Sandra's. Throughout her youth, Jesse was vibrant and joyous and readily handled the normal ups and downs of life with relative ease. As she grew into a young woman, she remained confident and self-assured, graduating from a prestigious university, and ultimately starting a successful business. Today, she is happily married to a loving man, with whom she raises their teenage daughter.

Jesse's life is exciting and wondrous, with new opportunities at every turn. Each day she is grateful for everything in her life and wonders how her life could be any better. As with Sandra, Jesse has fully embodied her conditioning and programming. However, Jesse has always believed she matters and that she can do great things. Her life, just as Sandra's, directly reflects her beliefs and her sense of worthiness. She, just as Sandra, has become what she was conditioned be. The difference is that Jesse was conditioned to believe she is worthy and has something to offer to the world, while Sandra was conditioned to believe she is worthless and will never amount to anything.

These examples show just how impactful our conditioning and programming can be to our self-worth. They also shed light on how our beliefs and perceptions of ourselves directly affect how we see our experiences. For instance, Sandra becomes very disheartened and extremely depressed when a relationship ends or she loses a job. For her this is just more proof she is a failure and doomed to live a worthless life full of disappointment and hardship. What Sandra has never realized is her belief that she is unworthy, a direct result of her conditioning and sustained abuses, is the root cause of her unfulfilling life, in addition to it being the measure by which she gauges all of her experiences.

From these examples we can see that events such as the ending of relationship or the loss of a job generally have a much greater impact on someone like Sandra than they do on someone like Jesse. This is in large part due to the differences in a person's beliefs and their resulting self-worth. Drawing again from our example we can see the stark contrasts. Where Sandra has a low self-worth and expects failure, Jesse has a high self-worth and expects success. Where Sandra sinks into despair and can't see new possibilities and outcomes, Jesse learns from her experiences and is open to new possibilities. She takes failures in stride knowing they are stepping-stones to success. So in the case of a dissolved relationship or the termination of a job, Jesse understands there are many factors that led to the ending, most having nothing to do with her. She also understands that regardless of how the ending came about there are life lessons to be learned and many more and grander opportunities awaiting her.

The take away here is that persons with a high self-worth more easily move through and beyond their negative feelings and challenging life experiences. Rather than hanging on and being dragged down, they acknowledge their feelings, learn the lessons, and let them go. This allows them to quickly and easily move forward to something equally as good or better than what they lost or gave up. On the flip side, persons with low self-worth tend to let their feelings of inadequacy control them. By maintaining a pessimistic perspective of themselves and life in general, they often spiral more deeply into a hell of their own making, a hell where they have given complete control of their lives to their demons.

How You Can Increase Your Self-Worth

You now know how to recognize your degree of self-worth. You also know a good bit about how you may have lost your self-worth. Most importantly, you know that regardless of where your self-worth stands at the moment (high, low, or somewhere in between), you are worthy of love and living a good life. And finally, you know there is a strong connection between your self-worth, your demons, and your feelings of wholeness. The reality is, the lower your self-worth, the stronger will be your demons' control, and the more broken you will feel. Therefore, one of the first steps to becoming whole again requires that your reclaim your birthright of worthiness.

With every increase to your self-worth you will find yourself less and less bothered by those pesky demons. You'll also notice yourself feeling more and more whole. Ultimately, your demons will be a thing of the past and you'll feel like the whole and amazing being you are.

So how do you go about increasing your sense of self-worth? To explain I'll use an analogy. Think of the impact of your negative conditioning and programming on your self-worth as if it were a personal computer with a virus.

When a computer has a virus detrimental things happen to the operating system, software programs, user files, and sometimes even the hardware. This occurs because of rogue and malicious programs that have been insidiously embedded into the computer's operating system. Their purpose is to manipulate, control, or destroy by corrupting some aspect of the system's programming. The end result is a poorly performing system that ultimately malfunctions. The typical symptoms are decreased processing speed, limited functionality, corrupted information, lost data files, and system crashes.

Depending on the particular virus, the process of corruption can occur quickly or slowly. Very often it occurs slowly, over an extended period, with the user experiencing an ever-diminishing ability to use the system productively.

Using this analogy, think of your negative conditioning and programming as a series of computer viruses that have been embedded into your mind. Some reside in your conscious mind, but most reside in your nonconscious mind where they have been freely running the show for most of your life. The longer they've been embedded, and the more often they've been run (both internally and from your outside environment), the more trouble they will have caused you, with the greatest impact being a significant and detrimental blow to your self-worth.

The trick in both cases, to restoring your self-worth and the proper functioning of the computer, is to eradicate the offending programming by reprogramming and if necessary reconditioning the system. Think of your mind as the operating system, programs, and files that have been infected. Think of your body as the hardware. And think of the state of your life as the result of having run the malicious programs countless times over the course of your life. Is it any wonder your self-worth suffers so greatly when you've been continually running damaging programs designed to bring you down?

Reflecting on Sandra and Jesse's stories it is obvious that Sandra had some very negative programming and conditioning that severely damaged her self-worth and thereby left her challenged to effectively deal with the ups and downs of life. In Jesse's case, her conditioning and programming was much more positive, leaving her with a strong self-worth that has given her considerably greater abilities to gracefully and positively handle life's ups and downs, including any potentially traumatic or devastating experiences.

Negative conditioning, programming, and life experiences can be overcome. Even better, they can be turned into positive attributes and personal qualities. Some of the most effective methods I know for achieving this change are described in this and the following four steps. Each step provides a specific method to help you reprogram and recondition your mind. By implementing the actions in these steps you will very effectively *overwrite* your negative programs and personal sound bytes with more positive and beneficial ones. With repeated application you will ultimately experience high self-worth.

In this step the focus is on loving and honoring yourself. Your ability to love and honor yourself says a lot of about your self-worth, which is directly reflected in the degree of self-confidence, self-esteem, and self-respect you experience.

As will be seen, the more worthy you feel, the more you will automatically love and honor yourself, and the more you love and honor yourself, the more worthy you will feel. When you have reclaimed your birthright of worthiness, your self-worth will begin to soar, with everything in life becoming noticeably easier. You'll find yourself more readily letting go of what has happened to you, and what is going on in and around you. You'll find yourself attracting good things into your life, as if by magic. And ultimately, you'll meet your true self – through whom you'll live a rich, meaningful, and fulfilling life as the whole and complete person you were born to be.

Love and Honor Yourself

You've paid a heavy price for living so long with low self-worth and a lack of self-love and honor, with the result being you don't really know or see you – your true self. Rather, you see an illusion you think is you. And since you don't like the illusion you see, you treat yourself badly and let others treat your badly as well. When you suffer from low self-worth you are often lonely and depressed, feeling as if you'll never really belong, experience real love in your life, or have the good things you desire.

Isn't it time you gave yourself back what is rightfully yours? Isn't it time to quit paying this heavy price? Why wait until someday? Why wait for someone else? Every day you wait to give to yourself what is rightfully yours is a day too long.

Look closely in the mirror. What do you see? Really look. See the person you really are. See the child you once were. See the child that still lives within you. Would you treat a child the way you are treating yourself? Would you say that child is unworthy of love? If your answer is an emphatic NO, as I suspect it is, then realize you are that child and you are just as worthy. It doesn't matter your race, your culture, or your religion. It doesn't matter what you've been taught or what you have experienced. By virtue of the fact that you are here, you are worthy of love. I implore you to have the heart and courage to see the beautiful child you are, to begin loving and honoring her today.

Open your heart and allow yourself to receive the most natural and abundant force there is in this universe – LOVE. The day you begin to truly allow LOVE into your life, will be the day you know you are worthy. On that day your guilt, shame, and fears will begin to subside, never to return. Return to yourself what has always been yours – love, wholeness, and self-worth. The only person who can actually deny you these things is you. There is no one to whom you need prove your worthiness. So don't let anyone let you think otherwise. Begin today to love and honor yourself. Then notice just how quickly your life improves.

In my opinion, being able to love and honor yourself is by far the most transformational piece of the wholeness puzzle. Once you are able to love and give to yourself, everything changes for the better. This transformation process starts with you accepting and believing you are worthy of love and wholeness. It's followed up with practices that teach you how to give to yourself what you need most – unconditional LOVE.

Put Yourself First

"You can look the whole world over and never find anyone more deserving of love than yourself." ~ The Buddha. We all deserve to be put first in our life and we all deserve to be loved and honored. As the Buddha put it, there is no one more deserving than you. Putting yourself first starts with you believing you are worthy: worthy of love, worthy of receiving, worthy of all the good things life has to offer. It is then followed up with you steadfastly loving, honoring, and giving to yourself.

If you can't put yourself first, how can you expect others to put you first? If you can't love, honor, or respect yourself, why would you expect others to love, honor, or respect you? Anything you can't give to yourself or receive with love and gratitude is a sign you feel unworthy.

Stop for a moment. Think about others you know who don't love, honor, or respect themselves. How often do you feel compassion and do things for them, but in time walk away because you've tired of their self-deprecating manner and inability to receive your gifts of love? Probably more often than you realize. Even if you haven't outright walked away from them, the likelihood is you've pulled away, giving them much less attention than you once afforded them. In these cases, the common tendency is to complain about, judge, and avoid the person in question, while wishing they would care more about themselves and feel more deserving.

It is my humble opinion that it is our duty to love and give to ourselves, just as we love and give to others. To be able to truly receive from ourselves, or anyone else, we must first see ourselves as worthy of receiving, be it attention, compliments, love, respect, or anything else we desire.

Understand that the love I am speaking of is not what is commonly referred to as narcissism; but rather, it is a healthy sense of self-respect and the type of self-love that makes us capable of truly giving and receiving whatever we need or desire to ourselves, as well as the ability to truly give to or receive from others.

Always remember, by virtue of the fact you are here, you are therefore worthy. It is your birthright. Remember too, it is cruel for those who raise us, however well meaning, to make us feel and believe we are so unworthy. It is my express belief that this is almost always the result of their own sense of unworthiness and inability to love and honor themselves. Therefore, they use others as their personal punching bags in order to make themselves feel more powerful and deserving.

The Benefits Of Loving and Honoring Yourself

Loving and honoring yourself are the keys to the kingdom of heaven on earth. Until you can love and honor yourself exactly as you are, with all of your perceived imperfections and so-called failures, you will always feel broken and tormented by your demons. Loving and honoring yourself opens the doorway to healing and wholeness.

When you feel whole, you will automatically feel worthy. When you feel worthy, you will automatically experience a greater sense of wholeness. When you love and honor yourself, you will feel worthy. When you feel worthy, you will love and honor yourself. When you love and honor yourself, others will love and honor you. When you deem yourself worthy, others will deem you worthy. Therefore, when you love and honor yourself you will feel worthy. When you feel worthy you will experience good things in your life. In fact, you will attract them with unimaginable ease.

It's all connected. Whether you realize it or not, your self-worth, self-respect, self-confidence, self-esteem, and the general state of your life are all interdependent upon one another. They are also all dependent upon your ability to love and honor yourself.

When you can truly love yourself, just as you are, your life will change in the most amazing ways. You'll feel freer and more confident than ever before. The weight of the world you've been carrying around will be lifted from your shoulders. Your whole world will greatly improve and it will happen very, very quickly.

One of the most amazing effects of loving and honoring yourself is having the feeling that your whole world has changed for the better, seemingly overnight, when basically nothing has yet changed except how you perceive yourself and the possibilities for your life. This feeling opens the door to the life you've to date only dreamt of. Shortly after having begun to regularly love and honor yourself is when you'll see the real changes occur. You'll begin experiencing your desires as your reality, seemingly by magic, all because you now feel worthy.

The magic I'm referring to has to do with who you are being. You can think of it as the energy (vibe) you are putting out. When we have low self-worth we tend to be pessimistic; we think and feel negatively about others, our prospects, and ourselves. In this state we emit a low-vibrational energy that very often repels the very things we really want. In the opposite case, where we have high self-worth, we tend to be optimistic, thinking and feeling positively about our lives in all its many facets. In this state we put out a high-vibrational energy that tends to attract the things we most desire.

Putting this in its most simplistic form, like attracts like. You, your thoughts, and your feelings are all forms of energy. When you are depressed or thinking negative thoughts you emit a lower-vibrational energy resonance than the one you emit when you are happy and thinking positive thoughts.

People who are happy and love their life don't tend to want to spend much time with people who are routinely miserable and hate their life. We see this played out in thousands of ways every day.

Individuals tend to hang out with others whose energy resonance is similar to their own. So if you don't like your circumstances, and you feel like you are continually attracting the wrong types of people into your life, look to your self-worth, your thoughts, and your feelings. Where do they fall on the energy spectrum? Do they tend to be low vibration (negative & pessimistic), high vibration (positive & optimistic), or somewhere in between? The higher they fall on the spectrum, the more good things you will attract into your life.

The energy emitted from your thoughts and feelings, from who you are being, is continually being released and picked up by others. Like energies tend to attract like energies. *Loving and honoring yourself raises your energy level. Therefore, when you love and honor yourself you will attract more desirable circumstances and people into your life. This is the magic.* Learn to love and honor yourself. Believe you are worthy of the best that life has to offer. It will change everything for the better. I know this to be true, because it has always been my experience. I have proven it to myself time and time again, and so will you.

Make The Effort To Love and Honor Yourself

Previously we learned that our self-worth, our ability to love and honor ourselves, and the state of our lives are all connected and interdependent upon one another. Since everything is connected it means we have the ability to improve the quality of our lives by making simple, but significant changes. The specific change I'm referring to is the practice of loving and honoring yourself, which begins with you loving and honoring yourself just as you are today. On the one hand this is as simple as repeatedly telling yourself *"I am worthy"* and *"I love myself"*. On the other hand, it of course takes a bit more effort. Rest assured this is 100% within your ability; with persistence you will be successful.

Improving your self-worth and learning to love and honor yourself just as you are takes time, but not nearly as much as you might think. Remember, you've been beating yourself up, taking yourself for granted, and feeling unworthy and unlovable for a very long time. For most people with low self-esteem, just saying the words *"I love you"* and *"I am worthy"* can be extremely challenging, especially in the beginning. Try it. See what happens? Did you want to argue with yourself and call yourself a liar? Did you experience negative or painful sensations in your body? Whatever occurred, my guess is you struggled and didn't find the words coming easily. However, with continued practice it will become both easy and natural, so much so you'll wonder why you ever found it to be so challenging.

Learning to love and honor yourself won't happen overnight. It's going to some time and practice. With commitment it will soon become second nature. How much time it will take you has a lot to do with how low your self-worth currently is, but more importantly it depends on how strongly you are committed to becoming whole again. The more committed you are the more quickly you will succeed. With the right mindset it is much, much easier than you could ever imagine.

When you love and honor yourself you are being different in the world. You have more presence. You give off a different energy signature. That presence and energy signature is what attracts good things and people into your life.

So put yourself first, know you are worthy, and give yourself the love and honor you deserve. When you can give it to yourself, you will receive it from others. You'll also give more freely to others.

While it may sound counterintuitive, the quickest way to receive love or anything else you desire is to first give it to yourself. By first giving to yourself you reduce or eliminate your clingy needs and expectations of others, which makes you more attractive and automatically draws to you more of what you desire.

As odd as this sounds, it is true. The more you reduce your needs and expectations on others by loving and honoring yourself, the more love and good things you will begin receiving from others. Best of all is the freedom you will experience from loneliness, isolation, and chronic feelings of injustice and depression. With this freedom comes a love unlike any you may have ever known; a love for your life that grows bigger and better each and every day, rewarding you with ever more joy and fulfillment in ways you cannot yet imagine.

I know you are skeptical; but as stated in the previous step, just be open to the possibilities. Stay with me. Believe you are worthy, because you are. Do whatever it takes to really and truly love and honor yourself, beginning with who and how you are right now. The rest will come.

At the end of this step you'll find a variety of practices designed to quickly rebuild your self worth. With dedicated use you'll be loving

42

and honoring yourself with ease in no time at all; thereafter you'll experience more and more of the great things life has to offer.

A Personal Reflection On Worthiness

To put what you've have learned about worthiness in a more tangible light, I'd like to share my personal experience with feeling unworthy, as well as the transformation that occurred when I learned to love and honor myself.

For most of my life I struggled with feelings of unworthiness without actually knowing I felt unworthy. Referring back to the *Signs of Feeling Unworthy* list, there were at least a dozen which were my constant companions. Some of the more predominant ones included 1) feeling like I had to do it all (over-achieving, perfectionism), 2) being overly responsible for others, 3) bullying myself with negative self-talk, 4) feeling unlovable, rejected, and ostracized, 5) feeling routinely criticized and blamed, 6) being defensive, 7) not acknowledging personal boundaries, 8) second guessing myself, and 9) feeling miserably unhappy.

The signs of unworthiness that ultimately got my attention were the ones that presented themselves when everything seemed to be going exceptionally well. In my late twenties, after putting myself through university, landing a very prestigious job, and being in the best relationship of my life, I became aware of a number of unexpected and unexplainable feelings.

Here I was with everything going fortuitously well, having achieved more than I had ever dreamed possible, yet I would routinely find myself feeling completely miserable. Month after month I was plagued with extreme bouts of loneliness, often feeling completely alone even when I was with those I loved. Additionally, I was experiencing chronic mental turmoil, periodic episodes of mild to moderate depression, and unexplainable physical pains that caused me untold fear and suffering.

The effects of my feelings of unworthiness wasn't just the pain and suffering I was experiencing; it was also the ongoing degradation to my self-esteem, self-respect, and self-confidence, which of course was affecting practically everything in my life, from my relationships and career choices to my vacation choices or lack thereof.

What awakened me to my feelings of unworthiness, and put my transformation into motion, was the impact of a few specific comments from a couple of close friends and co-workers, coupled with the abrupt ending of a significant relationship. Two of the comments that shook me to my core were that I was morose and I always got defensive when given a compliment.

The comment about my being morose came from a close co-worker whom I deeply respected. His comment really disturbed me. In fact it completely shocked me. More than anything in the world I wanted to be happy and enjoy life, and now one of my best friends, someone I admired for how fully he lived his life, was telling me I was morose. That one comment was a wakeup call that something significant was going on within me that desperately needed attention. It struck me so deeply that I vowed I would stop at nothing until I understood why I felt so miserable and had turned my feelings around to the point where I loved my life. What I didn't understand at the time, and sadly it took me many more years to realize, was that to succeed at being happy and loving my life I first had to improve my self-worth, which ultimately meant loving and honoring myself.

The second comment, about my becoming defensive when given a compliment, is one that was recurring on a fairly regular basis. Until my early thirties I was extremely challenged with accepting compliments and praise. I would almost always deflect them in some manner. The idea that someone could genuinely compliment, praise, or admire me was a completely alien concept. Until this point in my life genuine compliments and praise were virtually unheard of, and what had previously passed for compliments and praise weren't to be trusted, because the people giving them were usually after something that would ultimately hurt me in some way, or their so-called compliment was derogatory and really meant as a put down. Yet, after hearing over and over again about my defensiveness, and being repeatedly asked why I didn't just say thank you when given a compliment, I realized once again there was something within me that desperately needed attention.

These comments, among others, as well as my less than fulfilling relationship experiences, coupled with my own internal drive to be happy and enjoy life, started me on a path of self-discovery. I dug in. I spent a lot of time on self-reflection. For years I studied the effects of various types of abuse. I also studied and applied a wide range of practices for improving self-esteem, self-confidence, and self-respect.

Along the way I finally learned that most of my pain and struggles were the direct result of a diminished self-worth. I also learned that nothing in my life would improve for long, and most definitely not in the way I desired, until I could love and honor myself.

As I continued my studies and self-reflection I saw vast improvements in the quality of my life and my relationships. However, there was one feeling that continued to plague me, the feeling that I was utterly alone in the world, so much so that I often felt invisible. No matter what I did this feeling kept rearing its ugly head; over and over again it would interfere with my life. I'd be making forward progress, with my life improving on the whole, but still I'd feel stuck. There was a huge hole; something was missing that I couldn't quite place. Whatever it was, I knew it was within me. There was some part of my being that seemed to be missing. The recurring feeling I had was that a key part of my being was irretrievably lost, or at least so well hidden I many never recover it.

As you can imagine, this feeling of being invisible and alone had a tremendous impact on my personal relationships. In all honestly, there were times when I truly wasn't interested in close personal relationships, at least not of the romantic sort. Truth be told, I was afraid to get involved because I didn't want a repeat of my previous painful experiences; in many ways I had effectively closed myself off, basically saying it was better to be alone than to be abused or be with someone and still feel alone.

The effect of this was that I consciously closed myself off to romantic relationships for an extended period, while inadvertently causing all of my relationships to suffer. On the one hand I wanted to have good friends and close relationships, yet because I felt invisible and alone, and wanted no part of a sexual relationship, I was putting out the *vibe* for everyone to stay away. In effect, my feelings, and my thoughts about invisibility and aloneness, were actually making me more invisible and alone. They were invariably keeping me from attracting what I very much desired, with the result being that I felt even more alone.

In time I felt I had overcome my fears and learned what I needed to learn in order to have the relationships I desired. At that point I opened myself up, and did in fact have a few much improved relationships; yet something was still amiss, because I found myself to be adversely affected by a few particular events. A case in point is how devastated I felt when practically overnight I lost my all-time, best friend, who was for me a soulmate; he was the type of friend you think you never want to lose.

The circumstances surrounding this loss don't really matter. What matters is how and why I was so adversely affected. My friend's abrupt exit from my life had little if anything to do with me. He had his own issues with self-worth that are the true source of his departure from my life. But because I was still challenged much of the time to feel worthy of love, and to love and honor myself, it felt very personal. During the course of our relationship I was also experiencing a number of significant challenges in my career. The combined effect made it feel like everything in my life was against me (although in truth it was all perfect, much like the storm that clears the way for amazing new developments that couldn't otherwise be seen or realized).

It was at this point, after years of concerted effort to reinvent myself and my life, that I came to realize that what I really wanted in life wasn't going to materialize until I changed me, or rather accepted, loved, and became all of me. This meant I had to move beyond my darkest secrets. I had to recover and love the parts of myself that felt utterly lost to my most horrific experiences. I had to overcome my demons and become whole again. I had to learn to trust myself, to trust others, to acknowledge my boundaries, to be honest about my feelings, to speak my truth, to be my *true* self, and to celebrate my life.

This realization was the biggest turning point in my life. It was at this point I made a huge decision; I decided I was going to put everything in my life, except for my job, on hold for a few months, while I learned to love and honor myself. And only after I could love myself would I return to pursuing anything else. Taking this tact had its risks, but the alternative of continuing to live with the effects of a diminished self-worth seemed completely unacceptable. As I saw it, nothing I did really mattered if I couldn't love and honor myself. Until I could truly love myself I would continue having similarly unfulfilling experiences across all facets of my life.

This decision was by far the most important and transformative of my life, the result of which has opened doors upon doors of possibilities and new opportunities. Within the span of a few months after making this decision, new people and amazing experiences began showing up in my life, while the less desirable ones quickly faded away. Best of all my feelings of being utterly alone completely dissolved. To be completely forthright, the decision to do whatever it took to truly love and accept myself was just the first step.

The real healing and transformation occurred in the coming months. In less than nine months of fairly regular practice, which included reading, journaling, working with a life coach, and attending a very profound workshop that got to the heart of who I am (where I had the opportunity to heal by sharing and learning to see my life experiences with new perspective), I emerged reborn.

The best way I can think to describe this rebirth is like a reptile after it has shed its skin. I had shed my old feelings of unworthiness and un-lovability, as well as the stigmatizing guilt and shame I had been carrying as the result of the sexual and psychological abuses I had suffered as a child and young adult. The old skin of restrictive feelings was replaced with the new, suppler skin of self-love, self-worth, and self-acceptance, which dramatically increased my self-esteem and self-confidence, virtually overnight.

One of the most surprising effects of this transformation was my newfound ability to freely share stories about my most traumatic and shameful experiences. Where before I had assumed that anyone who knew the truth of my experiences would either reject me or think badly of me, even though I had little if any power to control or stop the perpetrators, the reality was just the opposite. When I opened myself up and allowed myself to be vulnerable, I was loved and accepted as never before. I took a chance and stood in my power. I allowed the real me to authentically and courageously emerge. Each time I've allowed this I've noticed it was becoming easier and easier. Additionally, the things I had previously felt unworthy of simply began showing up. But most surprising of all was the discovery of how much allowing myself to be vulnerable and courageous was helping others to open up, heal, and transform their own lives.

It's an amazing feeling when you can freely give and receive real love, in all of its various forms. Most amazing of all is the feeling you get when people recognize and appreciate you for being the inspiration that moves them to take action and heal themselves, all because you were courageous enough to love and honor yourself, and thereby be the person you were born to be.

I hope that sharing some of my personal experiences has given you a healthy sense of why your level of self-worth and your ability to love and honor yourself is so fundamental to you overcoming your demons and becoming whole again. I freely admit this was one of the most challenging pieces of the puzzle for me to come to terms with. For me this was the piece that completed the picture. You might even say it was the cornerstone. Until this stone was put into place I was constantly spinning, searching, and rebuilding because none of the other pieces were strong enough to support the rest.

This missing cornerstone is like a house that is missing a piece of its foundation. The missing piece causes weakness in the integrity of the foundation, which in turn creates ongoing instabilities that constantly cause stress-induced damage and disrepair to the rest of the structure. Despite repeated attempts through temporary abatements and patchwork, the damage continues to worsen until the underlying foundational problem is resolved. Your self-worth is that foundation. You repair it by loving and honoring yourself.

Actions To Increase Your Self-Worth

"He who is plenteously provided for from within needs but little from without." ~ Goethe. As stated earlier in this step, to feel worthy you must love and accept yourself. When you love and accept yourself, others will love and accept you in turn. Loving and accepting yourself is what allows you to live a life of wholeness. Start today. Believe you are worthy. Make the decision to love and honor yourself.

By applying the following practices you will create a solid foundation for the rest of the steps in this program.

1. **Repeat the following declarations, with feeling, at least five times each morning and evening. Put as much emotion into it as possible. Really feel it.**
   - I am worthy of love.
   - I am worthy of all the good things life has to offer.
   - I deserve to be treated well.
   - I am loved.
   - I love and accept myself just as I am.
   - I love myself. I really love myself.
   - I am whole.
   - I LOVE MY LIFE!

2. **Tell yourself I LOVE YOU.**

Look at yourself in the mirror. See the child within. Show compassion and love for that child. Tell her how much you love her. Repeat to her with lots of feeling "I LOVE YOU *your name*." Tell her again and again how much you love her, just as she is. Tell her she is worthy and you will take care of her.

Don't worry if you don't believe yourself. Just keep telling yourself I LOVE YOU. In a brief time it'll become very, very easy; so easily you'll wonder why you found it to be so difficult.

3. **Acknowledge your feelings.**

Be honest about your feelings. Your feelings are your feelings. Accept them without judgment. You feel what you feel. Almost all feelings are a variant of glad, sad, mad, or afraid. Learn to understand exactly what you are feeling and why.

Knowing what you feel and why you feel it will improve the quality of your life. When you are honest about your feelings you will make better decisions. Being aware of your feelings, understanding them, and honestly expressing them will allow you to effectively respond to the events in your life, rather than habitually reacting to them nonconsciously.

Don't be surprised if you aren't sure what you feel. This is common to those who feel unworthy. Because of conditioning and programming, and the various coping mechanisms we've put into place to deal with traumas and abuses, we often hide our feelings and emotions; sometimes we will learn to depend on a particular emotion, such as anger, to stand in for all of our emotions. Over time this causes us to lose touch with what we are really feeling.

One of the best ways I've found to explore and work through your feelings and emotions is to keep a journal. When you have feelings and emotions that trouble you, or that you don't understand, take a few moments to write about them in your journal. Just let it flow. You'll be surprised at what you discover. Your true self is always speaking to you, but you've learned to ignore the voice. Journaling helps you to hear and ultimately reconnect with that voice.

4. Acknowledge your personal boundaries.

Define the ways in which it is safe and permissible for people to behave toward or around you. It is your right to protect and defend yourself. Acknowledging your boundaries will help you to do this. It also tells other people the ways in which it is acceptable to treat you.

Boundaries are meant to protect us; they help us take care of ourselves. Boundaries vary from soft to rigid, with flexible boundaries being the healthiest. People with soft boundaries are easily manipulated and hurt; they may also manipulate others. They allow almost anything in. The more extreme in this category will completely lose themselves in others; they don't recognize any boundaries at all between themselves and other people. On the other hand, people with rigid boundaries tend to be closed off physically and/or emotionally. They keep everything and everyone out. Between these two groups are people with spongy boundaries. These people fluctuate between the soft and rigid extremes not knowing what to let in and what to keep out.

Ideally you want to have flexible boundaries that give you control without being overly soft or rigid. You want to decide specifically what is allowable to let in and what must be kept out so that it is difficult for anyone to manipulate, use, or violate you.

Without well-defined boundaries it is difficult to define yourself as an individual. You tend to be unsure of yourself, including your likes, dislikes, thoughts, feelings, and opinions. Knowing and acknowledging your personal boundaries puts you in control of your life; it communicates to you and others that you respect yourself and have a healthy self-worth. Demand that you are worth it. Start by demanding it from yourself.

5. Give and receive fully.

Whenever you are giving to yourself or someone else it is best to give fully. The same goes for receiving. This is a practice that will take some effort since you are not used to giving to yourself, or truly receiving what is given to you from someone else. For now, start with little things like accepting and giving compliments, and giving and receiving hugs.

When someone gives you a compliment just accept it with grace. No defensiveness, just say *thank you,* or, if appropriate, *I really appreciate that.* When giving a compliment or praise be sincere.

Give and receive as many real hugs as often as you possibly can. Make sure you feel safe; then go for it. Hold the hug for at least six seconds to experience the positive benefits. If hugs are outside of your comfort zone then push yourself. Don't wait for someone else to give you a hug. Go up and ask them if you can give them one.

Real and heartfelt hugs are amazing healers. Research has proven that hugging dramatically improves our physical, emotional, and spiritual well-being. It releases the hormone oxytocin, which increases our pain threshold, our feelings of optimism, and our self-esteem, as well as a long list of other positive and beneficial effects, some of which include reduced stress, decreased levels of depression, and a reduction in social anxieties.

We are social beings and physical touch is a necessity for our well-being. It is such a necessity that many psychology journals have reported that we need on the order of four hugs per day just for survival, eight for maintenance, and twelve for growth. It is a well-known fact that babies who are not touched do not flourish, and many perish. As adults, we have many of the same needs. Give hugs a try. You'll notice an immediate improvement in your well-being.

6. Celebrate!

Celebrate small achievements by rewarding yourself. You deserve it.

You're used to being beaten up, by yourself and by others. By celebrating your small victories you will quickly increase your self-esteem and your self-worth. Celebrating is a way to show you respect yourself. When you respect yourself, others will also respect you.

Celebrating is simple. There are thousands of possibilities. Find those that speak to you and give you pleasure. A few of my favorites include going for an evening walk at sunset, getting a massage, visiting museums and art galleries, and reading for pleasure. When I'm pressed for time, I enjoy a spending a few minutes outside with a cup of tea, or putting on music and dancing for 10-15 minutes.

Celebrating doesn't have to cost much or take much time. There are countless ways that cost absolutely nothing. The point is to take some time for just for you, just because, just for fun. You don't need a specific reason. Being alive is reason enough. Remember, you are worth it.

The following list provides a variety of free or inexpensive ways you can celebrate you. Feel free to use this list or create your own. Starting today, begin making celebrations a regular part of your life.

a. Take the day off and do something you enjoy
b. Go for a walk
c. Pursue your favorite hobby
d. Get a massage
e. Have a date night with a girlfriend (or guy friend)
f. Spend time with a loved one
g. Visit a museum
h. Play on the beach
i. Take a bubble bath
j. Have a cup of tea
k. Give yourself quite time with a good book or your favorite music (or both)
l. Get takeout and watch a movie
m. Buy yourself a new outfit
n. Take a nap
o. Take yoga or tai chi class
p. Watch your favorite TV program
q. Play with your children – allow yourself to be a kid again
r. Enjoy a few minutes in the great outdoor
s. Visit a botanical garden
t. Meditate
u. Dance – just for the fun of it
v. Sing – as if only 'God' could hear
w. Play a long neglected instrument or sport
x. Spend an afternoon volunteering – doing something that enlivens your spirit (perhaps a pre-school classroom)
y. Call a friend to catch up
z. Plan a trip

Until you make the unconscious conscious, it will
direct your life and you will call it fate.
-Carl Jung

Step 3 – Cultivate Awareness: Trust Your Inner Guide

Lisa's Story

Lisa's life has largely been one of mistrust, of herself and of others. As a result of her youth being fraught with neglect and all sorts of physical, psychological, and sexual abuse, she became extremely hypercritical, hypersensitive, and hypervigilant. With her nervous system in a state of constant overdrive, she became increasingly anxious, stressed, and overwhelmed. Additionally, because she was so used to living in a threatening and chaotic environment, she had the habit of nonconsciously recreating many of the painful circumstances of her youth because it felt 'normal', which roughly translates as feeling alienated, used, and never being good enough.

By her mid-thirties this pattern had become a vicious cycle that would leave her feeling physically ill and psychologically drained, to the point where she was frequently unable to cope with the day-to-day demands of life. At times Lisa wondered if she was going crazy, because she just couldn't understand why she was becoming more and more fearful, distrustful, and depleted. On the surface Lisa's life appeared to be great, but deep down she was so traumatized she couldn't see her own beauty or the goodness in her life.

In a misguided attempt to feel better, Lisa began periodically disappearing without word for days to weeks at a time. During these periods she would isolate herself, hoping the down time would help her to cope with her ever-intensifying pains, fears, and anxieties. However, rather than recuperating during these down times, Lisa found she was in fact becoming increasingly more anxious and depressed.

As a mostly nonconscious counter-measure to her depression, Lisa fell into the trap that is common to many people suffering from increasing anxieties or depression. She slipped into a number of self-destructive behaviors, including endless sleeping, excessive drinking, and taking high-doses of sleeping pills and painkillers, as a desperate measure to escape her pain. The result of this vicious cycle was increased self-loathing and an ever-greater mistrust of herself and humanity, much of which was brought on by the whispers and rumors being circulated about her being psychologically unstable and a significant risk to the project she currently worked on, as well as to her friends and co-workers.

The turning point in this cycle occurred following her most significant and lengthy disappearance. Having become so completely depressed and despondent, Lisa ended up locking herself in her room for nearly two months, during which time she completely ignored all of her friends, family, and responsibilities.

During this particular shutdown, several of Lisa's anxieties very nearly became self-fulfilling prophecies. Having ignored all of her responsibilities so completely, she very nearly lost her highly prestigious job, and in due course was evicted from the home she had shared with her best friend for the previous eight years. One of the key reasons she wasn't fired can be attributed to her housemate, a respected employee and co-worker, who intervened and explained that Lisa was suffering from what appeared to be a nervous breakdown.

Because of the nature and length of her absence, Lisa's employer required that she submit to a period of psychological counseling before returning to work. During her counseling sessions Lisa learned she had a very negative self-image, many self-destructive habits, and a cornucopia of coping mechanisms that were no longer working. Ultimately she learned to recognize the sources of her anxieties and mistrust, the very same sources that were now causing her to spiral out of control so completely that she was frequently and increasingly unable to function in any seemingly normal capacity.

Over the course of several months Lisa learned to see herself and her life in a whole new light; she also learned how to listen from within. Today she is increasingly able to trust her intuition and her instincts. Through the practice of mindful awareness, Lisa has learned to recognize her self-defeating patterns of thought and behavior, and is now able to respond to her thoughts, feelings, and the various situations in her life in a healthful and productive manner. Additionally, she has gradually been learning to love and respect herself; as a result she has vastly improved her self-image. Equally as important, she has learned to acknowledge and enforce safe and beneficial personal boundaries that have dramatically reduced her mistrust of others and her need for hypervigilance.

Today, Lisa very quickly recognizes when she begins falling into any of her old, self-destructive behaviors. She understands these self-destructive behaviors are nothing more than misguided reactions to old triggers being set off by painful thoughts, feelings, or situations that resemble those she previously had little power to understand or control. She also realizes the childhood coping mechanisms she had developed to handle these situations no longer serve her best interests.

Whenever Lisa catches herself reverting to any of her old self-destructive behaviors, she stops, takes a deep breath, and listens within. By listening within she is able to take measure of what is really going on, after which she can consciously respond in an appropriate manner, as opposed to nonconsciously reacting in one of her previous habitual fashions.

The Importance Of Awareness

Awareness is a vital step in the healing process. In fact it is absolutely essential. Without it, you are beholden to the whims of habit and your own misunderstandings and misperceptions of yourself and the situations in your life. With it life is full of wonder and possibility. Awareness gives you the power to effectively change what doesn't serve you.

In this step, we begin to peel the layers so you can become reacquainted with your true self. To do this we will employ the essential practice of mindful awareness. Through mindful awareness you will learn to a) spot when and how your demons are in control, b) recognize the messages received from your inner guide, whom you typically ignore, and c) begin trusting yourself, possibly for the very first time.

Before we dive in please take a moment to congratulate yourself for having come this far. Well done. You've made a big decision and have shown true commitment, which tells me you believe you are worthy of overcoming your demons in order to restore your innate wholeness and live the extraordinary life you were born to live.

I know for many of you the thought of getting to know your *true* self is a scary proposition. I'll venture to guess that just mentioning it invoked some fear. Let me assure you this is a common reaction and one you will ultimately find unwarranted.

To provide perspective on this fearful feeling let's look at a few of the common reasons why we often feel getting to know ourselves is such a scary ordeal:

1. We've been blindly assuming we *do* know ourselves, and are afraid to find out that our assumptions are wrong.
2. We've been lying to others about who we are, and are afraid the truth will come out.
3. We've been being the person others expect us to be or think we should be, and now fear disappointing them by choosing to be who we know in our heart and soul we really are.
4. We know we don't really know ourselves, and now we'll finally have to admit it and do something about it.
5. We're afraid if others find out who we really are, they won't like us.

These reasons are nothing more than negative thought patterns that reflect the hold our demons have on us. Instilled through our conditioning, programming, and various life experiences, these insidious thoughts will continue to bully us for as long as we continue to give them validity. By cultivating an awareness of our self-image, thought patterns, physical and emotional feelings, and various coping mechanisms, which include our habits, we can quickly break free of our demons' shackles. And when we break free we see there is nothing to fear.

This means getting to know and understand yourself, so that you may more effectively respond to your thoughts, feelings, and desires, both the positive and the negative. When you know and understand yourself, you will make better and more informed decisions. You will understand why you think and believe as you do. You will know why something makes you happy or sad. You will know why you like or dislike like something. And you will understand why particular things influence and motivate you, while others do not, which will allow you to effectively change the things you don't like about yourself and your life.

By cultivating mindful awareness you will learn to trust yourself, trust in others, and ultimately change how you respond to the situations and circumstances in your life. In short order you will recognize and understand your coping mechanisms, your personal boundaries or the lack thereof, your personal self-image, and your self-defeating habits and thought patterns, including those you use to dull or temporarily escape your chronic fears, pains, and anxieties. You will also begin to recognize how each of these have played out in your life to date, and thus understand why your life is as it is.

Awareness is a powerful tool. In many ways it is the most important of the healing tools, because without awareness none of the other tools have a chance of providing a lasting effect. With awareness your demons, whose favorite pastime it is to continually torment you in every conceivable manner, will quickly begin to fade from your life. Used in conjunction with the tools provided in the remaining steps of this book, your demons don't stand a chance.

Since awareness is so crucial to healing and becoming whole again, I'd like you to consider this quote from Pema Chödrön: *"The most fundamental aggression to ourselves, the most fundamental harm we can do to ourselves, is to remain ignorant by not having the courage and the respect to look at ourselves honestly and gently."*

What came up for you when you read Pema's words? Was there an awareness that wasn't there before? What were your thoughts? Did you have an epiphany, agree with the sentiment, or go into denial? I hope you had an epiphany, or were at least in agreement, because that means you are totally open to making mindful awareness a regular part of your life. If you were in denial, that's ok – it just means your demons are asserting their control and you have yet to recognize their true face.

If you are in denial, even a little bit, restate your commitment to becoming whole again. Begin focusing on all the benefits you will receive by becoming consciously aware. This puts you back in control, which is vitally important to your health and well-being, because being in denial is much the same as turning a blind eye. As illustrated in Lisa's story, turning a blind eye can make us spiral out of control, leaving us at the complete mercy of our demons.

Cultivating awareness opens the door to freedom: freedom from pain, freedom from self-doubt, and most of all freedom from those pesky demons that incessantly bully you. So let's get started bringing awareness into the forefront of your life. In no time at all you'll be skipping with joy and excitement for all of the newly emerging possibilities you see for your life.

Recognizing The Controlling Faces Of Your Demons

Our demons are quite insidious. They subtly, stealthily, and often alluringly trap and ensnare us into their control through their cunning and seemingly innocuous ways of getting us to repeatedly turn away from our true selves. Through their whispers and tricks, little by little they steal away our lives. Their control shows itself in many ways. Here we will look at just a few of the more obvious and common ways they can easily be recognized through the practice of mindful awareness.

Poor Self-Image

We all have a mental image of ourselves that depicts how we see and think of ourselves, both mentally and physically. Our self-image often also includes how we perceive others as seeing us. This image typically results from our conditioning, programming, and life experiences. Internalized criticisms and judgments from others are probably the two most influential factors involved in creating our self-image. However, nothing is cut and dry, and anything and everything from the media to major life changes can and do affect our self-image over the course of our lives.

Self-image describes the traits and characteristics we see in ourselves. These traits can be either positive or negative. Positive characteristics include seeing ourselves as smart, intelligent, talented, resourceful, attractive, beautiful, kind, loving, etc. They focus on our assets and potential, while simultaneously being realistic about our limitations. Negative characteristics include seeing ourselves as dumb, stupid, ugly, misshapen, selfish, worthless, a screw-up, and so on. They focus on our perceived weaknesses and faults, with a tendency to distort small imperfections and failures.

The characteristics we collectively put together to describe ourselves, based on our experiences and what is mirrored back to us from peers, friends, family, and other personal relationships, becomes our self-image. However, that image may not be an accurate representation of who we are. In fact, most often it is not. Most often our self-image is nothing more than the misguided way we have learned to see ourselves, and thankfully we have the ability to change that image.

Whether you realize it or not, your self-image is critical to your well-being. It directly affects how you think and feel about yourself, as well as how you respond to the events in your life. It's the key factor in determining the quality of your relationships, including your relationship with yourself. It plays a significant role in your successes and your failures. It's largely responsible for your overall outlook on life. In short, your self-image affects every aspect of your physical, mental, social, emotional, and spiritual well-being. Lisa's story is a prime example.

As your self-image is so important to your well-being, it's a very good thing you have the power to recreate it. And that power begins with awareness.

Recognizing a Poor Self-Image

Truthfully answer the following questions. They will provide you with a fairly accurate picture of your personal self-image. Pay close attention to how often your responses cast you in a negative light. The more negatives you have, the unhealthier your self-image, and therefore the more critical it is for you to become skilled in the art of awareness. If you are fortunate enough to have a healthy self-image, you will very much want to continue nurturing it.

- What do I believe people think about me?
    o Is it positive or negative?
    o Does it focus on my strengths, assets, and successes, or my weaknesses, imperfections, and failures?
    o Does it match what I know about myself?

- How do I describe myself?
    - What characteristics do I list? Are they positive or negative?
    - Do I focus on my assets and possibilities, or my weaknesses, limitations, and failures?
    - Do I routinely compare myself to others I believe are more gifted, talented, intelligent, or successful? If so, does this comparison make me feel like a failure or does it inspire me?
- How do I describe my body?
    - Do I focus on perceived imperfections?
    - Do I constantly compare myself to others I see as more beautiful or attractive?
    - Do I tend to use food, alcohol, or drugs to cover up or change how I feel?
    - Do I tend to use clothes, cosmetic surgeries, or other means to hide from the world or feel better about myself?
- Am I routinely hard on myself?
    - Do I routinely put myself down and think negative things about myself, or my life?
    - Do I have difficulty accepting compliments?
    - Am I overly humble about my achievements?
    - Do I give myself credit for my achievements or do I discount them?
- Do I pretend to be someone I'm not so others will like me or give me attention?
    - Am I always giving up myself for others?
    - Am I doing what I'm doing to please others or to live up to their expectations of me?
    - Am I putting on airs and falsely puffing myself up?

Don't despair if you currently have a poor self-image. Before the end of this process you'll have the awareness you need to create a beautiful self-image that will support you in creating the life you desire.

A word of caution: Most of us tend to be resistant to changing our self-image, even when that image is inaccurate and harmful to our well-being. Understand your resistance is nothing more than your demons doing what they will to maintain their control. Be brave. Step into your power. With a little practice using the tools provided throughout this book you will overcome them, while simultaneously creating a healthy and supportive self-image. As your self-image improves so will the quality of your life.

Self-Defeating Thought Patterns

Thoughts are a constant part of our lives. Research shows we have somewhere on the order of 60,000 thoughts per day. Most of these thoughts are nonconscious and repetitive. When we have a negative self-image and low self-worth our thoughts tend to be pessimistic and self-defeating. Thought patterns, be they self-serving or self-defeating, are learned behaviors most often linked to our early conditioning, programming, and life experiences.

Self-defeating thought patterns are typically irrational. They come in all shapes and sizes. The following provides a few of the more common patterns you should find familiar.

1. **All-or-Nothing Thinking:** Seeing things as all black or all white; total failure or complete success. There is no in-between, no gray area. It is either perfect or you have failed. A single bite of cake and you've blown your diet, so you might as well eat the whole thing.

2. **Assumptions and Jumping to Conclusions:** Interpreting something negatively with no facts to support your conclusion. For instance, you decide custard tastes bad without having tried it, or you conclude a friend is avoiding you when in fact they are busy taking care of their ailing parent and have no idea you'd like to get together.

3. **Discounting Accomplishments:** Discounting, overlooking, or rejecting your accomplishments and positive experiences. To your discounting mind they either don't count or don't meet some impossible standard you've set for yourself. For example, you do an outstanding job and get promoted. You tell yourself and others *"it's nothing, anyone could have done it"*. You didn't even think you did a particularly good job.

4. **Overgeneralizing Events:** Turning a single negative event into the pattern of your life. A single criticism becomes *"Everyone is always criticizing me."* A single rejection becomes *"I'll never have another date."* Overgeneralizing is recognizable through the use of defeatist statements containing *always* or *never*.

5. **Would, Could, and Should Statements:** *Would, could, should, must, ought,* and *have to* statements are all ways of expressing expectations and judgments. We commonly use these statements with the misguided purpose of motivating ourselves or other people. In reality the use of these types of statements usually backfires making us want to do anything but what is stated. Most often we get upset at whoever issues the statement, feeling rebellious, guilty, frustrated, angry, or disappointed depending on the expectation set or not met.

6. **Selective Mental Filtering:** Focusing and obsessing over a minor negative detail buried amongst many positive details. For example, you pull off a lavish reception for your best friend's wedding. It's a total success. Everyone compliments you except for one person who makes a snide comment about your positioning of the guests. That one negative comment, buried among hundreds of positive ones, has you in an uproar and feeling down for days; you've completely ignored all of the positive feedback to the exclusion of one minor criticism.

7. **Predicting Failure:** Predicting negative outcomes for future events in your life. For instance, before an upcoming job interview, you tell yourself *"I know I'm going to blow it. What am I going to do if I don't get the job? How will I feed my kids?"* or before going on a ski trip you tell yourself *"I'll probably break my leg. Who do I think I am anyway? I'm not a skier."* when you've never even tried it. Hey, you might be a natural.

8. **Magnifying Realities:** Exaggerating the size and importance of your problems and shortcomings, while most often minimizing your desirable qualities and attributes.

This is the equivalent of making mountains out of molehills while simultaneously making yourself out to have little to no capacity to deal with the situation or make a positive contribution.

9. **Labeling – Both Ourselves and Others:** Labeling is a form of nicknaming that comes with a negative side effect; we tend to treat people, including ourselves, based on the labels we give them. Labels are very often given as a result of some action that rubs us the wrong way. For instance, we make a mistake and call ourselves a fool, loser, or failure, with the consequence being we lose confidence and continue to think of ourselves as such. Or, we resort to calling the woman in the next office a *"whiny bitch"* because we find the tone of her voice annoying, and thereafter we treat her as such.

10. **Unfairly Comparing Ourselves:** Unfairly comparing ourselves to other people without having sufficient information to make the comparison. Example: You believe your neighbors have all the things you desire and are living the good life without knowing what their lives are really like. Examples abound. We think we lack something that others have, when the reality is we just have it in a different form, or we falsely compare apples to oranges in complete ignorance of our blunder.

Since our thoughts have such a dramatic effect on our well-being they will be covered in detail in the following step. For the moment, becoming aware of your repetitious and self-defeating thoughts is sufficient.

Negative Habits and Coping Mechanisms

Whether you realize it or not, you have a number of negative habits and coping mechanisms. Almost everyone has at least a few. But those of us with a multitude of merciless demons typically have a lengthy list, the majority of which we developed as children to protect ourselves from the stresses, anxieties, and disappointments that were a routine part of our lives. At the time, they were beneficial.

They helped us deal with things we didn't understand, had yet to develop the means to handle, or had little to no control to change.

As adults, most of these habits and coping mechanisms have become albatrosses we are unaware are encumbering our lives. They are so ingrained and automatic it is as if they have become a part of who we are. However, the reality is they are nothing more than habitual behaviors we still employ because we have yet to learn effective means for dealing with our feelings, emotions, and the various stresses in our lives. Recognize these habits and coping mechanisms are not who you are. Realize you have the power to change them whenever you choose. If you feel like you can't change them, understand this is nothing more than your demons standing their ground. They don't want you to replace these habits and coping mechanisms because they would lose their favorite playground, along with their control.

For the purposes of this discussion, habits and coping mechanisms are defined as the nonconscious physiological actions, learned behaviors (often nonconscious), and purposely developed skills we employ to reduce our stress and anxiety levels, as well as many of our intense emotions. These are most often applied to what are referred to as negative stresses and emotions, but those who have been excessively abused or traumatized will often apply them to their positive stresses and emotions as well.

On the surface these habits and coping mechanisms sound like a good thing. Some in fact are, but many as we will see are downright detrimental to our well-being, especially when employed long-term. A good example of this is highlighted in Lisa's story. When Lisa became extremely overwhelmed her depression intensified. When she reached a certain threshold she would withdraw from life. But withdrawal, a form of disengagement, didn't solve Lisa's problems; it only served to exacerbate her underlying anxieties and create new and bigger problems for her to deal with (remember, she nearly lost her job and was evicted from her home, both of which are major stressors on their own).

Habits and coping mechanisms employed as a means of escape only increase our demons control. Although avoiding our stresses, responsibilities, and problems may at times provide temporary relief, it is never beneficial over the long run. Repeated and long-term avoidance only brings us more of what we are so desperately trying to escape. Taking back your control begins with awareness.

The following are some of the more common negative habits and coping mechanisms we employ to manage our feelings, emotions, anxieties, and stresses. Some are equally a form self-defeating thoughts.

1. **Addictions (TV, Food, Alcohol, Drugs, Shopping, Video Games, Gambling, Exercise, Social Media, Sex, etc.)**
    The use of these activities or substances most often begins as an inconsequential means of releasing stress, tempering anxieties, or dulling physical pain. Through their repeated use they often become an addiction. At their extreme, they can take complete control of our life. A few even masquerade as seemingly healthy activities, such as exercise. However, if it has taken over our life to the point that we neglect family, friends, and responsibilities, it's no longer a healthy activity.

2. **Disengagement (Excessive Sleeping, Fantasizing, Daydreaming, Isolating Oneself)**
    Disengagement is the act of disconnecting, detaching, or withdrawing ourselves from something we find boring or unpleasant. Brief periods of disengagement are actually normal, such as with daydreaming. However, any excessive form of disengagement has in effect become a coping mechanism for something we are unwilling to deal with.

3. **Passive-Aggressive Actions**
    This type of action is an indirect expression of a thought or feeling we fear expressing directly. It involves expressing our aggressions in subtle, passive, and indirect ways. It manifests itself in a variety of ways, such as learned helplessness, sullenness, resentment, joking to cover hostility, and deliberately failing to meet obligations.

4. **Denial**
    Denial is the refusal or inability to accept some aspect of our reality. In effect, we put blinders on, pretending something is different than it actually is in order to make it more acceptable, such as only seeing the good or bad traits in a child or spouse. Examples include choosing to believe your

husband is working late on a project when you know he is having an affair, seeing only the good traits in your partner when in fact he frequently beats you, and being convinced you are gaining weight because your mother was heavy, not because you have a double mocha latte and sweet roll every morning.

5. Rationalization

Rationalization is the process of making up reasons to justify our emotional choices (e.g., going shopping), because we don't want to accept the real reasons (i.e., it's how we cope with disappointment or anger despite the consequences – such as buying a new pair of shoes when we couldn't really afford them or didn't actually need them).

6. Blame (including self-blame)

Regular blame is the act of making someone or something else responsible for our thoughts, feelings, and actions. Self-blame is the act of making ourselves responsible for the thoughts, feelings, and actions of others. Self-blame is very typical of those who have been or are being abused or manipulated. It is a key feature of someone with a victim self-image. Blame of either type gives away our control. It leads to helplessness, hopelessness, and despair.

7. Intellectualization

Intellectualization is the process of dealing with something unpleasant by focusing all of your attention on it, such as reading everything you can on the grieving process after the loss of a parent or child.

8. Excessive/Misplaced Humor

This is the habit of frequently using humor to deflect unpleasant thoughts and feelings. It can include laughing in inappropriate situations or using humor that is inappropriate to the situation. It is most often used to draw attention away from ourselves, our lack of confidence or preparedness, or some blunder we have made.

9. **Excessive Talking**

   Excessive talking is a common coping mechanism associated with incessant stress and anxiety caused from living in an environment that exposes the excessive talker to frequent or prolonged abuse, neglect, violence, hard deadlines, natural disasters, or other extremely high stress situations. The affected person will talk and talk and talk, often about nothing in particular, as a means to quell their anxiety.

10. **Workaholism**

    Workaholism is the tendency to avoid dealing with various problems and other unpleasantness in our lives by burying ourselves in our work. The workaholic most often sees their devotion to their work (office) as their duty, rather than their choice.

Recognizing and Trusting The Guiding Messages From Within

You are the most important person in your life, but how often do you really pay attention to the real you? How often do you hear and pay attention to the messages coming from your inner guide? Probably not very often.

You may be wondering just who this inner guide is. She goes by many names, but you can think of *her* as your spirit, soul, intuition, higher self, or guiding angel, whose purpose is to make available the inborn natural wisdom that is programmed into your being.

We are all born with the wisdom and knowledge we need to love, reach our potential, and lead meaningful and fulfilling lives. This wisdom and knowledge is buried within our bodies and the recesses of our subconscious. Our inner guide helps us to access this wisdom and bring it into our consciousness. Her messages are most often received through nonconscious feelings such as hunches and flashes of insight, as well as physical sensations, including the infamous gut reaction.

These messages are typically direct, straightforward, and brief. They frequently show up as strong, straightforward energy feelings that translate in our minds as *"YES!"*, *"GO!"*, *"You have got to do this!"*, *"Do this..."*, *"Now do that..."*, *"NO"*, *"Stay away"*, and so on.

There is no explanation, no elaboration, and no justification. Neither is there any worry about the opinion of others.

The messages from our inner guide are attempting to lead us in the direction we need to go in order for us to be the person we were born to be. They are an expression of love that comes from the heart (or soul). Yet we often experience them as scary and contradictory to the path we are currently on. This occurs because the direction they are leading us may be unfamiliar; it can also appear they are directing us away from the safety and security that has become our rational mind's preoccupation.

One of the greatest rewards we receive when we follow the guidance of our inner guide is how much more alive we feel. Even with uncertainties and new challenges, we feel less resistance; we are more aligned and harmonious with ourselves, which leads to more excitement about our lives. Following our inner guide requires no struggle or will power. When we are truly following our inner guide we feel as if we are going with the flow of the river rather than against it. The best way I know to illustrate this is with a personal example.

While attending a three-day, personal-growth conference some years ago, I received what may be the most powerful and emphatic message I have ever received my inner guide. At the time I was mentally and spiritually in a very low place, not particularly wanting to be where I was, despite having been extremely excited about attending the event for almost a year. On the morning of the second day a gentleman spoke who touched me in ways I can't begin to describe. As with most of the speakers he would at the end of his presentation make an offer for a product or follow-on workshop. Knowing this, what happened next totally took me by surprise. My inner guide screamed at me *"You must go! It doesn't matter what the offer is or how much it costs. Just go!"* all before he had even begun to make his offer. In a moment of complete and utter clarity I got up, went to the back of the room, and signed up for his 3-day program, still having no clue what it was about, when it would be held, or even where it would be held (which was a very risky proposition given my work schedule during at that time).

Understand, this type of seemingly rash decision-making was way out of the norm for me, given that my typical MO was to mull the offer over, look at all of angles and possibilities, and only then make a decision, regardless of the messages my inner guide might be sending me. But not this time, this time I listened and acted upon the wisdom of my inner guide. And I could say the rest is history. Listening to my inner guide that day dramatically changed my life for the better. Somehow my inner guide knew that my attending this man's workshop would transform my life. Thank goodness I listened, because not only did attending transform my life in a big way, but in the course of that one weekend I healed some of my deepest and most profound wounds.

One of the greatest gifts I experienced that weekend was a newfound trust in my inner guide. For whatever reason I seriously began to trust her wisdom. Within just a few short months of following her guidance I began loving my life, despite nothing much having actually changed except for how I saw myself, and the world around me. Another gift that came as a result of my transformation was the discovery of the purpose and direction I had been actively seeking for over a dozen years. Somehow everything just started coming together, and it continues to do so in ever more amazing ways provided I trust my inner guide. In fact, it seems the only time I run into any significant hardship is when I don't heed the wisdom of my inner guide.

Your Body Speaks – Are You Listening?

Our bodies are worthy of our attention. They are wise beyond our imagination. Not only are they imbued with the wisdom to repair and renew themselves, but they also send us all sorts of helpful signals telling us what we need, what we should avoid, and when we are on or off track with our lives. These messages most often appear as physical sensations, aka gut reactions. Most are subtle and barely noticeable, while a few are loud and forceful, giving us little ability to ignore them. However, because of our conditioning and coping mechanisms we have learned to ignore these messages, having in the process lost touch with the natural order and functioning of our bodies, as well as the wisdom it imbues upon us. Interestingly, the longer we go on ignoring the messages our bodies send us, the more loudly they begin to speak. Just as a child that is routinely ignored or neglected will do anything it can to get the attention it so rightly deserves, the wisdom from within us will do the same if we ignore it long enough. And its manner of getting our attention is typically anything but pleasant.

A simple example is when we ignore the signals that tell us to stop eating because we are satiated. The body has specifically told us it is full, yet we keep eating out of habit or distraction until we are stuffed, or worse yet ill. In both cases the body has sent us helpful messages. In the first case it said, *"Stop, I'm satisfied."* In the second it said, *"You've hurt me, please don't do it again."* It might have even said, *"Please (take a walk, drink some ginger tea, play for awhile, take a nap...) to make me feel better."*

Ignoring the messages from our bodies is a habit most often formed in early childhood. We are told we must eat everything on our plate. We eat or drink to feel comforted. We are told to hold it when we need to relieve ourselves. We are told to be still so often that we learn to ignore our body's natural need to move. We are told we don't feel certain ways, so we learn to ignore our feelings, often to the point of numbness. We are told to be nice, so we stew over disagreements without ever resolving them, thereby causing deep-seated resentments. We are abused and hide it away in the recesses of our memories; or worse yet turn the abuse back onto ourselves. And so on.

Over time, these and similar habits dull our awareness of the messages being sent to us via our bodies. Repeatedly ignoring these messages creates suboptimal feelings of well-being that become our norm. We live with low energy, chronic tension, headaches, pain, allergies, digestive complaints, sleep disorders, or worse, never realizing these sub-optimal feelings are messages from our inner guide telling us we need to change what we are doing and deal with the unpleasantness we are ignoring.

Since we don't recognize the messages for what they are we continue to ignore them, doing everything in our power to suppress them, which most often creates a vicious cycle of ever worsening symptoms that sometimes turn into full-blown physical or psychological disorders. At the point of diagnosable dis-ease (heart problems, cancer, chronic fatigue, phobias, etc.) our bodies have reached their threshold and are now screaming to get our attention.

Am I saying that all mental and physical maladies are caused as a result of our ignoring the messages we receive from our body (our inner guide)? No, not at all. However, research and personal experience have shown that many of these maladies are a direct result of our continually ignoring these messages. Chronic pain conditions are probably the most common. These maladies in particular have been linked to living in an ongoing state of stress, tension, and anxiety for periods ranging from months to years. Yet all is not lost. When we re-learn to hear and trust our body's messages these disorders and many associated conditions readily improve, which in turn improves our overall well-being.

Awareness, as previously discussed, is one of the primary keys to overcoming our demons to heal and become whole again. The main point of the overeating example was to illustrate how readily we ignore so many of the helpful messages we receive from our inner guide, in this case the messages received via the body. The secondary point was to give you an obvious place to start your awareness practice. Paying attention to the messages from your body will help you learn to tune in to your inner guide. The more practiced you become at hearing and trusting the messages from your body, the easier it is to hear and trust the messages from your heart, soul, and intuition, many of which come to you through bodily sensations.

The reality is our conditioning has caused us to ignore and mistrust our inner guide, ultimately losing trust in ourselves. We have closed ourselves off to our inborn wisdom and now look anywhere and everywhere outside of ourselves for the answers that can only be found within. It's time to reconnect. Look within and learn to trust the wisdom you were born with. Think seriously about the example. It makes clear the relationship between the messages we are sent, the messages we ignore, and the effects we experience (i.e., feeling stuffed or ill). While the relationship between the ignored messages and the resulting effects is not always so direct, there is almost always a negative effect when we ignore these messages, especially when they are repeatedly ignored for an extended period.

Begin listening to your body. Learn to trust and act on its messages. Doing so will lead you in a direction that is personally right for you. Don't worry if you initially misunderstand or misjudge the messages; if you are like most people you've been ignoring them for so long that you barely notice them, much less understand them. The important thing is to just start listening, interpreting, and acting upon the messages. Soon you will find yourself hearing, trusting, and understanding them with ease. The more often you listen and act upon them the more dramatically your life will improve.

Your Thoughts Provide Direction – What Are They Telling You?

We previously learned we have on average some 60,000 thoughts per day. Sadly, the vast majority of these thoughts are repeats of previous thoughts, such that we have very few new and unique thoughts throughout the course of a day. We also learned that many of these thoughts are extremely negative and self-defeating. And if that weren't enough, our thoughts love to play tricks on us, so much so they are often our greatest deceiver. This is especially true for those of us suffering from demon overload brought on by our conditioning and programming, as well as the various traumas, abuses, and other forms of negatively perceived experiences we hold on to and thereby use to inadvertently torture ourselves.

Of all the inner messages we receive, it is only the messages from our mind that ever contradict themselves and lead us astray from what is best for us. I'm sure you've noticed how your mind frequently goes round-and-round, arguing points, only to make you doubt yourself and choose to do things you later regret, or knew before doing were not healthy or fulfilling. This most often occurs as a result of our lack of awareness and our learned distrust of our inner guide. In effect, our conditioning and programming have given the control of our minds over to our demons, who'll stop at nothing to maintain their control. Think of it this way. Our demons utilize the injurious thoughts and beliefs that have been conditioned and programmed into our minds. Some 90% of these thoughts occur below the surface of our awareness. This adds up to a lot of harmful thoughts going completely unnoticed that are directly impacting the quality of our lives.

Now you may be wondering what if anything you can do if most of these thoughts are occurring in your nonconscious mind. How can you observe them? How can you improve them? That's where the practice of mindful awareness comes in. You can observe your thoughts both directly and indirectly. The direct method means becoming intentionally conscious of what you are thinking. You give direct and focused attention to your thoughts. You notice exactly what you are thinking, when are you thinking it, and what brought the thought on. Additionally, you keep track of the various types of thoughts you have, both the negative and self-defeating ones, as well as the positive and self-affirming ones. In time you will reflexively catch yourself thinking a negative and self-defeating thought and replace it with a more positive and empowering one at the moment the thought is occurring.

The indirect method for paying attention to your thoughts involves being mindful of your feelings and behaviors. Very often we outright ignore our feelings, when in fact we very much need to acknowledge them. Acknowledging them allows them to pass through us. Not acknowledging them keeps them hanging around and festering, causing untold problems until we finally acknowledge and let them go.

There is a high correlation between our thought patterns and the state of our lives. Research has shown our thoughts lead to our feelings, which in turn lead to our behaviors, and ultimately to the results we experience. Roughly it goes as follows: The more optimistic are our thoughts, the more favorable are our feelings, actions, and life results. The more pessimistic are our thoughts, the more unfavorable are our feelings, actions, and life results. While this is the typical flow, it is beneficial to recognize there are multiple influences occurring between our thoughts, feelings, and actions as depicted in Figure 2.

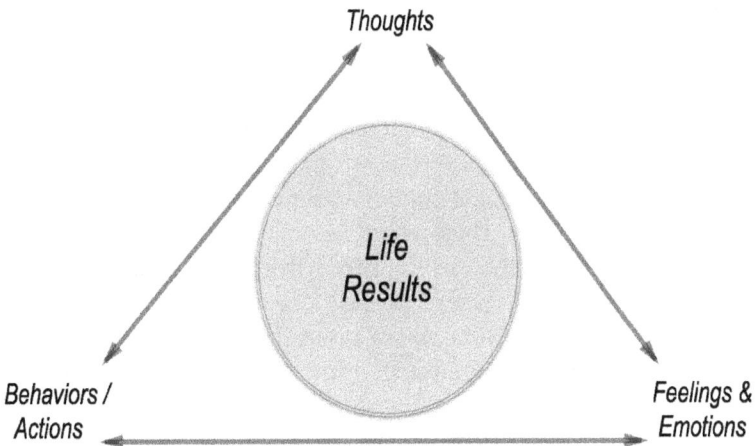

Figure 2: Thoughts, Feelings, & Actions Relationships

Your Feelings Are Powerful Indicators – How Are You Responding?

We can easily discern the type and quality of the thoughts we have been having by paying attention to our feelings, behaviors, and the results we are experiencing.

If you want to discover your predominant thought patterns, examine your results. If your results are typically positive, fulfilling, and rewarding then you can be sure you are predominantly having more optimistic and empowering thoughts than you are pessimistic and self-defeating ones. If your results are more often negative, dissatisfying, or self-destructive then you should have guessed by now that your predominant thought patterns are more often pessimistic and disempowering.

Take heart. Regardless of your predominant thought patterns to date, you have the power to change them for the better. The more thoroughly you improve your thoughts, the more satisfying and fulfilling your life will become. In the next step we'll look more deeply into how you can improve your thoughts. For now, the goal is to become aware of the thoughts you are having and the effects they are having on your life (with specific attention being given to the feelings and actions that follow a particular thought or thought pattern).

Our feelings are powerful indicators that provide significant clues to our behaviors. They are brought on by various internal or external stimuli that involve our physical senses, our thoughts, and our emotions. For our purposes we mainly care about the feelings resulting from our thoughts and emotions, as it is these feelings that provide the strongest clues about how we have responded or are likely to respond to the events in our lives if we chose to continue living in a predominately oblivious state.

As feelings and emotions are often described interchangeably I feel it is beneficial to discuss the differences between them before covering the behavior side of the equation. The key distinction is that emotions are primal, while feelings are more evolved and subjective.

Emotions are our bodies' natural response to threats and opportunities. They have predictable triggers that can be objectively measured through blood flow, brain activity, facial expressions, and body posture. They are typically over in a matter of seconds to minutes. Think about the fight or flight response. It is a primal state that occurs in cases where a perceived danger (real or imagined) could mean imminent harm to our being or that of someone we love. It is our emotions in action.

Feelings on the other hand are a conscious interpretation of the emotions we experience. They reflect the meaning we give to our emotions and are therefore our personal impression of an experienced emotion, hence their subjective nature. They also tend to stick around for an indefinite period, especially when we don't acknowledge them or let ourselves really feel them.

In summary, emotions happen to us. They are nearly universal across all people and cultures. They occur in the body; they are visceral, intense, and short lived. Feelings are their flip side; they are the conscious meaning we give to our emotions. They occur in the mind. They are often culturally or environmentally influenced. They may vary widely from person to person. And they tend to linger at a sustainable level of intensity for an extended period. They also tend to evolve over time (both at the individual and cultural levels).

In short, emotions are brief. They bring on particular feelings, which often stick around for a while, may be culturally influenced, and tend to shift with time.

Since our feelings are such strong indicators for how we tend to respond to the events in our lives it is important to understand the link between our thoughts and feelings. Whatever thoughts we have will provoke some type of emotion and therefore a given feeling. In turn, the feeling will give rise to a behavior (or at least the desire to act in a specific fashion), with the particular behavior being heavily influenced by our underlying conditioning and our level of awareness.

Table 1 provides a few examples of some of the more common behaviors associated with various feelings. The behaviors illustrated are a sampling of those common to typically unaware individuals who generally act on autopilot or from a state of disempowerment (which is more common to the negative emotions than it is the positive ones).

Paying attention to your feelings and how you react to life (your behaviors) will help you to overcome your demons, while simultaneously opening you up to hearing and trusting the more subtle and beneficial messages coming from your inner guide. The more you recognize the links between your thoughts, feelings, and behaviors, the more control you will have over your life, the more empowered you will feel, and the easier it will be for you to retire your demons to a place of wisdom. With a little practice you will begin recognizing the triggers that have you binge eating a pint of ice cream, vegging out to TV or romance novels for hours at a time, shopping your life savings away, avoiding good opportunities that come your way, repeating poor relationship choices, etc.

Emotion:	Feelings:	Common Behaviors:
Joy	Happiness, Centeredness, Cheerfulness, Contentment, Enthusiasm, Fulfillment	Eating healthfully, Exercising, Dancing, Singing, Spending time with friends and family, Being on time or early, Getting things done well and on time
Love	Affection, Compassion, Open Hearted	Forgetting to eat or overeating, Helping others, Volunteering, Treating others kindly and with respect
Fear	Nervousness, Worry, Unsettled	Avoidance of people, things, opportunities, tasks, etc., Eating unhealthfully, Excessive sleeping, Excessive TV watching, gaming, or web surfing, Excessive talking or shyness, Procrastination
Sadness	Disappointment, Depression, Despair, Fatigue, Hopelessness, Shame	Overeating, Eating unhealthfully, Excessive sleeping, Excessive TV watching, Excessive drinking, Experimenting with drugs, Being late, Not completing tasks
Anger	Bitterness, Disgust, Dread, Empowerment, Frustration	Pettiness, Picking fights, Acting out, Eating unhealthfully, Binge drinking, Treating others harshly and disrespectfully

Table 1: Common Relationships Between Emotions, Feelings, and Behaviors

Begin noticing the events, thoughts, and emotions that preceded your feelings and the actions you took shortly thereafter. Also notice how your feelings and actions lead to other thoughts, feelings, and actions. Begin recognizing your particular patterns to determine whether they are personally beneficial or self-destructive. If they are self-destructive try to make a connection as to why you are acting in such an injurious manner. It could be that it is the way you have learned to respond to certain feelings and situations. Regardless of the reason, you can learn to behave in a more empowering and wholesome manner.

Understand that emotions are pure, and that your feelings are your feelings. You feel what you feel. There is nothing inherently good or bad about any emotion or feeling. Also understand that allowing yourself to feel what you actually feel is a good thing. If you allow yourself to experience your feelings and emotions, the extreme highs and lows you experience will typically dissipate much more quickly, with the result being that you return to a peaceful state of equilibrium, neither being too up or too down. Recognize too that it is not the feelings and emotions you have that are causing you problems, but rather you're not allowing yourself to experience those feelings and emotions, coupled with the particular behaviors you choose to engage in after having a particular feeling or emotion.

To put this into perspective, consider the following. Let's say you are really angry about something your boyfriend did. You are disappointed at his lack of respect for your feelings and are afraid to say anything to him for fear he will find you too demanding and leave you. To dissipate your uncomfortable feelings you decide to binge on wine and chocolate while watching several hours of TV. Later you feel really miserable, cry yourself to sleep, and feel like a complete failure for making yourself ill, wasting so much time, and not having resolved anything with your boyfriend.

In this example can see that you didn't really allow yourself to fully experience your anger, fear, and disappointment? Can you also see that you didn't take any actions that would actually lead to a healthy resolution of the situation, which means the pattern is therefore likely to repeat itself? Can you see that what you actually did was to stuff your anger and choose to act in a way that was more self-destructive than nurturing, which effectively prolonged your feelings of fear and disappointment? And can you see that your specific actions are what led to your feelings of disappointment and disgust with yourself?

I hope you now recognize that it is not the initial emotions and feelings we have that are the problem, but rather how we chose to deal with them. That is, problems occur when we dismiss our feelings and emotions and choose to act in ways that are effectively a disservice to our well-being, as these types of actions do nothing to ultimately provide a resolution to the perceived problem that brought on the feelings.

Allow yourself to really feel your feelings. Become aware of them. Explore them. By doing so you'll learn a lot about yourself, and in the process take back much of the control you inadvertently relegated to your demons. Without attention (mindful awareness) you are like a puppet on a string. With attention and exploration you regain control. Little by little you'll recognize your emotional triggers and the manners in which you typically respond to them. Awareness gives you the freedom to change how you feel about and respond to the various situations in your life.

Remember, your feelings are neither good nor bad, but suppressing them and acting from a disempowered, autopilot state will cause you tremendous pain. For many this cycle of suppression and disempowering actions leads to a downward spiral of ever worsening pain and chaos in their life. Don't let this be you. Use the power of mindful awareness to heal yourself and improve your life. I promise you won't regret it. With a little practice it becomes completely natural and effortless.

Actions to Cultivate Awareness and Self-Trust

You are now aware of the most obvious ways in which we receive helpful and guiding messages from within. You are also aware of how we tend to ignore and distrust those messages, as well as the resulting pain that often ensues when we do. It's now time to turn that knowledge into a full-blown practice of awareness that will have you once again trusting in yourself and your inner guide.

Only by practicing mindful awareness can you effectively discern the real you from the demon voices in your mind. Remember, without awareness you are effectively a puppet on a string. So start your practice of mindful awareness today. It'll put you firmly on the road back to wholeness, while simultaneously allowing you to begin living a much more rewarding and fulfilling life.

Recognize that mindful awareness is essentially a skill you turn into a habit. Just as with any skill it takes a little time and practice to become proficient. The following activities provide a number of ways you can develop your powers of awareness. Use them alone or together. Create an awareness section in your journal to track your observations. You'll be using what you learn from these exercises in some of the following steps. For instance, in the next step you'll begin transforming your disempowering thoughts and beliefs so they better serve you, which first requires that you become aware of them.

1. **Awareness & Self-Trust Declarations**
    Repeat the following declarations for at least 30 days. Say them aloud and with feeling.
    *   I am aware of my thoughts and the feelings they provoke.
    *   I acknowledge my emotions and feelings. I give them the respect they deserve.
    *   I am aware of the causal links between my thoughts, my feelings, and my behaviors.
    *   I listen to and act on the wisdom expressed by my body.
    *   I listen to and trust my inner guide.
    *   I ask my inner guide for help and inspiration. When I ask she answers.

2. **Record The Messages From Your Body**
    Begin noticing the sensations within your body. They are helpful messages. Notice where they are located and how intense they are. Determine if you understand them. If you don't understand them, explore them. Think about their connections to what you have been thinking, feeling, doing, or not doing. See if you can put two and two together.

    Understand the messages you receive are sometimes delayed responses, so you might need to do a bit of detective work. For instance, you eat something that disagrees with your body, but your body doesn't send a noticeable message for a day or two so you don't immediately make the connection. In these cases you've likely felt the sensations numerous times before, but have chosen to ignore them because they are a nuisance you think will go away, or they are so common throughout society you think they are normal when in fact they are not. For example, every time you eat ice cream you wind up with a stuffy nose the next day.

Another example might be recognizing a particular physical pattern, such as when you think certain thoughts you always tense up. Maybe you clench your teeth, raise and tighten your shoulders, or hunch over while tightening your shoulders, your gut, and your buttocks.

Specifically notice if the sensations you feel are a gut reaction (i.e., a message from your inner guide - your intuition). If you commonly ignore your gut reactions thinking they are irrational, try going with them for once rather than ignoring them. Your gut is rarely ever wrong.

Finally, notice your most common bodily sensations. Notice when and where in your body you become tense, when and under what circumstances you breathe shallowly, when and why you have headaches or backaches, etc. Also notice when and what relieves your tension, when and why you breathe more deeply, and what relieves your other ache and pains. Become aware of the triggers. Try to determine if the sensations you feel are because of a particular thought, feeling, or emotion; an action you did or didn't take; a habitual stress response to an external stimuli; or something else altogether. Keep track of your observations. They'll help you see things and make connections you were previous oblivious to.

A note about tension: Chronic tension is unnatural. It is the result of our locking a lifetime of fears and traumas into our muscles, which in turn blocks our energy and holds us back from our potential. Our muscles are meant to be pliable and giving, the same as a dog or cats are when you apply gentle but firm pressure. For example, gentle but firm pressure to a cat's leg muscle will give way all the way to the bone, without so much as a wince from the cat. This is because the cat's muscles are relaxed. Ours only hurt because we hold on to tension to the point of turning our muscles into rocks. Know that if you clear the tension you will not only move more easily and gracefully, just as our pets do, but you will also free yourself from your past. I mention this since so many of us carry tremendous amounts of tension in our bodies, and becoming aware of it is the first step to releasing it.

3. **Record Your Thoughts**

Become aware of what you are thinking. Track how often you have particular thoughts and when they occur. Notice whether there is an underlying belief associated with the particular thoughts. Look for the triggers that bring on your various thought patterns, both the positive and the negative. Notice how your thoughts and beliefs affect your feelings, emotions, and actions, as well as your breathing, moods, and tension levels.

Remember, we think some 60,000 thoughts per day, most of which are nonconscious and repetitive. Use the power of mindful awareness to help you illuminate the thought patterns that are routinely escaping your consciousness. When you are conscious of your most dominant thoughts you can then transform or retire those that harm you and more effectively utilize those that help you, which is the topic to be explored in the next step.

4. **Record Your Feelings**

Become aware of what you are feeling. Let yourself experience your feelings. Explore them. Track when they occur. See if you can recognize their triggers. Set about determining what the underlying thoughts and emotions were that led to the feeling, and what actions you took in response to the feeling. Also, track any actions you desired to engage in even if you chose otherwise. Think about what made you choose the alternative action.

For example, say you were really disappointed about something and felt like pouring your sorrows into a pint of ice cream, but instead chose to go for a run. What made you choose to go running over eating the ice cream? Was it to relieve your tension and help you gain perspective, or was it to punish yourself? It's critical what the why is. Notice too if the initial feeling or resulting action spurred any follow-on thoughts, feelings, or actions. For instance, maybe you thought to yourself, *"Wow, I'm really glad I went for a run. I feel so much better. If I'd eaten the ice cream I'd be beating myself up right now. That jerk cancelling on me isn't worth making myself ill. I'll have to remember how empowering it is when I take constructive actions."*

Be sure to look for common patterns you tend to repeat. Also, pay careful attention to when and why your feelings (and your moods) shift. Shifting feelings and moods are often the instigating force for why we spontaneously choose to do one thing over another (such as forgoing a more healthful choice for a less healthful one).

5. Record The Messages From Others To Which You Have A Strong Reaction
While the messages we receive from others are external rather than internal, there is an internal component to those for which we react strongly. With that in mind, record any external messages that incite you either positively or negatively. Note the thoughts, feelings, and emotions the message provoked, as well as any action you may have taken. Try to discern why you reacted so strongly. Realize the reaction is often the result of our denying some part of ourselves that we see in the other person. The denied part can be something we consider good or bad, moral or immoral, a vice or a virtue. It's important to understand that whatever this part is, we react strongly to it because it exists within us. The primary difference is typically in how we choose to exhibit it.

Let's say you react very strongly, possibly even irrationally, to your spouse periodically backing out of planned engagements the two of you made, even when he has a legitimate reason. You feel he is lying to you and being terribly inconsiderate and uncaring of your feelings. To gain a better understanding of your irrationally strong reaction, take a look at where in your life you aren't showing up as you promised. Maybe it's at work. Maybe it's with your children. Maybe it's with a friend. It may even be with yourself.

6. Record Your Habits
Your habits say a lot about what's going on within your mind. They provide clues to your thoughts, feelings, and emotions. Most often, the more negative and disserving are our thought patterns, the more negative are our feelings and emotions. Negative thoughts, feelings, and emotions are energetically lower than positive ones. When we are in a lower energy state we tend to have poorer habits than when we are in a higher energy state.

Take note of your habits. Determine whether they are healthfully serving for you, or not. Look for clues as to how and why you formed the habits you have. A few examples to explore include your eating, drinking, exercise, sleeping, breathing, posture, work, organization, TV viewing, web surfing, shopping, relationship, and communications habits. Track when and why you engage in your particular habits, both the positive and the negative.

Note: If you once had more positive habits and now have fewer positive ones, see if you can uncover when and what caused you to veer off course and fall into a less healthful pattern. Examples are all of a sudden drinking more, sleeping more, or watching several hours more TV per week than usual. If you have gone from less positive to more positive habits, please congratulate yourself and document what instigated the change. It's just as important to be aware of the reasons for positive changes, as it is the negative ones. You can use this newfound awareness to benefit you in ways that wouldn't otherwise exist.

7. **Practicing Listening To and Trusting Your Inner Guide**
All of the information that comes to us through our senses is accessible. However, only a small fraction of that information is directly accessible through our conscious mind. The rest, stored within our nonconscious mind and our body, is only accessible through our inner guide, via our heart, soul, and intuition. Ask your inner guide for help in finding the direction, answers, and solutions that are right for you. Be open to receiving her guidance. Be confident she will provide the information you seek. Trust the feelings and hunches she sends you (especially if they seem contrary to, or are extremely supportive of, the direction, answers, ideas, and solutions your rational mind comes up with).

If you are new to hearing and trusting your inner guide, start small. Begin with things that have little if any negative consequences, such as asking your body the best choice of what to eat or how to spend the hour of free time you have. When you feel comfortable with the small things, begin working on the bigger things you desire to change or improve in your life. In time you will trust yourself and your inner guide with the big decisions. Give your inner guide a chance. You've given your demons and numerous external sources a chance and you've seen firsthand where they've led you.

No one I know who trusts their inner guide has ever said they were led astray. On the contrary the story I hear over and over again is that when they trusted themself and their inner guide they were always led to exactly where they needed to be, even when the path seemed scary and unfamiliar. Also, when they trusted themselves and their inner guide, things turned out far better than they could ever have imagined.

Intuition and the other messages from our inner guide fills the gaps that remain when we examine all of the other information and evidence we have at hand. Case and point: a few years ago I had two job offers to choose from. On the surface they seemed virtually the same. The pay was the same, the work appeared very similar, and the two positions were for the same company, so the environment was also much the same. After fretting for days about which to choose, I finally listened to my inner guide who I had been ignoring. She spoke loudly. For one position she said, *"Take it."* for the other she said, *"What are you thinking? Are you crazy?"* My decision was made. I took the position my gut told me to take and I never regretted it.

Your beliefs become your thoughts. Your thoughts become your words. Your words become your actions. Your actions become your habits. Your habits become your values. Your values become your destiny.
-Mahatma Gandhi

Step 4 – Challenge Your Thoughts and Beliefs: Change Your Thoughts to Improve Your Life

Kathy's Story

Kathy's mind was always churning. She'd get excited about an art show she had planned or a potential job opportunity that came up, and shortly thereafter she would become depressed or overwhelmed. Her thoughts routinely alternated between being super-positive and overly optimistic to being extremely negative, degrading, and intensely pessimistic, which had her mood following suit – like a yo-yo on its string, up and down, up and down.

After awhile, Kathy felt like her life was falling apart. She kept wondering what was wrong with her. Why couldn't she get it together? Why on one day would she be a hotbed of emotion, worrying, doubting, over-analyzing, and becoming super-sensitive to the smallest of things, and yet on another day be calm, focused, and confident, able to accomplish whatever she set out to do. She really did feel like a yo-yo on its string, one day blue and procrastinating, the next day enthusiastic and productive.

This pattern became so disabling that Kathy began to wonder if she was bi-polar or had some other type of neurological disorder. Wanting very much to improve the quality of her life and feel confident enough to take on a big art project that would require a lot of energy, sustained enthusiasm, and positive belief in herself, Kathy decided to get professional help to determine the cause of her so-called yo-yo syndrome. What she learned was that her problem stemmed from her thoughts and beliefs, all of which she could change to better serve her.

Relieved she didn't have a neurological condition that would require being medicated, Kathy began feeling more optimistic about her future. She followed her therapist's suggestion to track her thoughts and note the beliefs behind the thoughts. What she discovered totally shocked her, yet it explained almost all of her ups and downs.

Through reflection and careful review Kathy discovered the majority of her thoughts and beliefs about herself, and life in general, tended to be negative. Additionally, she discovered that a large percentage of her beliefs, in reality, weren't even her own. They were those that had been gifted to her by her most influential mentors, friends, and family, through their repeated expression of them as a matter of truth.

Kathy's yo-yo syndrome stemmed from many of her thoughts and beliefs being in direct opposition to one another. In affect her thoughts and beliefs were so incongruent they 1) kept her moods and actions swinging wildly from one end of the spectrum to the other, or 2) cancelled each other out leaving her bewildered as to why she couldn't move forward.

Upon further reflection Kathy realized she believed, no, in fact she knew, she was highly intelligent, a very gifted and talented artist, and had the capacity to be super successful in the art world. However, much of her conditioning and programing had her running a nonconscious soundtrack that said she wasn't nearly as talented or gifted as she thought she was, that people like her weren't given the kind of opportunities she was interested in, and there was no way she could ever make a living as an artist, so she had better be sensible and get a real job.

While Kathy knew in her heart she could succeed, her old conditioning and programming constantly had her doubting and worrying if maybe her friends and family weren't right. Even more devastating to her was how her old conditioned and programmed beliefs had affected her ability to maintain a healthy relationship. As an adolescent Kathy had been made to believe she was ugly and that no man would ever want her, or at least no man of any worth. In truth, Kathy is very attractive, so attractive that many of her peers are insanely jealous of her. Yet the damage had been done. The constant teasing and putdowns Kathy received from jealous and insecure peers and family members left her with a poor self-image that had her projecting herself as an ugly duckling. The result was she rarely had a relationship that lasted longer than a few weeks, and the few that lasted for any extended period were fraught with deceit and mistreatment, which left her even more untrusting of herself, men, and people in general.

In time Kathy learned to catch herself when the old soundtracks started playing. She now knows the thoughts she tells herself are only true if she decides they are. Today, when a disempowering thought or belief surfaces she tells her mind *"Thank you for sharing, but I choose to think a more empowering thought that better serves me."* She then consciously instills a more beneficial thought, which she repeats several times so that the new thought will in time overwrite the old one.

Using the practice of mindful awareness and intentional thought replacement, Kathy has put a halt to the yo-yo thought patterns that were hampering her success and sabotaging her relationships. Today she is thriving as an art director for a major magazine, showing her personal work in a number of high-profile galleries, and enjoying a very fulfilling relationship with the man she is engaged to marry.

Understanding the Power Of Our Thoughts and Beliefs

Kathy's story is a familiar one. Her story, like many of those in the preceding steps, highlights just how important our thoughts and beliefs are to our well-being. These stories demonstrate that no matter what we have been taught or have experienced, it is what we think and believe about ourselves, our experiences, and the world at large, that ultimately determines our destiny. This is a very important concept to grasp, and one that is vital to you becoming whole again. It is also the key to you getting the most out of the remaining steps outlined in this book.

The main point you will discover in this step is just how impactful your thoughts and beliefs are, including how it is they create the circumstances of your life. You will also discover that your thoughts and beliefs are where the most insidious of your demons hide. Take heart, because by the end of this step you will know exactly how to expose and retire the demons that delight in manipulating you through your thoughts and beliefs.

Our Lives Are A Reflection Of What We Think and Believe

Thoughts and beliefs have no real substance, yet they are immensely powerful. They can, all on their own, lift us up and bring us down. Their power comes from the emotional charge we attach to them and the consistency with which we think them. This is both how and why we become what we think and believe. The following quote by Henry Ford is a perfect reflection of this natural law: *"Whether you think you can, or you think you can't, you're right."*

It should now be obvious from the stories and quotes we have explored thus far that our mind has a major influence on the quality of our life. It stealthily affects our mood, determining the level of joy or disappointment we experience, while simultaneously giving rise to most of our circumstances, both the good and the bad. It can even make us sick or help us get well depending on the flavor of our predominant thoughts and beliefs. And if you haven't caught on just yet, it is largely responsible for our feeling fragmented and inadequate – in a word unwhole.

In the previous steps we learned that approximately 95% of our thoughts and beliefs take place in our nonconscious mind. This means our nonconscious mind is almost always calling the shots, based on the thousands upon thousands of repetitive thoughts and beliefs we are unaware we are having. We also learned that we have on average some 60,000 thoughts per day, with the majority of these thoughts being nothing more than repetitions of previous thoughts, the bulk of which are most commonly fear-based thoughts. That's a lot of nonconscious fear repeating itself in our demons favorite playground.

Now for the kicker that brings it all together. The more we think a particular thought the more it tends to become our reality. The stronger the belief behind the thought, the more frequent and powerful is the thought. The more frequent and powerful the thought, the more likely we are to act on it (which includes non-actions like procrastination). Repeated thoughts and actions (or non-actions) in turn become our habits, and our habits ultimately determine our results.

Putting this in more familiar terms, if you continually think you will fail at something, the likelihood is you will fail. At best you probably won't do very well. On the other hand, if you continually think you will succeed at something then you most likely will. At a minimum you will likely do well. This holds true whether you are taking a math exam, completing an assignment for your job, parenting your children, or building a business. It doesn't mean everything turns out exactly as you desired just because you thought it would. What it does mean is if you believe your desire will turn out well, and you keep believing and applying yourself, then the desire or something better will most often be your result.

Let's now apply this to a specific example: Let's say you very much desire to be offered a particular job for which you have just interviewed. Do you see that if you were to continually tell yourself *"I'm not good enough", "They'll never hire me",* or *"I'll never get the kind of job I really want"* that the job you desire will never come to pass. At best the employer may offer you a much less desirable position. However, the probability is they won't give you an offer at all, after which you'll think your thoughts and beliefs were true. Ultimately you'll feel down on yourself and likely end up taking whatever job you can find. Yet, if you do the opposite and repeatedly tell yourself, *"I will get the job I desire or something better",* chances are you will do just that, if not with this company then with another.

By way of another example, look at the effect of constantly telling a small child she's stupid and never does anything right. The result is rarely if ever good. Most often the child matures with low self-esteem and diminished self-confidence, believing she isn't any good as a person, at what she does, or both. These beliefs will affect her thoughts and actions, ultimately making it challenging for her to perform even the simplest of tasks with confidence.

Understand we are each that child. As we grow up our thoughts and beliefs often take on the flavor of what has been dished out to us, with the result being we take on the role of self-judge and persecutor. No longer do we require anyone else to tell us we are stupid, lazy, or pathetic, because regardless of the validity of these statements we have come to believe them to be true. And through the constant reinforcement our thoughts provide we in turn give rise to our circumstances through the actions our thoughts put into motion.

The reality is, the more we tell ourselves we are something the more disposed we are to become it. The more we say we are going to do something the more probable it is we will do it. Our repetitive thoughts become our realities because in time we come to believe them. Therefore, whatever we strongly believe and repeatedly think will inevitably become our nature, drawing to us whatever we most consistently think about.

Taking this a step further, think back to the vibe discussion in Step 2. If you'll recall, our thoughts and feelings are forms of energy. Our negative thoughts, feelings, and emotions put out a lower vibrational energy, while our positive thoughts, feelings, and emotions put out a higher vibrational energy. If you'll also recall, each energy level attracts to it other thoughts, feelings, people, events, and circumstances that emit a similar vibration. This means the lower thought forms such as negativity and pessimism will tend to draw negative types of circumstances into our lives, whereas the higher thought forms that are positive and optimistic will tend to attract more favorable circumstances into our lives.

Our Mind Has A Habit Of Playing Tricks On Us – Exploring The Playground Of The Nonconscious Mind

There is much more to our mind's power than we know. So let's look at the big picture to gain perspective on what it is about our mind that so often leaves us feeling helpless, defeated, broken, and out of control.

So far, we've learned several important things about our minds:

1. Our nonconscious mind is the favorite playground of our demons.

2. Our mind is continually speaking to us in an ongoing dialogue. It produces some 60,000 thoughts per day, with 95-98% of them occurring within the nonconscious (thereby falling below the radar of our awareness). This means we are generally only aware of about 1200 of our daily thoughts.

3. The vast majority of our 60,000 thoughts are repeats of previous thoughts. Research estimates the repeat level to be about 80% (~48,000 of 60,000), with most of the repeated

thoughts being fear-based thoughts. That's a lot of reinforced fear.

4. Our thoughts produce specific energy vibrations. Negative thoughts produce a low-energy vibration and positive thoughts produce a high-energy vibration. We attract to us in kind what we energetically vibrate through our thoughts, feelings, emotions, and behaviors.

5. Our thoughts and beliefs affect our health and well-being, as well as the overall state of our lives.

Two additional, but very important, points to make about our mind and the role it plays in our well-being are the following. First, our nonconscious mind (often referred to as the subconscious or unconscious mind) makes up approximately 90% of our total mind. It consists of the processes of the mind that occur automatically. These include, but are not limited to, the processes of thought and memory. You can liken this portion of the mind to the submerged portion of an iceberg. See Figure 3 to get a glimpse of some of what goes on under the radar of our awareness.

The nonconscious mind contains a composite of everything we see, hear, and experience, much of which is information the conscious mind could not immediately process or make meaningful sense of. You can think of it as disassociated information that would otherwise have caused the conscious mind to overload, some of which includes repressed memories and even false memories that emanate from our traumatic experiences and early conditioning.

Both the conscious and the nonconscious mind later utilize this stored information to help us generate ideas, solve problems, form opinions and conclusions, and so on. Additionally, the mind uses this stored information to help protect us from harm. However, our recall of this stored information is often faulty. It is also easily manipulated through the repetition of our thoughts and various external inputs. But as we will see, we can use this manipulation feature to our advantage.

Secondly, the thoughts our mind produces release a variety of chemicals throughout our body that are continually affecting our mental and physical well-being. Two of the most easily recognizable signatures of these chemicals are the influence they have on our moods and energy levels.

The breakdown of this chemical effect roughly goes as follows. Limiting thoughts and beliefs induce limitations in the body, mind, and spirit, with the limitations often being expressed as depression or other debilitating mental and physical conditions. On the other hand, more expansive thoughts and beliefs create health, healing, and good energy.

We characteristically observe the effects of our more expansive thoughts as expressions of joy, enthusiasm for life, and the feelings of love, satisfaction, and fulfillment. Whatever we choose to accept, the reality is the state of our health and our life is unequivocally connected to and continuously being affected by our thoughts and beliefs.

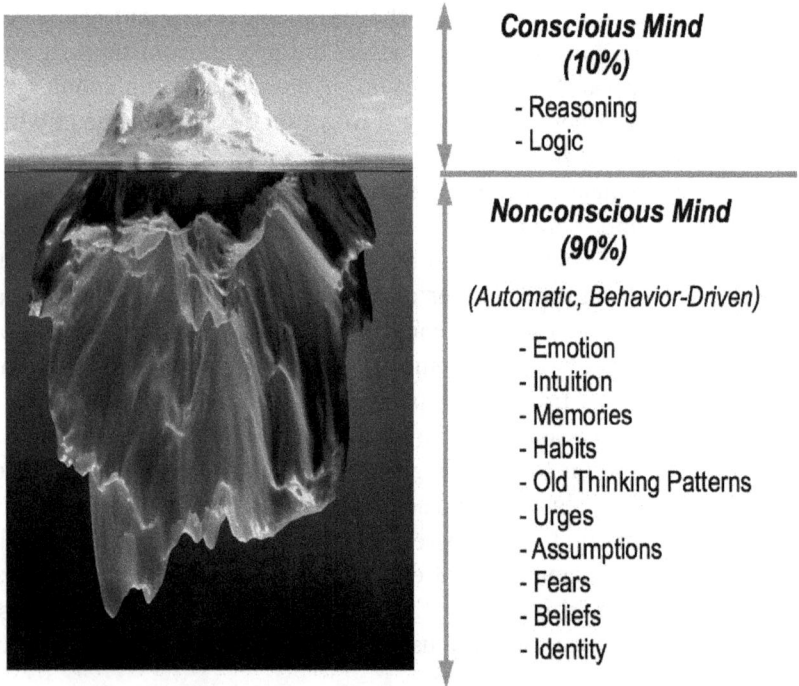

Conscioius Mind (10%)
- Reasoning
- Logic

Nonconscious Mind (90%)
(Automatic, Behavior-Driven)

- Emotion
- Intuition
- Memories
- Habits
- Old Thinking Patterns
- Urges
- Assumptions
- Fears
- Beliefs
- Identity

Figure 3: Iceberg Representation of the Mind

Knowing what we now know we can begin exploring how the mind plays tricks on us, as well as how it is that not all these tricks are necessarily bad. We'll start with a breakdown of some of the key differences between the conscious and the nonconscious mind.

The conscious mind, as brilliant as it is has very limited processing power. Over 95% of the minds processing power resides in the nonconscious mind.

The conscious mind likes to focus on the past and the future; it finds it very challenging to be in the present. The nonconscious mind on the other hand is present-oriented, yet it forever remembers everything we have ever experienced through any of our senses.

The conscious mind operates and helps us function through memory recall, reasoning, perception, intuition, and imagination. The nonconscious mind operates based on habits of thought, belief, and action; it controls over 96% of our perceptions and behaviors.

From this we can discern that our nonconscious mind helps us perform many routine activities without our needing to call on the limited resources of our conscious mind (think walking, driving, dressing, eating, and bathing). Patterns and habits of thought, belief, and repeated actions kick in to let us perform routine activities without conscious thought. However, depending on how our mind has been programmed and conditioned these ingrained patterns and habits of thought, belief, and behavior can also spell trouble for us, as we've been observing. Thankfully though, we can reprogram our mind to our advantage. *The beauty of the nonconscious mind is that it will believe anything we tell it provided it is sufficiently reinforced.*

Now that we've seen several examples of how our habitual thought and belief patterns can play undesirable tricks on us, such as making us believe we are less than we really are, and thereby creating our less than desirable circumstances, let's now look at a brief example of how this feature of the mind can be used to our advantage.

Athletes frequently employ a technique called visualization to overcome their limiting thoughts and beliefs. Their visualizations are often the only factor giving them the edge they need to beat out a competitor by differences of only a fraction of a point or second. These athletes program their mind and therefore their actions by repeatedly visualizing themselves performing their routine perfectly.

To picture this technique in practice, imagine a gymnast visualizing (mentally walking through and feeling) every move of her routine on the balance beam from the mount, to the landing, and finally the standing ovation she will receive. Imagine her going through every move in her mind as if she were doing it for real. Imagine her feeling in her mind what her body will be feeling during her performance: the spring of the floor mat under her feet, the solidness of the wood of the beam under her hands, the wind being created by her moves as she somersaults through the air, and the sticky feel of the chalk on her hands and feet.

Athletes perform this type of visualization time and time again. The more often they perfectly visualize their play or routine, the more it improves their confidence and their actual performance, regardless of how often or how well they have executed the play or routine in practice.

Think about it. How often has there been an upset because 1) a favored athlete had a brief lapse in concentration or a last minute thought of slipping or falling, 2) a less favored athlete who wasn't expected to place at all wins because she visualized herself performing flawlessly and taking the gold, or 3) some combination of the two? You are no different than these athletes. You use these same techniques all the time. The difference is in how you use them, which is more often nonconsciously and without a specific intention or purpose.

Later in this step we'll explore how you can systematically begin reprogramming your nonconscious mind to effectively transform some of your most oppressive demons into an internal support committee, thereby realigning your mind to resonate with your helpful and supportive inner guide, and ultimately your most authentic self. But first we need to explore a bit more about the origins and effects of these oppressors that make a playground of our nonconscious dialogue.

Discovering The Mental Bullies Who Make Us Our Own Worst Enemy

You're likely already aware that many of your thoughts are extremely self-brutalizing. But in case you aren't, or aren't sure, let's look at a few examples. Think about the following question in relationship to yourself. How often have you felt hurt or experienced a barrage of disserving thoughts because of a particular expression on someone's face, someone not having acknowledged your presence, or the tone of voice someone used when making a comment that wasn't even directed toward you? How often have you thought I'm not good enough, I'll never fit in, I'm not pretty enough, I'm not slim enough, I'm not talented enough, I'm not smart enough, I'll never be loved, no one likes me, or something of the sort in one of these situations?

Think about it and answer truthfully. Was it rarely, frequently, all the time? Whatever your answer, it's time to recognize these are self-limiting and self-brutalizing thoughts your mental demons are conjuring up because of your poor self-image.

Now ask yourself the following questions. Where did your barrage of critical thoughts come from? Why did you feel hurt? What specifically triggered the thoughts and feelings you experienced? Were you actually being criticized, judged, or overlooked, or did some unidentified force within you step in and begin to validate your unhealed feelings and the demeaning beliefs internalized by your inner child? Remember, until we retire our demons, which will heal our inner child, those negative thoughts, beliefs, and feelings will stay with us, being easily triggered by even the most insanely trivial of events.

This is a sad reality for the majority of us having grown up in an abusive, neglectful, or traumatic environment. That is, our habitual, nonconscious dialogue has turned us into our own worst enemy. The reason for this is our childhood conditioning and programming has trained our nonconscious mind to see the negative side of almost everything, and therefore become extremely critical, judgmental, and pessimistic toward ourselves, others, and life itself. As a result, our nonconscious mind has effectively become our most oppressive demon, which I will henceforth refer to as the inner critic.

All of us have an inner critic from whom we experience some degree of bullying. This is true even if our childhood programming, conditioning, and experiences were predominantly positive. The key to the degree with which we experience this bullying is the age at which our negative experiences occurred, coupled with the severity and duration of those experiences.

Generally, the more negatively we were treated and spoken to as a child, the more negative and pessimistic we become in our thoughts, beliefs, feelings, and behaviors as we mature. Whether the words and actions aimed at us in our youth were true or not, many of us have internalized them to the point where we now believe a) we aren't good enough in some way, b) we don't deserve to be treated well or to have good things in our life, and c) our needs just don't matter.

Taken to extremes our inner critic can turn us into a martyr. Martyr or not, most of our suffering is of our own making. It is the direct result of the nonconscious dialogue put into action by our inner critic.

The Inner Critic and Her Supporters

We've just met the inner critic, but there's significantly more to her story. What we know so far is that she is born out of our conditioning, programming, and the negative perceptions and beliefs we formed as a result of our experiences. The more negative those perceptions and beliefs the more fodder she has with which to attack us.

We also know our inner critic has a penchant for attacking us in ways that make us feel inadequate and unworthy. However, our inner critic is much more insidious than one might think, as she has a whole committee of ardent supporters helping her in her quest to undermine our self-confidence and wreck our self-worth.

As it is, our inner critic and her supporters love to criticize, judge, ridicule, tease, and otherwise beat us up. This has the negative effect of making us doubt ourselves and feel wrong, bad, guilty, or shameful about the things we think, say, and do (or don't say or do). And when this group isn't attacking us directly they are often attacking someone else.

One way to think of this cohort is as critic, judge, prosecution, and jury all rolled up in one. They are quite the band of thugs. Who outside of your inner critic do you know who so fervently attacks you with such harsh, unyielding, and unforgiving voices? Probably no one.

Taking a closer look at this committee will shed some light. If you begin observing your own committee's voices as an objective bystander you will begin to see they show an astonishing resemblance to a number of particular people from your past, who for whatever reason had a predilection for attacking you by means of harsh words; hurtful or frightening expressions; painful, disrespectful, or harmful physical actions; and even through the act of ignoring you and your needs.

Each of these forms of attack tends to have a negative emotional effect that very often instills within us a number of degrading and demoralizing beliefs about ourselves. This is especially true when we are young and have not yet matured enough to recognize a true attack from one we only perceived as an attack. For our purposes, perceived attacks are misunderstood verbal and physical expressions and actions that we have internalized as a degrading truth about our abilities or our worth.

Think about it. How often does your inner critic or one of the voices from her committee sound just like the rants of your alcoholic father, the mocking judgments of your enabling mother, the putdowns of your older sister, the taunts of your elementary school classmates, the cruel and derogatory remarks of your high school peers, the deflating criticisms and judgments of one or more of your teachers, or even the accusing sermons of your religious leaders.

Think back to your childhood. How did your parents, teachers, religious leaders, siblings, and peers treat you? What kind of verbal dialogue did they have with you? How often did they ignore you and your needs? How much of what you experienced did you internalize as an absolute truth about your abilities and your worth as a person?

Internalizing the real and perceived insults to our character causes our mind (aka our inner critic and her support committee), to become obsessively focused on reinforcing what we have come to believe is true, that we are unworthy of being our true self and experiencing the things we desire. In fact, our beliefs, especially the negative ones, become the critic's fodder. Time and time again she and her committee use these beliefs against us, constantly bombarding us with a litany of negative and pessimistic thoughts, such that we come to seriously doubt ourself and our abilities based on nothing more than an inconsequential look or remark. This then becomes confirmation to our mind that our beliefs are in fact true, so much so that even a kind word or praise is often perceived as an attack.

Adding insult to insult, our mind, under the control of the inner critic, will frequently conjure up the worst possible outcomes for a given situation despite there being little to no evidence to support the prediction.

One of the most devastating fallouts we experience from these inappropriate internalizations is the learned denial of our needs. By denying our needs we disown parts of ourselves, become fragmented, and in effect lose touch with our true self. Often we become a mere shell of a person who has no idea who we really are. We may think we know, but the sad reality is our demons are keeping our true self locked deep behind a false facade, which is but one of the reasons it is so critical to commit to peeling the proverbial onion. The more layers we peel away, the more we expose our true self, a being who is infinitely more amazing and powerful than the shell of a person our demons have made us believe we are.

Inner Criticisms and Judgments In Disguise

For the purposes of this discussion we will be focusing on what are commonly referred to as negative criticisms and judgments, as opposed to the more constructive and beneficial forms of criticism, since it is the negative ones that cause us so much harm. Now that we are clear about the types of criticism and judgments we are referring to, let's explore what those commonly dished out by our inner critic and her committee tend to sound like.

Criticisms and judgments dished by this cohort sound very much the same as those we hear from other people, although they are frequently even more harsh and almost always more relentless than those received externally. Think about it. How often do you berate yourself about something, going on and on and on about it, even finding others to repeat your personal berating to (like it's not enough that you berated yourself, but now have to make sure someone else is aware of how terrible or stupid you think you are)? These are the voices of your inner critic and her committee doing their utmost to dismantle your well-being. But wait. There's an even more insidious side to these bullies, which is what I will refer to as inner criticisms and judgments in disguise.

Ask yourself, how often do you criticize, judge, or blame someone else? How often do you hear someone else criticizing, judging, or blaming another person? I'd bet it's pretty often. But why? Why do we criticize, judge, and blame others so routinely? The answer may surprise you. The main reason we criticize, judge, and blame others is almost always to deflect some inadequacy we feel about ourselves. We do this by projecting our negative feelings about ourselves, or our lives, onto someone else.

And now we reveal the insidious side of this action. To criticize, judge, or blame another requires we first criticize, judge, or blame ourselves even more harshly than the recipients of our wrath. The disguise then is that we are generally, if not completely, unaware of the self-criticisms and judgments taking place. So when we criticize, judge, or blame another we are actually harming ourselves much more than we are the intended recipients.

What this means is we are disguising our inner bullying as external bullying. Sadly, we rarely if ever see this bullying for what it really is until we have learned to understand the ways of the inner critic. So, while the projection of our wrath to an external recipient seems to deflect, or at least dull our pain, the reality is it only compounds it.

Therefore, does it actually make us feel better to criticize, judge, and blame someone else? Not really. On the one hand it may make us feel more powerful in the moment, but deep within us it is stirring up a hornet's nest of future pains and troubles. This is because criticizing, judging, and blaming another is tantamount to a double-edged sword that inflicts multiple wounds, with the person wielding the blade being the one who receives the most significant wound of all, a wound that will continue to fester and grow until the inflictor learns to dispel their inner critic and her committee of supporters.

Before moving on, let's look at some of the unintended negative effects we sustain as a result of our criticizing, judging, and blaming others. Henceforth, judgment applies equally to criticizing and blaming.

1. Judgments make us feel heavy. They weigh on our consciousness.
2. Judgments are a double-edged sword. We can only judge another for something we ourselves are guilty of in some fashion. In effect we are actually judging ourselves.
3. Judgments create our experiences. However we choose to judge someone or something is how we will experience the person or the event (e.g., judging someone or something as bad, terrible, or awful, tends to create a bad, terrible or awful experience for us).
4. Judgments create separation between others, and us, as well as between our desires and us. Think about it. When we judge someone for the car they drive or the house they live in because we consider it extravagant and wasteful (for instance, they could be using the money to feed starving

99

kids in Africa), we are creating a separation between us and our having their degree of wealth, as well as a separation between us and the individuals themselves. Sadly, these types of judgments are what help to create the haves and the have-nots, cast systems, prejudices, stereotypes, etc., which as history has shown have a tendency to lead to hostilities, ongoing conflicts, the suffering of many, and oftentimes war.

5. Judgments (especially self-judgments) lock what is being judged into place. Example: By judging yourself about having gained a few pounds by saying *"My butt is so fat."* you are in effect telling your butt, *"I'd really like a fat butt thank you very much"*. And guess what, your mind and body will go out of their way to increase the size of your buttocks. The same is true for a thousand other things. Judge yourself for losing things by repeatedly saying *"I'm always losing things. I lose my keys, my money, my jobs... It never ends."* and that is exactly what you will experience, losing things.

6. Judgments separate us from our true self. When we are being judgmental we are out of alignment with the person we are at our core, our true self.

7. Judgments cut off our awareness and block from us anything that doesn't match the judgment.

Recognize too that some of the judgments we dish out may indeed be another person's judgment of themselves. Because we humans tend to wear our self-judgments on our faces and our bodies like neon signs, with our thoughts, feelings, and emotions being broadcast like radio signals, we will sometimes pick up another person's self-judgment as our judgment of them, just as the receiver in our car radio picks up the radio signals broadcast by a radio station. One of the ways to recognize this form of judgment is to notice your self-judgment for having judged them. If you are beating yourself up because you have judged another, see if you can determine if it was really your judgment, or their judgment of themself that you were just reflecting back to them.

Beliefs That Don't Really Belong To Us

Would you believe me if I were to tell you that many of your beliefs aren't really your beliefs at all? I'm guessing probably not. Really, why should you believe me? Logic says that if you believe something then it has to be your belief, right? Wrong! Wrong! And wrong again! OK, I'll explain. Hopefully, you will then believe that not all of your beliefs are indeed your beliefs.

By now you should have a pretty fair understanding of how environmental conditioning and programming effects our well-being and therefore our lives, especially the conditioning and programming that occurred in early childhood (for our purposes age 12 and under, but especially the years between birth and age 6 – the unfiltered, human sponge years).

Throughout our lives we are gifted a multitude of beliefs, some harmful, some beneficial, and some that directly conflict with our true beliefs (those not gifted; the ones that come from our inner guide, or true self if you will, and those that are born of our personal experiences). I say gifted, because you didn't have the opportunity to make a decision about whether something was in fact true for you or whether you indeed desired to believe in something. Rather, you were force fed (in effect hypnotized or brainwashed into believing) something that a parent, a teacher, a sibling, a peer, a religious leader, or the media told you was true about yourself or the realities of life. However, in some cases, they may not have even told you these so called truths directly, but rather through their actions, fears, and the conversations held between themselves. In these cases, you indirectly picked up their beliefs without having any experiences of your own to justify the beliefs.

By the way, your parents, teachers, and the many other significant influencers in your life were gifted many of the beliefs they in turn gifted to you in exactly the same way. So, hopefully you are beginning to realize that not all of your beliefs are in reality your beliefs. In case you're still in disbelief or on the fence about some of your beliefs not really being your beliefs at all, I'd like to share a couple of personal examples I hope will remove your doubts.

Example 1:
I grew up in a family where money was considered a scarce resource that was difficult to obtain. My parents argued and

worried about it incessantly. They even considered conservative types of investing, such as Certificate of Deposits (CDs) and U.S. Savings Bonds too risky to take advantage of. For all practical purposes they didn't even have a basic Savings Account. A few of the family mottos centering on money included *"money doesn't grow on trees", "if you want something you have to work hard for it",* and *"everyone is out to take advantage of you".* The ingrained and habitual thought patterns and beliefs of my parents in turn became a mostly nonconscious soundtrack continuously running in my own mind, despite my having no actual experiences to support their validity. The fact is we had more than enough of all the necessities, in addition a great many things that more than debunked these family mottos. And while we were far from being financially rich, we certainly weren't poor by any stretch of the imagination.

These external thought patterns and beliefs of my youth were so consistent and ingrained that I internalized from a young age that I would indeed have to struggle and work hard my whole life in order to mostly just get by. In effect, the mantra both from within and from various well-meaning people became, you have to get a job, keep your nose to the grindstone, and save what little you can for a rainy day. Life is hard and you can't trust anyone, so you'd better suck it up, get tough, and make the best of what you've got. And those grand dreams you have, well that's all they are, just dreams, so get your head out of the clouds and get back to work.

This mantra was in stark contrast to some of my actual beliefs, which told me I could do whatever I set my mind to and that if making money and growing wealth is easy for some people then it can be easy for me as well. I just have to learn how it's done. Yet, as you can imagine, those gifted beliefs running on auto-repeat took their toll. In effect they were muffling and drowning out my more serving beliefs.

I'm sure you can see how ingrained beliefs like these can radically affect a person's life. I'd venture to guess you've experienced at least a few similarly ingrained beliefs yourself. In my own life, these gifted beliefs have definitely had an impact on the quality of my life and the ease with which I have accomplished a great many things. That is, despite my having become a very successful professional, having done quite well financially, and having gained a full understanding of the tricks my mind plays, I still periodically contend with my mind worrying about whether I will be able to make ends meet, especially in my later years, and that I must work harder if I want to live the life I desire (when in reality I need to work smarter and take more play breaks – to live life if you will).

As a result of my gifted beliefs I've often sacrificed my dreams for a *perceived* security that I know doesn't really exist. Although having plenty of money is helpful, it is in reality my mindset, that is my positive, optimistic, and unwavering thoughts and beliefs about myself, and my abilities, where the real security lies. I know and believe that as long as I have the right mindset I can lose everything I have and then recover with relative ease, even surpassing where I was before the loss. However, with a limiting mindset, like the one I was gifted, any loss could be devastating, thereby making it a daunting challenge to restore myself and my life to their former status.

Example 2:

For years and years I desired to break out on my own and do something that would directly improve the lives of men, women, and children from all walks of life, but especially the lives of women, children, and senior citizens who have been marginalized, made to believe they are worthless, or have been pushed in to being someone they are not (e.g., a children's storyteller at heart being prodded, coaxed, and coerced to become a prosecuting lawyer, or an actor at heart being forced to become a heart surgeon), thereby suppressing, subduing, or outright extinguishing their passions and their spirit.

From a very young age I've had a keen interest in human behavior, as well as a strong desire to help people become the person they were born to be so they could live happy and fulfilling lives. Not only have I had the interest and desire, but, as it turns out, I'm naturally good at a great many things that fit perfectly into a number of congruent vocations.

Yet until recent years, because of my own limiting beliefs, many of which were gifted, I felt as though I had nothing of any particular value to offer. After all, who was I? A nobody. For as long as I can remember I'd been told to shut my mouth and be quiet. I'd also been told I didn't speak very well. Add this to having been made to believe that my feelings and opinions were of no importance or consequence and you can easily understand how I honestly couldn't see how I could make a difference, much less take on anything as daunting as writing a book, becoming a professional speaker, holding my own workshops, or starting my own business.

Some of my more repetitive and disabling mind tracks included *"What do I have to say?"*, *"Why would anyone listen to me?"*, *"I don't know how to get published."*, *"I don't have the time or the money to write a book."*, *"I don't know how to start a business."*, *"I'm a lousy speaker."*, *I'll have to work even harder than I do now."*, and *"What if I fail?"*

On the one hand these are essentially nothing more than excuses, but behind the excuses are a series of gifted and limiting beliefs that had very effectively eroded my self-confidence and self-worth, while very nearly extinguishing my innate gifts and passions. You see, I had inadvertently picked up a multitude of my parents', teachers', and other influential peoples' limiting beliefs about how risky and dangerous it is to go for your dreams.

The result was gifted fear and a serious sense of unworthiness. My mind had become my worst enemy by very effectively convincing me that I didn't deserve or have the fortitude to live the life I really desired. So, doing the best I could given my limiting mindset, I meandered down a number of seemingly random paths, attempting to accept my life as it was, replete with all the meaningless frustrations that made it so intensely dissatisfying.

Thankfully, my near constant dissatisfaction with the status quo, along with a growing feeling that something was missing within me, and my life, kept me searching. In time I stumbled upon books, workshops, mentors, and coaches who helped me discover and understand the effect my thoughts and beliefs were having on my life.

Armed with a little knowledge I began paying closer attention to the exact nature of my thoughts and beliefs, deconstructing where they came from and the specific effects they were having on my life. In time I recognized just how limiting they could sometimes be, after which I began in earnest the practice of mindful awareness and conscious thought and belief replacement, where I would not only replace the limiting ones with more empowering ones, but reinforce the empowering ones until they became habitual.

Over time I realized that to have any chance of living the life I truly desired, as the whole and gifted person I really am, I would have to eradicate the bulk of my fear based thoughts and beliefs and take a chance, regardless of what others choose to think about my choices, because it's my life, not theirs.

Using this book as an example, whether it's a best seller or only sells a single copy, I can honestly say I have triumphantly diminished the stranglehold of my inner critic and her bullying gang of supporters. The act of writing and publishing this book is a major victory in and of itself. And for each person it helps in any way at all only magnifies that success.

Just as I have succeeded in putting my mental demons in their place, retiring many of them into the wisdom that now *supports* me in all I do, so can you. You have the capacity to be successful in whatever endeavors you choose, especially if it is something you love doing or are very passionate about. It starts with you being mindfully aware of your thoughts and beliefs, in addition to the effects those thoughts and beliefs are having on your self-worth and your life. Remember, all creations first begin as a thought (an idea). They are only later realized because of a solid belief, a lot of reinforcing and supportive thoughts, and finally keen and focused attention to specific actions that bring the creation to life.

If you're still having trouble wrapping your head around this concept, think for a minute about Thomas Edison and the commercially viable incandescent light bulb. It took him over a 1000 different tries before he finally succeeded in finding a suitable filament material. All along the way people were telling him he was a failure and he'd never succeed, even his staff was discouraged. He didn't have it easy. He had many challenges throughout his life, yet he, like all successful people, began with a thought and kept going with an unwavering belief and repeated actions, taking into account what he learned along the way, until he finally succeeded. A summation of his belief that he would triumph is expressed in this quote: *"I have not failed 1,000 times. I have successfully discovered*

1,000 ways to NOT make a light bulb." And the rest as we say is history.

Believing We Are Unwhole Is An Illusion Of The Mind

We've already discussed at considerable length our programming and conditioning and the effects it has on our lives. But to make the point of this section clear I will reiterate how vitally important it is to remember that we have been programmed and conditioned by the outside world since birth, and in fact we continue to be programmed and conditioned by the outside world each and every day of our lives. This makes it all the more difficult for us to listen to what is inside, especially since almost everyone and everything in our environment is doing their utmost best to draw us away from our true self and the wholeness that exists within us.

You see, from birth we have been programmed and conditioned to believe we are unwhole. We are taught that as humans we are sinners, which in and of itself leads us to believe we are unworthy and in turn unwhole. We are taught that specific types of experiences rob us of our wholeness, such as when we are sexually violated or psychologically abused. We are taught that we are lesser beings and therefore unwhole because we were born with a particular color of skin, grew up on the *wrong* side of the tracks, or were born into or associated with a particular religion, cast, sect, or other marginalizing group.

Every day we are bombarded with messages whose purpose is to make us feel we are lacking something that we must have if we are to be whole. These missing components range from the perfect job, a life partner, children, a perfect body, a certain drug, a lifetime in therapy, the big house of the American dream, a hefty bank account, a specific religious affiliation, the newest toy or gadget, and on and on and on. No wonder we feel so fragmented and incomplete.

Yet the reality is we are whole. We were born whole and we continue to be whole. The reason we feel unwhole is because of our conditioning and programming, and the inadvertent walling off of various aspects of ourselves in order to fit in (out of desire or necessity), survive in an abusive environment, or cope with our traumatic experiences.

But what of those who program and condition us, doing whatever they can to draw us away from our true self and our wholeness of being? Why would they do this? For the most part it is an outgrowth of their fears and self-serving interests; that is, it is the result of the disharmony existing between their inner and outer worlds, as they themselves do not understand the ruthless tricks of the mind. Therefore, being fearful of looking within, they do not see the wholeness and perfection that already exists within them and the other living souls that inhabit this planet.

For most people it is a scary proposition to discover that their whole way of being and thinking is built on false beliefs and perceptions. Yet it is the very act of listening within that would set them free from their misguided thoughts and beliefs.

Largely, that's what this book is all about. It's about listening to what is inside of us. It's also about reprogramming and reconditioning ourselves so that we may live in harmony with the natural order of our being (the harmonious integration of body, mind, and spirit). However, true listening takes commitment of heart and dedication to the practices of awareness, introspection, and thought replacement. Just as with building and maintaining a healthy body, or perfecting the art of playing an instrument, we must implement habits and rituals that train our minds to be our most avid and effective supporter. Only then will we have harmony between our inner and outer lives.

Transforming Our Mental Bullies Into Supportive Allies – Let The Healing Begin

We've explored a lot thus far, so let's recap just a bit. What have we learned? The key points from this step are 1) we've been conditioned and programmed to believe we are inadequate and unwhole, 2) many of our thoughts and beliefs aren't in actuality our own, although we have internalized them as though they are, and 3) our minds are great tricksters, who hold us hostage, beat us up, and sabotage our efforts and our dreams. We've also learned that our lives are indeed a direct reflection of our predominant thoughts and beliefs.

Additionally, we've hinted that we don't have to put up with our mental bullies, that with a little guidance and repetition of effort we can turn our most vicious of demons (the inner critic and her support committee) into our most ardent and supportive allies.

Before you decide this is an overly daunting task you aren't sure you're up for, let me assure you that you *can* train your mind to get out of your way, such that it will quit lying to you and allow an opening through which your true self will emerge to take the forefront in your life.

Once you understand and accept how the mind works, everything will begin changing for the better. No longer will you be routinely controlled by the vagaries of your mind. With each passing day your inner critic and her gang of malcontents will wield less and less power. More and more the real you, the whole and integrated you, will govern the direction and outcome of your life. With the real you in control you will live more and more harmoniously, regardless of what actually transpires in your life.

So how to do you go about learning to turn your mental bullies into your most ardent allies, the supportive coaches and parents you may never have had? First, believe you can. Then, apply the practice of mindful awareness to root out your predominant thoughts and beliefs (if you did the exercises in Step 3 you should already be familiar with this piece of the puzzle). Next, reflect on the nature of your thoughts and beliefs and the effects they are having on your life. Finally, replace your negative and disserving thoughts and beliefs with ones that are empowering and supportive. In a nutshell, that's it. However, to really make this process rock you'll need to listen within and get to know the real you. For now, you can continue doing the exercises outlined in Step 3, especially the ones that focus on listening to the messages from your inner guide. In Steps 7 through 9 we will explore more ways for you to get to know your true self.

Following these guidelines you will create the most supremely valuable of support teams that will be available at your beckoned call. In a brief time, your most notorious demons (the inner critic and her committee) will become your most trusted and valued allies; they'll begin *working for you* as effectively as they once *worked against you.*

Does this mean you'll never again experience the criticisms and judgments once dished out by the inner critic and her demoralizing committee of troublemakers? No. What it does mean is 1) you will experience fewer and fewer hurtful criticisms and judgments from the machinations of your nonconscious mind, 2) you will know how to peel the onion to discover the underlying truth and positive intentions behind many of your most disserving beliefs and thought patterns (be they gifted or of your own making), and 3) you will know how to reprogram your nonconscious mind so it very effectively supports you, the real you.

Confronting The Inner Critic

There are lots of ways we can confront our inner critic and effectively put a halt to her denigrating antics. Some will seem almost childish, some will definitely take you out of your comfort zone, and others will be easy peasy. By the way, if they seem childish or take you out of your comfort zone, know this is your inner critic and her gang trying to fool you in to letting them stay in control.

For each of the following I will only refer to the inner critic. However, the technique applies equally to her gang of supporters and should be applied to them as well.

Naming and Describing The Inner Critic:

Recognize your critic as an entity, a voice that is within you, but who is not you.

By naming and describing your inner critic you make her easier to confront. It's much easier to confront something you can visualize than it is some vague and unfriendly voice emanating from the recesses of your mind (just as it was easier for Dorothy to confront the Great and Venerable Oz once Toto had pulled back the curtain and revealed him to be nothing more than an ordinary man preying upon the fears and desires of his visitors).

1. **Name your critic:** Give your inner critic a name. If she reminds you of someone specifically, say your Aunt Martha, then maybe Auntie or Martha would be a good name.

2. **Describe what your critic looks like**: Give your critic dimension and style. If she looks like your overly critical teacher, then describe her that way.

3. **Describe what your critic sounds like:** Give your critic a voice. Maybe she sounds like your bellowing father, spewing all sorts of vile and unkind words.

Capturing What the Critic Says:
It's important to really get to know when and what your critic is saying to you so that you can put her words into the proper perspective, because sometimes she really is trying to protect you.

4. **Write down what your critic says:** Capture in your journal exactly what your critic says, when she says it, and in what context she goes off.

5. **Look for patterns in your critic's diatribes:** Just as it is good to recognize our habits it is good to recognize your critic's habitual rants.

Decoding the Critic's Comments:
Decoding the critic's comments provides perspective, thereby easing the sting of her blow.

6. **Look for underlying fears:** Analyze what your critic has said. Dig below the surface to determine if there are underlying fears. If there are, try to understand why these fears exist. Are they because of your experiences or are they inherited fears that were gifted to you?

7. **Recognize when your critic's intention is protection:** Analysis of what your critic says, when she says it, and in what context she says it will shed light on whether her intention is protection. It may be that you do not need to be protected, but because of imagined or inherited fears your critic feels justified in doing what she can to keep you safe. Recognizing her intention will help you make conscious decisions for moving forward, regardless of her warnings. Over time she will back you up and become more supportive, especially when it has become clear there is nothing to fear.

8. **Determine whose words your critic's comments sound like:** Mindful awareness of your critic's words may reveal they are in actuality the words of an unwitting donor, such as your mother, a teacher, a best friend, etc. Recognizing whose words your critic is reciting will effectively reduce the power they have over you.

Putting The Critic's Words Into Perspective:
Recognize that most of the time your critic's words are unfounded and exaggerated, often being repeats of your unwitting donor's thoughts and beliefs (e.g., those of your mother). Take the time to put them into the proper perspective.

9. **Exaggerate your critic's comments:** Be playful. Make the critic's comments sound as ridiculous as you can. Intentionally blow them out of proportion. Keep exaggerating them until you can see the utter ridiculousness of them.

   For example: Say your critic says, *"You know you won't get the job. What are you going to do then? You're almost broke now. Soon they'll be coming to take your house."*

   Now exaggerate it to the maximum. Be totally ridiculous. For instance, you might say, *"You know your right. I won't get the job. And yeah I'm almost out of money. And if I don't get a job soon, they'll take my house. Then the kids and I will have to live in the car. And next, they'll take the car too. And then you know what, they'll come and take our clothes, then our hair, and then our teeth. Wow, were going to be penniless, homeless, bums running around naked gumming our way through the day."*

   OK, hopefully you get the idea. By making it utterly ridiculous you not only gain perspective, but you also empower yourself rather than wallowing in the fear your critic induced.

10. **Role-play with your critic:** There are several options for role-playing with your critic. Here are a couple of options:

   a. Have someone sit across from you and act the part of your critic so that you may more readily observe and confront them.
   b. Have someone act as a coach who shines a light on what your critic is saying through questions and thoughtful feedback that helps you to see your critic's comments for what they are.

   Note: You can play the parts yourself if you don't have a partner or coach to work with. It takes a little practice to

111

switch places with your critic or to act as your own coach, but it can be very beneficial, much like when you exaggerated her comments.

Other Methods For Confronting and Quieting The Voice Of Your Inner Critic:

11. **Just Say STOP:** Look at yourself in the mirror and forcefully say STOP! ENOUGH IS ENOUGH. Often this will shut the critic up, at least for a while. She's not used to you standing up to her. So tell her ENOUGH! NO MORE! If you don't have a mirror that's OK. Tell her to stop anyhow.

12. **Imagine your critic has an off switch:** When your critic gets going just flick her off, the same as you would a room light or a battery operated toy. The only difference is you are flicking the switch in your mind. If it helps, use a hand gesture to represent you flicking the switch to the off position.

13. **Imagine your critic's comments going up in smoke:** Imagine the words your critic says going up in a puff of smoke. They're going, going, gone. See them evaporating before your eyes, just as the smoke from a candle dissipates into thin air to be seen no more.

14. **Thank your critic for sharing:** Thank your critic for sharing with you. Tell her you understand her point of view and that you realize she is just trying to keep you safe. Then find something good in your life to really appreciate (it's helpful if it's related to your critic's comments). This empowers you and makes it difficult for your critic to argue. Afterward, let your critic know what you're going to do, whether she agrees with you or not.

15. **Practice loving and honoring yourself when your critic starts up:** Do something to love and honor yourself when your critic gets started. This goes against what she expects and empowers you in the process.

Overwriting the Inner Critics Lies With Positive Thought Replacement (Reprogramming the Nonconscious Mind)

For the purposes of discussing thought and belief replacement we will continue using the inner critic as their voice. Understand this process of replacement applies equally to any and all of your disserving thoughts and beliefs.

Replacing your disserving thoughts and beliefs is very much a process of intentional thought replacement. Sometimes it is nothing more than emphatically stating the opposite of a given thought or belief. Other times it is more tailored, such that you replace the disserving thought or belief with one that is expressly what you want to think or believe, or one that is specifically relevant to the given situation.

The following sums up the basic process of thought replacement, of which there are a few minor variations. Use the one that is most relevant to your given thought or situation.

1. **State the opposite of the negative or disempowering thought, belief, or accusation.**

   Examples:
   - *I hate my life.* Replace with *I love my life.*
   - *I'm such a dope.* Replace with *I'm a genius.*

2. **Create a powerful, meaningful, and empowering statement to replace the negative thought or belief.**

   Examples:
   - Disempowering belief*: I'm unlovable. No one cares about me.*
   - Empowering belief: *I am lovable. I am love itself. I love myself. I have lots of people who love and care about me. My mother loves me. My friend Sally loves me. My partner John loves me. In fact, everyone I know loves me.*

   Another way to do this is to say *"Thank you for sharing, but I choose to think the following, more empowering thought!"* Then replace the disempowering thought with an empowering thought that truly serves you.

3. **Create a list of personal declarations, which are positive statements asserting or declaring the truths you desire for your life.**

Examples:
- I love my life.
- I am a kind and loving person.
- I am loved by many.
- I am healthy, happy, and whole.
- I live in the present moment, here and now.
- I trust myself.
- I always find a way to achieve my dreams and goals.
- I am a generous giver and an excellent receiver.
- I succeed in spite of everything.
- I am an attractive, powerful, and loving woman.
- I am confident, charismatic, and courageous.
- I live with purpose and passion.
- I live in joy.
- I am a powerful creator.
- I make this world a better place.

Regardless of the method you choose to use, be sure to repeat your new and empowering statements several times per day. The reason for this is it takes time to overwrite your old programming. Those old, disempowering thoughts and beliefs have worn some pretty deep groves, so it's going to take time to make the new, empowering ones stronger and more prominent than the old, disempowering ones. In time the old ones will fade away, just as a photograph fades in the sunlight, with the new ones becoming your stewards of well-being, proudly exhibiting themselves like a happily engaged woman exhibits her engagement ring.

This is one of the key reasons for regularly utilizing declarations. They help to accelerate the process. To get the most benefit repeat your declarations daily for an extended period (e.g., when you wake up and before you go to bed, for a period of at least 90 days). Also, be sure to add as much positive emotion and passion as you can muster.

The more emotion you put behind them, the more quickly and deeply they become ingrained.

The Critic Becomes The Coach

You'll know you have effectively reprogrammed your nonconscious mind when your inner critic has become your most admiring advocate. Where previously your thoughts seemed to do nothing but berate you, you now find them supporting and encouraging like a really good coach. This doesn't mean your thoughts will always sound kind, because they will in fact still criticize you at times, but now the criticism will tend to be useful and constructive, like the constructive criticism a good athletic coach gives an athlete to help her improve her technique and gain the confidence she needs to push beyond her self-imposed limits and reach her true potential.

To assist your inner critic in transforming herself into an empowering coach it is helpful to employ the following two techniques on a regular basis:

1. **Journaling:** Journaling is especially beneficial for transforming your inner critic because it really helps you to peel the onion. Two key things happen when we journal. First, we tend to go deeper and deeper, uncovering hidden treasures, even when we weren't trying to. Things surface, coming into our awareness, that fill in the holes of the bigger picture, just like when we piece together a jigsaw puzzle. Little by little we see the whole picture in all its brilliant and glorious splendor. Secondly, we tend to ask ourselves more useful questions, which stimulate the digging process that ultimately uncovers our true self and leads to inspired solutions to our so-called problems.

2. **Role-Playing:** Role-playing as already mentioned helps us to tame the inner critic, but it can also retrain her. In this usage of role-playing you want to basically have the inner critic play the role of coach. You can do this in one of three ways: 1) partner with someone and have them play the role of coach to your inner critic, redirecting her to be more encouraging; 2) play the role of critic yourself, again redirecting her to be more encouraging; and 3) journal how

you would like the critic to sound, such that you directly show her how she should treat and support you.

Note: All of the techniques described under *Confronting the Inner Critic* and *Replacing the Inner Critic's Lies* will support this process. If you want to expedite the process, make sure to regularly employ journaling and role-playing as part of your strategy.

∴

Discovering our nonconscious thoughts and beliefs, and transforming those of our inner critic and her rag-tag band of supporters into supportive allies, is very much a process of peeling the proverbial onion. By routinely following the techniques outlined throughout this and the following few steps, you'll effectively transform your most ruthless of demons (your inner critic) into a friend and ally in no time at all.

Keep in mind, when our inner critic is in control, although we may not believe much of what others say about us, our nonconscious mind still believes what we tell ourself; so be very aware of what you are telling yourself.

Actions To Turn Your Nonconscious Mind Into Your Most Ardent Support System

Remember that ~95% of the time we are thinking and acting on autopilot, being led wherever our nonconscious thoughts take us. Remember too that most of those automatic thoughts and many of our beliefs are fear-based and limiting, and that it is these thoughts and beliefs we draw from to create our everyday experiences. This is but one of the reasons that mindful awareness and intentional thought replacement are so vital, both for the healing process, and for regaining control of your mind from your most notorious of demons, your inner critic.

It's time to take action. Quit turning a blind eye to the machinations of your mind. You *are not* a victim unless you choose to be. You *can* take control of your thoughts. No matter how you grew up, no one is making you think the thoughts you think or have the beliefs you have. You have the prerogative to change your thoughts and beliefs any time you choose.

The following actions provide several methods for turning your nonconscious mind into a full on support system. Use them in conjunction with those described earlier in this step.

1. **Declare You Are Already Whole**

   Use the following declarations or create your own. Repeat your wholeness declarations for as long as it takes for you to feel and believe you are whole.

   • I am already whole. I was born whole. I need only to retrain my brain.
   • I am healthy, happy, and whole.
   • There is nothing missing. I am complete just as I am.
   • Wholeness comes from within. I need nothing to complete me.
   • I feel whole when I love myself. I LOVE MYSELF! I AM WHOLE.

2. **Discover Your Predominant Thoughts, Beliefs, Feelings, and Actions**

   As we've already learned, we all have many thoughts and beliefs we aren't aware of. In Step 3 we explored a number of the more common self-defeating thought patterns we frequently employ, especially when we have grown up in a negative and demoralizing environment. In this step we learned a lot about the inner critic and the power of our thoughts and beliefs. We've learned that all limiting thoughts and beliefs create obstacles and impediments for us. As such it is important for us to implement a discovery process that systematically employs the practices of mindful awareness and intentional thought replacement for the thoughts and beliefs that don't serve us.

   Taking what you learned in this and the preceding step, begin rooting out your predominant thoughts and beliefs, as well as any associated feelings and behaviors. If you did the exercises in Step 3 you can use what you captured there to begin the discovery process for thought predominance, causal links (between thoughts and beliefs, feelings, and actions), and inherited beliefs. Make sure to also capture when the thoughts occur, what sets them in motion, and whether they are positive or negative (e.g., empowering or disempowering).

Some additional information you should consider capturing is what type of thought patterns you regularly have (see *Self-Defeating Thought Patterns* in the previous step for examples), and what area of your life your thought and belief patterns relate to (money, your abilities, your self-image, relationships, spirituality, etc.). This will help you to understand the results you are experiencing in particular areas of your life.

If you didn't perform the exercises in Step 3, begin now. The sooner you start, the sooner you will be able to transform your mind into a trusted friend and ally.

Once the discovery process is complete you will more effectively be able to determine the best course of action to take for reprogramming your mind.

3. **Discover When and Why You Are Being Judgmental**
    In this exercise you will want to pay special attention to when you are criticizing, judging, or blaming, either yourself or someone else. Again, using your journal note your criticisms, judgments, and blames, capturing who the specific recipient was (you, your spouse, etc.), as well as what instigated your diatribe. Additionally, note the following two things: 1) who, if anyone, the diatribe reminds you of (e.g., a parent), and 2) how you felt before and after your diatribe.

    Be especially mindful of how you are actually berating yourself when you criticize, judge, or blame someone else. See if you can discover what it is about yourself you are unhappy with. And don't cop out. It's incredibly rare for us to go off on someone else without there being some underlying dissatisfaction we have with ourself that sets us off.

    To help you eliminate your judgments, criticisms, and blaming employ the following practices:

    a. Ask whom does this judgment belongs to? Keep asking until you're sure. Remember, we're like the receiver in our car radio picking up the broadcasts of those around us.

    b. Ask yourself, What if there was nothing judgeable about me? About X, Y, or Z?

c. Ask yourself, What if I didn't have the capacity to judge? How would I feel? How would I interact with myself when I am upset or dissatisfied? How would I interact with others?

d. Choose how you respond to the situations in your life based on your awareness, as opposed to reacting in judgment. You'll feel a lot lighter.

e. Play a game with yourself. Tell yourself you're not going to judge anyone or anything today, just for today. Then follow through. If you do judge, let it go and begin again.

4. **Recognize Beliefs That Aren't Your Own**

As already mentioned, a fair percentage of our beliefs are not really our beliefs at all. These beliefs have been gifted to us through our programming, conditioning, and environment. Sadly, many of these beliefs are disserving, compete with, or contradict some of our more empowering beliefs, and thus cause us a load of problems.

The purpose of this exercise is to look closely at your beliefs and discover whether they are in fact your own, or ones you have inadvertently inherited. Secondly, you want to determine if the belief serves you or disempowers you. If the belief disempowers you then it's time to let it go, replacing it with a more empowering one if need be.

Using the information you captured in Action 2 (of this Step), see if you can determine whom each of your beliefs sounds like. Next, determine whether the beliefs are beneficial to you, or not. Finally, if a belief is not beneficial to your well-being, decide what belief you'd rather have in its place. Make sure to make note of the replacement belief(s) so you can use them in the reprogramming process.

Take special care to note if you start defending a belief you don't actually believe. We sometimes do this because something is so ingrained within us, that is, because we have habitually heard it over and over again throughout our life, more than it is something we really believe. Other times we defend a belief because in effect what we don't believe in is ourselves.

5. **Reprogram Your Thoughts and Beliefs**

Have you ever noticed how a bully on the playground will continue to pick on someone, continually punching them and knocking them down over and over again until the victim learns to stand up to the bully and exert their own power. Well life has a way of treating us in much the same way until we learn to take control of our mind. Think of your mind like you would a wild horse that kicks and throws the rider until it has been tamed, or an untrained dog that pulls and leads you wherever its senses take it until it has been trained. Your mind is that untrained horse and dog. It is also the bully on the playground. Until we tame and train our mind, it acts just like the crazed and untamed animal, or the insecure bully, constantly making noise and threats by spewing meaningless and destructive chatter.

The time has come to learn how to quiet your mind, to effectively transform it into your trusted friend and ally. This means it's time let go of your disempowering thoughts and beliefs. Much of this will be accomplished through the process of reprogramming your mind, where you systematically replace your old, disempowering thoughts and beliefs, with new, more empowering ones.

Reprogramming your mind can be accomplished in a variety of ways, several of which have already been explored. However, since this is such an important piece of the puzzle for cutting through your illusions, and regaining your sense of wholeness, I'll reiterate some of the more fundamental methods for reprogramming your thoughts and beliefs. They are:

a. **Intentional Thought Replacement (aka Affirmations & Declarations)**

Intentional thought replacement is much like reprogramming a computer with a faulty program or a virus. You first discover the offending code (Step 4, Actions 2-4). You then replace it with code that will provide the results you desire. The key difference between your mind and the computer is your mind takes considerably more replacement cycles. You'll need to repeat the replacement process frequently until it has become ingrained and you find yourself regularly manifesting the results you desire, or something better.

For specific examples see those given earlier in the section on *Replacing the Inner Critic's Lies*.

b. Change Your Perspective

Sometimes we don't so much need to change our thoughts and beliefs as we do our perspective. For instance, you just got laid off and you see the loss of your job as something bad, despite the fact you were miserably unhappy with the job and desperately wanted to make a change. So rather than looking at the loss as something bad, begin to see it as an opportunity to finally take some time for yourself and go for the dream job you've been fantasizing about for the last few years.

c. Visualization

Recall that visualization is seeing the result you desire in your mind's eye. Recall too that the nonconscious mind can't tell the difference between what we visualize and what we actually see, hear, and do (hence why our memories are sometimes false). Realize this is a very powerful tool.

You can perform visualization with just your imagination, through role-playing, or through a variety of writing exercises, some of which are described in Step 6 (*Tell Your Story*). If you are unclear how to visualize, think back to the example given earlier of the Olympic gymnast doing a flawless routine in her mind. Clearly see yourself being the person you desire to be, living the life you desire to live. Add as much detail and emotion as you possibly can. Make sure your visualization is true for you today, not someday. You want to visualize yourself and your life the way you desire it to be, as if it is true for you today.

d. Coaching

Coaching can be a very effective process for both recognizing and replacing your disserving thoughts and beliefs. Coaching is a coactive partnership between you and the coach, in which both of you must be truthful with yourselves and each other. One of the most beneficial aspects of working with a coach is their ability to act as a mirror, illuminating your blind spots and providing you with new perspectives in a non-threatening manner.

Since coaches aren't generally emotionally linked to you or your success, they have a greater capacity than your friends and family to act as a mirror. Additionally, coaches are typically excellent at guiding you to discover your own empowering solutions, whereas your friends and family may not want you to find these solutions for fear of being left behind. Through the use of a specialized type of questioning, coaches can very effectively teach you to quickly retrain your mind. Additionally, they can help you to discover your true self, your passions, your gifts, and your life direction.

If you are being significantly challenged with taming your mind consider working with a coach.

∴

Please understand you will never have 100% positive and empowering thoughts, so don't fret when you feel like you are having too many negative ones. The reality is, with thoughtful application of the practices described within this book, you will likely have a relative balance of positive and negative thoughts, regardless of how much work you do. There are two fundamental reasons for this phenomenon: 1) everything in the universe has its opposite. Just as day has night, and hot has cold, we have positive and negative thoughts. 2) Certain portions of our brains are predisposed to negativity as a safety mechanism, which becomes severely overblown in today's modern world that is largely devoid of the dangers experienced by our cave man ancestors.

The trick is to notice where your attention is. Is it more often on the positive or the negative? Learn to spend more and more of your time focusing on your positive thoughts and beliefs rather than disregarding them in favor of the negative ones. Tending to focus on the negative is nothing more than a product of your conditioning and programming.

Anyone or anything we can't be grateful for shows us the boundaries of our box. Ungratefulness closes us down, shrinks us, and creates states of fear and guilt. What we can't love or feel gratitude for limits, stagnates, or blocks us. We are all created to love. Everything that transpires in our life is designed to teach us to love, both for ourselves and for others.
-Dr. John Demartini

Step 5 – Make Peace With Your Personal History: Express Gratitude to Experience Freedom From Your Demons

Natalie's Story

Natalie had tried what seemed like every possible method to let go and heal from some of her most horrific experiences. She had been in therapy for years, had done lots of forgiveness work, and had even tried hypnotherapy and regression therapy.

After years and years of work she felt she had made little progress, as she continued to be afflicted by periodic episodes of hysterics, self-loathing, and extreme feelings of being all alone, especially when she found herself in or observing situations that triggered her painful memories. These episodes typically left her feeling depressed and wondering why she tried at all. During her depressed periods her thoughts would become so pessimistic she would begin thinking *"there just aren't any real solutions to be found; I'm doomed to continue living this nightmare, forever alone, unfulfilled, and never experiencing real love or true happiness"*.

With years of therapy and what seemed to be hundreds of failed attempts to make peace with her past, Natalie was beginning to think that all of the so called healing methodologies were nothing more than hopeful theories presented by basically well-meaning doctors who had no real idea how to effectively help themselves or their patients. She'd tried it all, time and time again, and to no avail. But being the stubborn and persistent person she is, Natalie decided she couldn't give up. Somehow, she would and could find a way to release the hold her past had on her to finally heal and be the whole person she knew she was intended to be.

The turning point for Natalie came when she attended a workshop that applied gratitude as one of its main healing modalities. Initially skeptical, but remaining open-minded, Natalie decided to give it her all. She thought, *"What can it hurt. It sounds a lot like forgiveness, but I said I wanted to find a way to heal, so I'm going to give it 100%. I'm going to believe there is something to it. If philosophers and spiritual traditions, from ancient times to the present, believe gratitude is so vital to our well-being then I'll give it a try."*

Natalie was astounded. Many of her programmed beliefs were obliterated. She came to understand that gratitude is not forgiveness at all, but is instead the feeling or attitude of being thankful or appreciative for benefits one has received or will receive. It is the acknowledgement of and gratefulness for those benefits, which often only exist because of the extreme challenges and horrific experiences we have endured. Natalie also learned that when we are truly grateful, love, forgiveness, and abundance are the blessings we receive for our gratitude; and the more grateful we are the more we receive.

While this sounded too simple and too good to be true, something told Natalie there is truth and wisdom in these words. Following the workshop, where Natalie learned various methods for applying gratitude in her life, she made it her mission to apply gratitude to everything in her life, but especially to the people and events that had so deeply traumatized her. For several weeks, one person or experience at a time, Natalie tirelessly made the effort to discover as many reasons as possible why she was grateful for the person or the experience. When she completed this one exercise, she'd already listed hundreds of benefits she'd received as a result of her abusive and traumatic experiences. She also found she was now able to really forgive and love several of the people she had previously thought impossible to forgive or love. More importantly, she was finally able to forgive and love herself.

Today Natalie expresses gratitude on a daily basis, from the smallest and most mundane of things to the largest and most impactful. If you were to ask Natalie what she considers to be the most fundamental and beneficial healing tool, she would emphatically answer *"the gift of gratitude; apply it daily to experience the phenomenal and immediate difference it makes to your life"*.

Gratitude – The Gift That Heals From The Inside Out

What if you learned the key to receiving more, and living a more fulfilling life, was to live your life in a state of gratitude? What if you also learned you could easily vanquish the majority of your demons, including the most pernicious of them, through gratitude? Would you not then choose to be grateful for everything in your life, no matter what?

Natalie's story gave us a glimpse of the power of this miraculous gift. Her story also defined what gratitude is. To reiterate, gratitude is defined as the state or feeling of being thankful or appreciative. It is an acknowledgement of some benefit one has received or will receive. Another way of defining gratitude, as stated in the words of Cicero, is *"Gratitude is not only the greatest of virtues, but the parent of all others."*

Gratitude is akin to a strong set of roots that anchor the tree. It is the foundation upon which all other healing modalities stand. Without gratitude, we are building on shaky ground. Most often, any relief and healing we experience is fleeting, which makes us think we've made little to no progress. When this happens again and again, no matter what we try, we wonder why we even bother.

It's not that we haven't made progress, it's just that we don't yet have a solid set of roots upon which our new ways of thinking, feeling, and being can rest, so we topple over now and again, floundering until we find another anchor point, at which point we once again reach for the sky.

But when we anchor with gratitude, the healing and everything else we desire comes much more quickly and easily. It also makes it much more difficult to uproot us. When we have strong roots, we more easily bend and sway with the events in our lives. Even in the throes of a gale force event we stand strong. We may be shaken and lose a few leaves or branches, but we remain strong and whole to our very core.

I hope by the end of this step you will not only believe that gratitude is a remarkable gift, but I also hope you will also be applying it in your daily life so that you quickly begin reaping its many rewards, not the least of which are improved health, increased happiness, and more prosperity.

In my personal experience nothing has fostered more healing, love, and life fulfillment than the practice of gratitude. If you were to only apply one step from this book I would make it this one, *the gift of gratitude.* Applied regularly, this one tool alone will make a phenomenal difference to the quality of your life.

Gratitude Changes Our Perspective

One of the greatest gifts of gratitude is its ability to change our perspective. When we change our negative and pessimistic perspectives to ones of appreciation, love, and abundance we immediately begin experiencing increased optimism, better health, and more joy and happiness, which leads to increased possibilities, opportunities, and life fulfillment.

To put this into perspective, consider the tendency we in the United States and much of the Western World have of looking at the glass as half empty, or worse. Many continually belabor and moan about what they do not have, as well as what they perceive as slights, no matter how large or how insignificant those slights may be. This tendency leads to pain and unhappiness, and worst of all it provokes jealousy, envy, and animosity, which in turn destroys our health, our relationships, and even the fabric of our country.

The reality is we each have so much more than we acknowledge. At the most fundamental level, no one has anything we don't also have. The only difference between us is the form the thing we think we don't have takes. By example, let's say you envy your neighbor because you feel she has it all. In your mind her life is easy and glamorous. She is rich and successful, with an exciting career, lots of money, fancy clothes, and exquisite home furnishings, as well as personal assistants to take care of the household chores and other routine tasks. And to top it off, she gets to travel the world on a whim. In comparison, you feel your life is mundane and ordinary.

When you compare your life to hers you tend to see it as nothing more than a non-stop marathon of juggling your children's activities, taking care of a home and family, and working the odd jobs for various non-profit organizations, even though these are things you typically very much enjoy.

Let's now add to your neighbor's picture. Yes, she is financially well off and can flit around the world on a whim. But underlying it all she is miserably unhappy, feels totally alone, and believes she is a failure, both as a mother and a wife. She puts forth a brave front and a false smile, because she doesn't want anyone to know her family life is a sham and all but nonexistent. Many of the so-called glitzy family trips she takes are actually taken alone as an escape from her unfulfilling home life. Her children are away at expensive boarding schools, where the youngest feels bullied and the oldest is frequently in trouble, and her husband is so wrapped up in his work and business deals she feels she doesn't even exist where he is concerned. Most of the time she secretly envies you the richness and love she sees within your family. She'd give up almost anything to have a close and loving family, most especially the glitz, glamour, and personal staff.

Now let's look at where you are rich and successful in your life. While you and your husband have a more modest income and seemingly less exciting jobs, you have a fantastic relationship with each other, and with your children. You are a leader in your community; you take the time and initiative to make the world a little bit safer and better through the various activities and organizations you support and lend a hand to. Your children feel safe and loved; they are growing up knowing exactly who they are. Seeing this gives you great pride, as well as a deep sense of self-worth and accomplishment. This lifestyle was your choice. When you graduated from college you had similar opportunities to those of your neighbor, but you chose instead to marry the man you felt was committed to you and your children, and to do work that used your skills and talents, while affording you a more flexible work schedule so you could be with your children as they were growing up. Acknowledging these realities and their blessings, would you really want to trade places with your neighbor?

From this example, it is easy to see how our perspectives can so easily affect the quality of our life. When we appreciate what we have we recognize we are much wealthier and more successful than we give ourselves credit for. If you feel lack in any area of your life, take a serious look at whether you are negatively comparing your life to someone else's and therefore jading your perspective, such that you are creating senseless animosity and pain for yourself and others.

Gratitude Dissolves Resentments, Leading to Lasting Forgiveness

Another of the major gifts of gratitude is its ability to dissolve deep resentments for personal injustices, whereby true forgiveness can ensue. With true gratitude resentments just melt away, not only because we see things from a different perspective, as illustrated in the previous example, but also because we recognize the part we played in the perceived injustice and/or the gifts we gained because of the experience.

To give credence to this gift, I'll use an example from my own life. For many years following a divorce I never wanted, I carried a deep hurt and bitterness toward my ex-husband. I felt drained and blamed what I saw as his betrayal for much of the state of my life: personally, financially, and professionally. I felt rejected, disempowered, and admittedly, like a victim. I'd lost so much of what I'd worked for years to build, with the outcome being I had to start over in almost every aspect of my life. On top of that I still had to regularly interact with him unless I also quit my job.

In most regards the feelings I was experiencing with respect to my ex-husband are all too common, especially for those who harbor a lot of inner demons. It all changed for me when I applied the gift of gratitude to our relationship. When I viewed our relationship through the lens of gratitude I became extremely thankful and appreciative for everything that had transpired, both the good and the bad. I acquired a much more balanced perspective. I saw how much I had grown and how we were both responsible, each in our own way, for what had occurred. Above all, I realized our relationship had very much outgrown itself, and so long as I continued to resent him he would continue to maintain a level of control over me, which would continue to affect the quality of my life. Additionally, I saw how so many others had supported me during that challenging time.

Finding the reasons I was grateful for all of my experiences with my ex-husband, including how things turned out, was a true blessing.

With the application of a few simple exercises that I completed within the course of a few hours, I melted away years of resentments, completely releasing myself from his hold. From that point forward facing him was easy.

Anytime thereafter, if I felt any impediment that was in some way related to my ex-husband, our marriage, or our divorce, I would look to why I was grateful for how things had turned out, which would instantly dissolve the blockage and allow me to more freely and confidently move forward.

Gratitude Creates Emotional Freedom

As demonstrated in the previous examples, *gratitude* is a powerful force. One of the things those suffering from the bullying effects of inner demons so often wish for is mental, psychological, and emotional freedom. They desire to be free of their fears, worries, anxieties, painful memories, and the negative beliefs, opinions, and judgments they have of themselves and others. Gratitude can and does provide tremendous relief from all of this and more. It is but of the reasons why gratitude is such an amazing gift.

Applied regularly, gratitude endows us with the emotional freedom we so desire. Emotional freedom in turn creates mental and psychological freedom. This occurs because gratitude elicits love. As love and gratitude are two of the highest vibrational states we can experience, we find we automatically act from a place of wisdom, have more peace in our lives, and experience more of our true spiritual nature when we are in a grateful and loving state.

No one in a loving and grateful state can simultaneously experience, anger, hatred, grief, or any of the other negative emotions. This is because we can't simultaneously be vibrating at a very high frequency (the top of the scale) and a very low frequency (the bottom of the scale). Whatever your beliefs regarding energy frequencies, the Law of Attraction, or spirituality in general, you can easily prove to yourself that you can not exist in both states simultaneously. You can also prove to yourself that a loving and grateful state is on a higher energy plane than are the negative states of anger, hatred, and grief.

One of the easiest ways to test this is to work yourself into a rage about something. Get really angry. Yell about how you hate someone or something. Threaten your revenge. Really feel the effects on your body and your mind. How does it feel? Is it heavy, draining, irritating, or worse? It uses a lot of energy, doesn't it? It also produces toxic chemicals within your body that continue to build up and eat away at you so long as the issue remains unresolved in your mind. That is, it will continue to poison your body and degrade your life so long as you continue to feel hurt, angry, disappointed, frustrated, or fearful in relation to the person or event; this applies equally to unresolved events for which you have suppressed your memories.

Remember, this is just an exercise for you to experience and understand the healing power of gratitude and recognize that you can't be in two very different states at the exact same time. When you were in the rageful state could you even think about being grateful or loving? Not likely, because anger, hatred, revenge, and the other negative emotions tend to consume us, especially when we are in the throes of their influence or the influence of our demons.

Now that you've experienced the low-vibrational energy state associated with the negative emotions of anger, hatred, and revenge, it's time to experience the high-vibrational energy state of gratitude and love. Think of someone in your life who you are truly grateful for, someone whom you dearly love (they can be alive or deceased, person or animal). Express your deep appreciation and gratitude for them and the gifts they have given you. List all of the benefits you have experienced because of them. Now express your deepest and most profound love for them and the time you've spent together. How did that experience feel? Did you feel a lightness of being? Did you experience feelings of happiness, joy, or bliss? Did you have feelings of contentment, hope, or optimism? Or did you perhaps feel appreciated and loved by remembering your experience with them.

Real love and gratitude are light. They don't expend much energy. Most of all they heal us by pouring nurturing chemicals into our bodies that offset the toxic ones created from our negative emotions. This does two important things: 1) it heals us in body, mind, and spirit, and 2) it increases our energy levels, allowing us to function more optimally, both mentally and physically.

I hope this experience has given you a glimpse of the power of gratitude. Whenever you feel down or negative in any way, look to gratitude. Find what you are thankful and appreciative for by recognizing the benefits you have experienced or will likely experience because of the person or event that has brought you down.

The Gratitude Path To A Harmonious Life of Abundance and Fulfillment

You've already learned a lot about the gifts of gratitude, but there are many, many more. A few of these include the following:

- *Gratitude fosters love for self, for others, and for the environment.* It teaches us to recognize and feel our connection to all that exists. When we feel connected our love grows. As our love grows we are all the more grateful for everyone and everything in our life.

- *Gratitude aids us in being our authentic, best self.* When we are living in a state of gratitude and love we more easily connect with our true self, our intuition, and our inner guide, which allows us to be the best of we are. When we are authentic we shine, bringing forth our natural gifts, talents, and brilliance. This in turn creates possibilities and opportunities we would never otherwise have recognized or accepted.

- *Gratitude allows us to love our life.* When we are grateful we automatically experience feelings of peace and harmony. These feelings in turn allow us to experience more satisfaction and fulfillment, which fosters contentment and love for our life, often just as it is.

- *Gratitude cultivates abundance in our life.* When we are grateful and appreciative for what we have, we receive even more of what we desire with much less effort. Often, it seems as though things just magically appear. The reason for this is that gratitude puts us in a receptive vibrational state that lets the universal intelligence (God) know in advance we deem ourselves worthy, ready, and appreciative for what we have and will receive.

At this point you should have a solid picture for how the application of gratitude can powerfully improve the state of your life, as well as how it will allow you to effectively retire many of your demons. Through gratitude you will not just retire your demons, you will also turn them into wisdom. At the end of this step you will find several exercises specifically designed to teach you how to effectively apply the gift of gratitude in your life so that you may experience its many benefits for yourself.

However, before you dive in there are a few items we need to address so that you may experience the full benefits of this step as quickly as possible.

Understand You Are Not A Victim, Nor Are You Forever Beholden To Your Past

One of the most difficult challenges most of us living with inner demons have is to accept we are not the victims we believe ourselves to be, especially if we have experienced excessive or horrific forms of trauma, abuse, or neglect. Just because we have experienced harm at the hands of others or through injurious events does not a victim make. Yes, we may have been harmed and we may even have been a victim at the given moment, but sadly many of us go through life believing we are still victims, sometimes decades later. Because of an ancient wound we experienced at the hands of another sometime deep in our past, we continue limiting ourselves through fear, guilt, and shame, in addition to making ourselves out to be less than we really are – to be broken and unwhole.

The real tragedy here is that we are in fact survivors, having received many strengths and blessings because of our experiences. But rather than recognize these benefits we instead focus on the infraction and what was done to us or taken from us. This focus weakens us, destroys our self-worth, and keeps us in a low-vibrational state that only attracts more of what we don't want. In effect, we make ourselves victims by broadcasting to the universe we are unlucky and good things rarely if ever come our way, so please, please, please, give us more of what we don't want because that is what we expect.

I can hear your protests now, so I beg of you to stay with me, because I once believed exactly as you do and therefore completely understand your protests.

Realize Everything That Occurs in Our Lives Serves Us in Some Way

As counterintuitive as it may sound, everything we experience does in fact serve us in some way. No matter what the experience there is always a benefit. The problem is we are often blind to the benefit because a) our conditioning and programming teaches us to play the victim and only look at the negative side of the equation, b) we are blind to the benefit being received, or are unwilling to admit it is a benefit because playing the victim fulfills a particular need we have, or c) the benefit doesn't manifest until sometime after the experience and we have yet to connect the dots.

I'm sure you can think of a crises or challenge that you, someone you personally know, or someone you know of has experienced, that initially seemed horrible and devastating, but with time and perspective were seen as blessings in disguise. As a direct or indirect result of the crises or challenge experienced you or this other person grew, became stronger, had new opportunities show up, and/or strengthened an existing relationship or entered into a new one. The point is there are always blessings and gifts received. Even in the immediate aftermath when we are totally blind to the benefits, we typically are experiencing numerous small blessings. They may show up in the form of a hug, a supportive friend offering to help out, or someone just listening to our story and our fears, when before these supportive acts may have seemed all but non-existent.

While there are many people's lives from which to draw from as examples, I'll use another personal one. Twice in my life, first as a child and then later as a young adult, I experienced sexual abuse that continued for an extended period. These experiences had devastating effects on my self-worth and my personal relationships, especially those of an intimate nature. As an adult these experiences continued to haunt me until I learned to be grateful for them by recognizing how they had benefited and served me, and continue to do so to this day.

Earlier I stated that I understood your protests. The snippet I just shared is only one example of the many horrific experiences I have endured in my life. Understandably I was a victim at the time, most especially as a young child. Sadly, like so many, I continued to feel like a victim throughout much of my life. So I unashamedly admit that accepting the idea that being grateful for everything in my life, no matter how painful or extraordinary, was initially a huge challenge for me. I questioned, how could I be grateful for all of the injustices I had suffered? And what could there possibly be to be grateful for about having been severely abused or mistreated by so many and for so long?

Reality check. I was tired of living as a victim. I was tired of feeling totally alone in the world. And I was tired of the constant mental and physical turmoil I was experiencing as a result of my bottling up and repressing my feelings and memories about these and other traumatic experiences. I had reached the point where I was willing to try just about anything to be free and feel whole again. This is where gratitude came into the picture. I had read a book and several articles on the subject of gratitude, which discussed the positive and immediate results we reap when we apply gratitude to the various aspects of our lives. Feeling I had nothing to lose, I put aside my skepticism and gave it a try. The results were immediate, profound, and lasting. I felt as if I had truly experienced a miracle.

One evening I sat and wrote page after page of reasons why I was truly grateful for every painful event I had experienced and to every person I felt had ever harmed me in any way. In a few short hours I felt as if the weight of the world had lifted from my shoulders. I cried happy tears for the joy of who I am and who I get to be, which is a result of everything that I've ever experienced. I found the benefits for taking the time to discover my blessings, the things for which I am truly grateful, are many. In just one evening I was able to release years and years worth of blame, shame, and guilt. And for the first time ever I was able to truly forgive not only my perpetrators, but also myself, which is often the most difficult thing for those who have been abused and violated to do. Very often we blame ourselves for the actions of others, or our inaction, when in fact we had absolutely nothing to do with the attack and most often had no means to prevent or stop it.

From that day forward many of my demons were no more. In a few short hours I had not only vanquished them, but I had also retired them into true and lasting wisdom. I recognized the strengths and gifts I had developed as a result of my experiences. I began to understand my path in life. And most importantly, I recognized that I truly liked the person I had become, and I wouldn't be that person without my first having lived through all of my experiences. This is the power of gratitude.

We Learn and Grow When We Acknowledge Our Blessings

Gratitude is one of the most effective methods for opening our eyes to the many benefits we have received from our experiences. When we find what we are truly thankful and appreciative for, including all of our experiences and all of the people in our lives, we recognize our strengths, heal our hearts and souls, regain our sense of wholeness, release the hold the past has on us, and very often discover our true calling, purpose, or path in life.

When we are grateful we no longer see the glass as half empty, but as full or overflowing. This is the blessing we receive when we express gratitude for everything in our lives, no matter how painful or horrific. There is always something to be grateful for, even when it is difficult to find, which admittedly can be especially challenging in the moment or immediate aftermath of a traumatic experience. When we find the blessings and learn from our experiences we grow as a person. The key is to accept that the blessings are there. Then apply the gift of gratitude to release the hold the event has on us. When we do this we open ourselves to the lessons and benefits received because we are now able to see the experience in a new light.

Gratitude isn't about finding the silver lining. It's about embracing the cloud with love and appreciation so that we are liberated from our self-imposed box. We have a choice in how we view our experiences and live our lives. We can see ourselves as victims of our circumstances and repress the best of who we are, or we can choose to liberate ourselves by finding our blessings and retiring our demons into wisdom, thereby stopping them from wreaking havoc on our lives.

When we recognize and acknowledge what we are grateful for, both in general and because of our experiences, we reap many benefits, many of which you will find to be immediate, lasting, and positively life-altering. The following is a sampling of some of the more common ones:

- Decreased physical pain
- Decreased mental turmoil

- Increased confidence and well-being
- Better relationships
- Increased feelings of wholeness (we feel more integrated and complete)
- A general feeling of happiness and fulfillment
- The ability to really love ourselves
- The ability to give and receive more freely and joyously
- A sense of purpose or direction

Use gratitude to help you learn and grow as a person. It's an experience you most definitely won't regret.

Take Responsibility For Your Life By Acknowledging and Accepting What You Have Experienced

The beauty of gratitude is its ability to help us acknowledge and accept what we have experienced in a positive way. When we acknowledge and accept what has transpired, we are in effect taking responsibility for our life: past, present, and future.

If you desire to experience a more fulfilling and abundant life, with more love, opportunity, and success, then give yourself the gift of gratitude. You're worth it. Begin being grateful for everything in your life and see what a difference it makes. See how quickly you begin to realize many more of your dreams and goals, how much more you enjoy each and every moment, and how much freer and more whole and complete you feel.

Don't underestimate the power of this simple tool. Put aside your fears and skepticism, take responsibility for your life, and apply the gift of gratitude.

You'll know when you are experiencing true and deep gratitude because it will bring tears of inspiration to your eyes, and your heart and mind will open up giving way to a more complete you. Gratitude equilibrates the positives and negatives in our lives by balancing our perspectives and expanding our consciousness. So I ask you, what is there not to be grateful for?

Remember, the choice is yours. You can continue to play the role of victim, or you can step into your power and reclaim your life. You *can* choose to liberate yourself and become the best you possible. When in doubt, realize you are still here – you survived. Since you are reading this book it's obvious you have a powerful desire to thrive. Honor your strength and your will to thrive. Gratitude will show you the way.

Personal Experience With Gratitude

I've already shared a few tidbits about my own experiences with gratitude. However, since I consider it to be one of the most important and beneficial steps in this book, as well as one of the most powerful healing tools known to mankind, I feel it is important to share a little more about how gratitude has helped me to heal and turn my life into a life I truly love. I do this because I very much want you to discover and experience the benefits of gratitude for yourself.

Before I began applying gratitude in my life, I really didn't like my life all that much, and sometimes I really hated it. Even though I had survived inordinate amounts of abuse, escaped my isolating childhood environment, and had become highly successful in ways beyond even my wildest dreams, I still felt miserable and unhappy much of the time. Everything seemed to be a struggle. I recurrently felt fearful, overwhelmed, and mistreated. I often blamed events and people from my past for the state of my well-being and much of my life in general. I didn't like a lot of things about myself. I was routinely as mentally abusive to myself as others had previously been. I pushed myself excessively. And I tended to suppress and hold back my anger, frustrations, and fears, which combined with the rest caused me to experience burnout, as well as a number of physical pains and maladies that were creating even more fear and unease.

Although I experienced some level of relief and healing through various other means and practices, it was the gift of gratitude that brought me the most immediate, in-depth, and lasting healing. Each time I have surrounded a painful event or circumstance in my life with love and appreciation I have experienced profound healing while simultaneously recovering another part of the person I know I was born to be.

Through the miraculous gift of gratitude, not only have I retired many of my demons, healed and returned to greater and greater levels of wholeness, but as mentioned earlier, I have also truly forgiven both my perpetrators and myself (something I thought impossible before experiencing the gift of gratitude).

Because of the gifts of gratitude I now love myself, and my life, in ways I never dreamed possible, despite very little having changed on the surface. Gratitude has helped me to recognize my calling in life. It has also allowed me to begin living in alignment with my true self. Does this mean I consider everything in my life to be exactly as I desire it to be or that I no longer experience heartache, pain, and other upsets? Not at all. What is does mean is the effects of the ups and downs of life are much less dramatic and much shorter in duration. Where once they may have lasted for days to years, they now typically last only a few minutes to a few hours (with rare cases lasting a few days), and then I'm back on top of my game, having recognized what it was that I needed to learn in order to continue my personal growth and healing.

May the gift of gratitude provide you with as much healing, peace, and understanding as it has for me and countless others.

In closing I'd like to share two additional quotes on gratitude. *"Gratitude is an art of painting an adversity into a lovely picture."* ~ Kak Sri. *"Grace isn't a little prayer you chant before receiving a meal. It's a way to live."* ~ Jacqueline Winspear.

It is my opinion that these quotes sum gratitude up in a way that provides incentive for making it a regular part of our lives.

Actions To Cultivate Feelings of Gratitude

We are only here in this life for a brief time. It seems only proper that we use everything at our disposal to make it the best life we possibly can. Gratitude is simple and effective. It costs you nothing more than a few minutes of your day. Apply it often for maximum benefit.

The following exercises provide a number of very effective methods for applying gratitude throughout your day and your life.

Try them all. Regularly employ the ones that work best for you and your circumstances.

1. **Your Morning 10**
   Every morning write down 10 things you are truly grateful for. They can be big, small, or even seemingly inconsequential, so long as you are truly grateful for them in some way. Use the form *"Today I am so happy and grateful for _____."*

Examples:

- Today I am so happy and grateful for the amazing dinner I shared with my best friend last night. It was great catching up and reconnecting. I hadn't realized how much I missed her. I'll make a point of keeping in touch and getting together because our time together always enriches our lives.

- Today I am so happy and grateful for the beautiful sunrise. Sunrises always give me a feeling of connection to the divine, as well as the hope that comes with the promise of a new day.

- Today I am so happy and grateful for Dan Millman's book *"The Peaceful Warrior"*. The wisdom contained within the pages of that book helped me to see how I have been making my life so much more challenging than necessary. Today I begin applying Socrates wisdom in my own life.

- Today I am so happy and grateful for the accident I was in yesterday. It was a real wakeup call. I now see how I've been so focused on do, do, do that I haven't actually been living. I'm making a point to stop and smell the roses each and every day.

Feel free to stop after stating what you are so happy and grateful for. Anything that follows isn't required. However, adding why you are so happy and grateful allows you to really acknowledge what it is you appreciate and thus discover why it is such a gift. Don't forget to look at both the positives and the negatives, as in the examples above, or you'll overlook some important lessons and benefits.

By performing this exercise each and every morning you will start your day with a positive outlook, even if you awoke in a less than stellar mood. Do it for at least 30 days before making a decision about its usefulness. Use your journal. Make notes about what you discover. At the end of thirty days, review what you have written. It will surprise you.

2. **Gratitude Discovery Session**
Write down all of the reasons you are grateful for a particular experience or person you feel has harmed you in some way,

especially if you still harbor any negative emotions towards the person or the event. Find the blessings. List how you have benefited and grown because of what you've experienced. Don't stop until you have listed at least 20 reasons (things you appreciate and are truly thankful for).
Example:

At the age of 7 your mother became seriously ill, such that she was often incapable of caring for herself or the family. Your father was away for weeks at a time on business; when home he was harsh and sometimes brutal. As a result of these circumstances you became the de facto stand in for your parents, acting as caretaker for your mother, your younger siblings, and the household, which stripped you of the opportunity to be a child or participate in most normal childhood experiences. Today you experience bitterness towards these events and your parents. You also feel insecure around your peers since you never really learned to associate with them. Even worse you're excessively hard on yourself, feeling you must take care of everything yourself, and that it must be perfect or you've failed. To top it all off, you're not sure who you really are.

A few of the direct and indirect benefits you've experienced and could be grateful for are as follows:
- Your ability to juggle many things at once without becoming flustered. You work extremely well in chaotic environments and know how to handle situations that many adults balk at or find extremely challenging.
- Your expertise as a cook. You learned to experiment and create all sorts of fantastic dishes. You now have a love of experimentation that excites the palates of many.
- Your ability to entertain yourself. You never get bored because you learned from a young age how to use your imagination, as well as your love for reading, writing, and drawing, to keep you entertained. Whenever you needed to escape or entertain your siblings you put these natural gifts to full use. Today they are well developed, even though you never had the advantage of professional instruction. People frequently express how gifted and talented you are.

The more things you can find for why you appreciate and are thankful to the person or the experience, the more the negative emotions and demons surrounding the person or experience will diminish. In short order you will see the person, circumstance, and yourself in a totally new light. You will gain new perspective, discover strengths and talents you hadn't previously recognized, and become a much happier, optimistic, and loving person.

The more you perform this exercise the more possibilities you will begin to see. Being aware of the possibilities creates more opportunity. But, more importantly, the more you do this exercise, the more you will begin to like, if not love, the person you have become. When you really like and ultimately love yourself, you will attract great things into your life.

3. Gratitude Letter

Write a letter of gratitude to someone whom you are sincerely grateful and appreciative. The person can be living or dead. Express everything you can think of as to why you are grateful to them. Be specific. Do your best to recreate the memories of how you felt. Describe why what they did meant so much to you both then and now. Share how it has positively affected your life.

Once you've finished you can either send the letter or not. Realize it's much more powerful if you actually send it. If the person is no longer living, just read it aloud as if you were reading it to them. Do this as well if you otherwise choose not to send the letter.

An additional way to use this exercise is to write a letter of gratitude to yourself. Describe all the reasons you are grateful for your past challenges, as well as your triumphs. (Do this version for 30 days. It is profoundly healing and will help you move forward both in love and in life. Another potential benefit is the discovery or solidification of who it is you would like to become.)

Once you've mastered this technique, try it with someone you feel has harmed you, or for which you harbor negative feelings. The benefits far outweigh the costs.

4. Gratitude Inventory List

Create a list of 100 things for which you are grateful. If you desire, you can divide the list into different categories to get you started. Some examples are personal possessions (things you own), relationships, personal qualities (character traits about yourself and others you admire), personal experiences (places you've been, things you done), financial assets, work (paid, volunteer), etc.

One hundred items may sound like a lot, but once you break your life into categories it doesn't take long. When you've come up with 100 items, take it to a new level by coming up with another 100, and then another.

Periodically repeat the exercise because new things will come to you.

5. **Gratitude Journal**

Keep a daily gratitude journal. You can include your Morning 10, your Gratitude Discover Sessions, and your Gratitude Inventory List. You might also include an Evening 10, listing what went well today and why you are grateful.

Remember, you have lots to be grateful for. Often it's the simple things, such as the joy of seeing a rainbow, having a cup of tea with a good friend, or taking a leisurely and relaxing bubble bath at the end of a hectic day.

As the days, weeks, and months go by, your journal will fill with all sorts of beautiful, hopeful, and optimistic feelings. Through the frequent and continued exposure to these feelings you will experience a positive inner shift that will be reflected in your outer reality. In a short time you will realize you are delighted with who you are and the direction your life is going.

∴

Gratitude brings forth the riches of life; complaint brings only misery and poverty. In which well spring are you swimming?

As you become more clear about who you really are, you'll be better able to decide what is best for you – the first time around.
-Oprah Winfrey

Step 6 – Tell Your Story: Share It, Understand It, Rewrite It

Cara's Story

Cara is a well-known, talented, and financially successful artist with many enthusiasts and admirers. Yet for most of her life something prevented her from creating the art she could see in her mind's eye. Technically she was always extremely proficient, much better than most, but for some unknown reason she never seemed to be able to capture the feeling and passion she felt her art needed to really touch the soul. To her it was good, but nonetheless lifeless.

As art is Cara's life, she found it devastating when she'd reached the point where she didn't feel she could continue if she couldn't portray the feeling and passion she desired. It seemed no amount of accolades or success was worth it if she couldn't visually express the passion and emotion she felt was missing.

What Cara didn't know at the time was how directly her childhood conditioning was affecting her art. As a child she'd been taught to never show her emotions or talk about the awful things that went on inside her home. This conditioning was so ingrained that Cara couldn't allow herself to express the magic spark of her soul – that essence a number of really great artists throughout history have captured so well.

Just at the point of giving up art altogether, Sam, one of Cara's close friends, took her under his wing. With his caring and understanding manner she gradually opened up about her early life. Without prying or pointedly asking her about her past Sam just comforted, listened, and suggested she take some time to explore why she had decided to become an artist and how she would feel if she gave it up.

Over the course of several months, Cara reflected on Sam's suggestion. Little by little she shared stories from her past with him about why she had become an artist. What Sam routinely noticed was how little emotion Cara showed when telling her stories, despite them being so sad and painful it was all he could do to hold back a flood of tears. In an attempt to help Cara, Sam asked Cara how a particularly sad and traumatic story made her feel. Cara looked him straight in the face, completely bewildered and said, *"I don't understand what you are asking. What do you mean how does it make me feel?"* Sam then proceeded to share with Cara how it made him feel.

This was an exciting turning point for Cara. She realized when she shared her life stories with Sam she felt lighter and more alive. Additionally Sam's responses opened her eyes to what had been stolen from her as a result of the repression of her feelings and emotions. She thought, *"It's no wonder I can't portray the feeling and passion I desire in my art, I've had them tightly locked away beyond the reaches of my brush."*

With these realizations Cara made a vow she would allow herself to talk about things previously considered forbidden. Additionally, she would relearn how to express her feelings and emotions. She'd do whatever it took to be whole again, so she could bring her art to life. If that meant sharing with the whole world, then so be it.

With Sam's help Cara quickly learned to feel, recognize, and understand her feelings and emotions, but expressing them was still a challenge. While she now intensely feels her emotions, the years of shutting them off had become so automatic that without someone letting her know she still showed little to no expression she had no awareness. Inside she was alive and overflowing with feeling, but outside she was continuing, mostly unbeknownst to her, to put forth her famously conditioned poker face.

Cara felt fortunate to have such a wonderful friend as Sam. She felt he saved her life and her art. The more Cara learned to feel and express her emotions, the more the passion and soul she'd previously felt were missing began showing up. Today Cara is even more successful as an artist. With each passing year, as she continues her healing journey, both she and her art have become more alive, passionate, and soulful.

The Healing Powers Of Telling Our Story

Telling our story is almost always healing, especially for those of us who have been taught or forced to suppress our feelings, emotions, and even our memories. When we tell our story, especially to a kind, compassionate, and understanding soul, who has the capacity to help us relearn how to feel our feelings, understand them, and ultimately to express them, we are simultaneously liberated and healed. Telling our story helps us to become reacquainted with our true self by helping us to reintegrate integral elements of our natural being, which have been relegated to some off-limit area of our mind or body, to be toyed with by our demons until we finally accept, acknowledge, and express what we feel.

Many reasons exist for why we suppress the parts of us that make us feel fully alive and whole. However, as with the suppression of our confidence, self-esteem, and self-worth, it's most often the result of the traumas, abuses, and neglect we experienced as children.

It is a disgraceful tragedy that so many of us are punished for expressing our true selves, which includes expressing what we think, feel, and remember. We are told or asked such things as *"oh no, you don't feel that way"*, *"what do you have to be happy/sad... about"*, *"we don't talk about those things in this family"*, *"don't you ever let me hear you talking about that again"*, *"that's not how it happened"*, *"you're lying"*, *"if I catch you crying again, I'll give you something to cry about"*, and so on. Sometimes we're even lied to about our memories, being told they are wrong, that it happened another way (the way we are expected to remember it), or that it didn't happen at all, it's just our imagination.

This occurs time and time again, frequently being delivered in a threatening or demeaning manner. The result for the majority of us on the receiving end is the shutdown of our feelings. Our survival instincts kick in to ensure we survive, which causes us to disregard our feelings and thereby suppress our emotions. For many it becomes so complete they couldn't tell you what they feel, even if they wanted to, just as Cara couldn't initially tell Sam. For others, they go so far as to also repress or alter certain memories in order to cope with the pain and unpleasantness of their past or current circumstances.

Benefits Of Telling Our Story

Telling our story has many benefits. For starters, it feels good to let things out; it's cathartic. When done in a purposeful manner the benefits derived are directed, in-depth, and lasting. A few of the most noticeable benefits of telling our story include the following:

1. **A Deeper Understanding of Ourselves and Others**
   When we share our story we learn a great deal about ourselves through the reactions and responses of those we share with. We discover things we had been completely unaware of, which have been affecting us both positively and negatively. We make connections that had previously gone unnoticed. Additionally, we gain a better understanding of those we share with, as well as those who are a part of our story.

2. **A More Realistic Perspective**
   Telling our story provides us with the gift of perspective. Often, just through the process of telling the story, we see things in a whole new light. This can occur even if we only write our story, rather than actually sharing it. However, when we share our story with another person we have the added benefit of our listener's reactions, thoughts, and perspectives to help us see things we've been blind to, misinterpreting, or beating ourselves up for.

3. **Increased Personal Wisdom**
   Just as telling our story provides us with a deeper understanding and more realistic perspective, it also enhances our knowledge base, strengthens our intuition, and improves our insight, thereby increasing our wisdom. Telling our story improves our ability to discern and judge what is true and right for us. Some of our most enlightening moments occur through the process of telling our story.

4. **True and Lasting Emotional Freedom**
   Telling our story is a release that provides varying degrees of emotional freedom. Through the process of telling our story we open the pressure valve that has kept our suppressed

feelings, emotions, and memories locked away. The more completely we open the valve and process what comes up, the freer we become.

Telling our story, both on paper and to one or more trusted individuals, is a great way to open our hearts and minds, and reconnect us with our true selves. Through repeated telling, and as we will see later, the rewriting of our story, we peel back layer upon layer of false representations of who we think we are or think we should be, until finally we meet our true spirit, which might possibly be the greatest experience we can ever have.

5. **Improved Health and Well-Being**

Telling our story has the added benefit of improving our health and general state of well-being.

One of its greatest benefits is its ability to reduce our stress levels. Remember the pressure value we just talked about. That valve produces a lot of stress. It takes a lot of energy to keep all of those feelings, emotions, and memories bottled up. Telling our story reduces the pressure and increases the flow of healing energy, thereby raising us up and lifting our spirits.

Other key benefits include the diminished symptoms of depression, anxiety, panic, and post-traumatic stress disorders, reduced substance abuse, and reduced pain from autoimmune and inflammatory disorders frequently associated with the long-term suppression of feelings, emotions, and traumatic memories.

And finally, telling our story leads the way to clearer thinking and improved problem-solving abilities.

Dangers Of Telling Our Story

It should now be obvious that telling our story has many benefits. But, what of its dangers? In truth there really aren't many. Most of the time it is way more dangerous not to tell our story, because as we've seen and research has proven it is always harmful to keep our feelings, emotions, and painful memories bottled up inside of us, especially for long periods of time.

It's not so much the events we experience that cause us problems, but rather how we process them (or in this case don't process them). The suppression of our feelings and emotions is a major factor in the creation of our demons and their playground. Processing and releasing them sets us free and heals us. Remember, long-term suppression has been proven to be a key link in the development of numerous life-threatening diseases and psychological disorders.

That being said, the only real dangers I'm aware of are 1) telling your story to someone who would use the information to harm you, 2) telling your story to someone who isn't supportive or understanding, and 3) digging into certain types of very traumatic experiences too quickly (e.g., experiences that have induced suicidal tendencies, PTSD, manic depression, or other serious conditions where the individual often desires to do harm to themselves, or others).

Danger number one should most definitely be avoided. Danger number two won't necessarily do much harm, but it certainly won't allow you to heal as quickly, and it could cause setbacks or regression. Danger number three is a hard one to call. It will require personal judgment from both you and the persons with which you are working.

If you are extremely depressed, have frequent or intense anxiety or panic attacks, have any form of PTSD or life threatening substance abuse habit, or are at all suicidal, then please consider getting professional help before embarking too deep into the stories surrounding the traumas that have brought on your debilitating disorder. We wouldn't want you to plunge any deeper into despair than you already have.

If you have any of the disorders listed above, please understand that effective methods, well beyond the scope of this book, exist to help you heal from these life-threatening disorders. Those with less severe cases of many of these disorders can definitely benefit from the storytelling methods shared in this step, as well as the actions provided in the other steps. However, I again urge caution, and recommend professional guidance from a psychiatrist, psychologist, or other qualified therapist if you see a marked increase in any of your symptoms. I want you to heal and become whole again, not plunge deeper into the pit of despair in which you currently find yourself.

NOTE: Brief increases in symptoms are often part of the healing process. This is due to the stirring up, surfacing, and processing of what we have long suppressed. It is also due to the grieving process; that is, we often grieve whom we have been for so long as we begin to step more fully into our authenticity.

In these cases, a life or personal empowerment coach, who is knowledgeable and experienced with the effects and healing stages of trauma induced demons, may be just the ticket to help you swiftly move forward and put your demons to rest. These individuals are typically more effective than a trusted friend or family member because they know how to guide you on your journey. They will also provide you with helpful feedback and supplemental exercises to more quickly and effectively move you through the healing process.

Ways To Safely Tell Your Story

There are many ways we can tell our story. When we think of telling our story, two forms automatically come to mind: 1) sharing it with another person or group, and 2) writing it down, as in a memoir. However, there are a variety of others to consider that are very effective for helping us on our journey to become whole again.

The methods we will cover are specifically meant to help you gain understanding and perspective, reintegrate lost parts of yourself, reacquaint yourself with your *true* self, retire your demons into wisdom, and become emotionally free, thus leading to inner peace, wholeness, and personal fulfillment.

These storytelling methods are extremely safe and effective for most individuals. They fall into two distinct categories: 1) various forms of solitary writing, and 2) various forms of personal interactions.

If you don't like to write or feel you aren't any good at it, please put aside your prejudices against the activity and give it a try, because it is truly one of the most incredible healing tools you have at your disposal. If you are afraid to share with another person, for whatever reason, please find the courage to give it a try with someone you feel you can trust, and whom you know to be compassionate and supportive. As mentioned earlier, it's best if they can also give you feedback that will help illuminate your blind spots. What you don't want is someone who is merely sympathetic, that is someone whose main objective is commiseration. The goal is to understand, heal, and grow, not commiserate about your wows and remain where you are. Remember, you are only a victim if you choose to be, and while sympathy on its own may temporarily make you feel better, its potential for any real healing or growth is severely limited.

Writing To Tell Your Story

Writing is free therapy; it's cathartic. It feels good to write. And it's also a great way to get a lot of stuff off your chest without the need for confrontation.

There are many ways to use writing to tell your story. The various forms discussed here are in effect different forms of journaling. Journaling is the act of recording and reflecting on one's personal experiences, thoughts, and feelings on an ongoing and regular basis. Journaling as you will see is far more than keeping a diary. It is in fact an effective problem-solving tool that opens the doorway to greater personal awareness, clearer perspective, and deep and profound insights about oneself, one's life, and one's relationships. The more you journal, the more benefits you receive. Journal regularly and take notice how much wiser and more integrated you are becoming; notice also how your relationships and sense of well-being are improving.

The following forms of writing are best done in a quiet place where you will have uninterrupted time for 15-60 minutes. Their principle purpose is to 1) improve your powers of introspection and self-reflection in order to gain personal understanding, new perspectives, and increased clarity; and 2) find empowering solutions and answers to your problems and challenges.

1. **Writing To Explore Your Feelings and Emotions**
   Writing about your feelings and emotions relieves stress, clears the mind, increases personal awareness of your self-defeating behaviors, and provides insights about your triggers. It allows you to face your fears and demons head on, and to have conversations with people you're currently afraid to or can't, all without repercussion. It helps you to better understand the people in your life, gaining perspective as to why they behave as they do, and even more importantly to understand why you react to them as you do. And finally, it

helps you become aware of your strengths, gifts, and talents, know what is most important to you, and recognize the things that make you feel good.

Whenever you experience strong feelings or emotions, either positive or negative, take some time to write about them and what brought them on. If you feel distraught, upset, or have something troubling you, take some time to write about it. Write about what you feel. Vent. Talk things out as if you were conversing with the person who upset you. Talk to your higher self and get her perspective. Ask yourself questions, such as *Why do I feel this way? What set me off?*

2. Freeform Writing

Freeform writing is nothing more than flow of consciousness writing. It is best done for a period of 10-30 minutes. All you do is write whatever comes up, without stopping, thinking, or editing; just write until the time you've set aside has elapsed. At the conclusion of the specified time, go back and read what you have written. You'll be surprised at the insights that surface. You'll also wonder where some of what you wrote came from. It came from you, your inner guide, the voice you so often ignore.

The more you practice, the more insights you'll have. The more specific and purposeful you are, the more readily they'll show up. If you'd like, pick a topic you want to explore and then let your thoughts flow freely through your pen.

3. Non-Dominant Hand Writing

Non-Dominant handwriting is the act of writing with your non-dominant hand (i.e., if you are right-handed you are going to write with your left-hand). The key benefit of this form of writing is its more direct access to the creative powers of the less used hemisphere of your brain (the one that's not accessed as much when you use your dominant hand).

You can use non-dominant handwriting for any of the writing exercises. You'll typically get significantly different answers, solutions, and insights from those you would receive from using your dominant hand.

Warning: Writing with your non-dominant hand will feel awkward. Don't let this stop you from applying it, because the benefits are far greater than a bit of discomfort. Remember, you are accessing infrequently tapped creative resources that will help you grow and heal.

4. **Guided Questions Writing**
   This process involves writing down a powerful and evocative question, to which you desire an answer, followed by the answers that surface. When you've captured your answer, repeat the process by asking a related or deeper question. Keep going until nothing else comes to mind. Review your answers and act on those that will take you and your life in the direction you desire.

   Example Questions:
   - What if I treated myself the way I should have been treated, rather than the way I was treated/am being treated?
   - What actions can I take right now to feel more empowered?
   - How could *this* turn out better than anything I have imagined or planned? (e.g., *this* = this day, my life, this interview)

   Use guiding questions whenever you desire a solution, have something troubling you, or just want to explore some aspect of your life. The answers you receive will astound you.

   The benefits of using guiding questions are many. For our purposes, they are threefold: 1) increased awareness, by uncovering what was previously hidden from your consciousness, 2) improved understanding and perspective, and 3) manifestation of beneficial solutions that will improve your life.

   All of the answers you require reside within. The trick is in asking the right questions in order to draw the answers out.

   NOTE: Your mind will answer whatever question you ask of it. So make sure the questions you ask are expansive rather than limiting. Here's an example: *What can I learn from this?* vs. *Why do I always fail at this?* The first question is expansive. It gives way to beneficial solutions and creates an opening for asking further probing questions. The second is limiting. It has a sense of finality about it that closes us down to the possibilities and opportunities that exist.

5. **Re-Storying Your Life**

The purpose of re-storying your life is to consciously alter the direction of your life. It means to *add* in purpose, meaning, and direction, where one of these may be completely missing or in short supply in your current life. It doesn't mean erasing your post or starting over in the sense of changing your family, friends, spouse, job, etc., although you may choose to make some changes in one or more of these areas.

The point is to add purpose, meaning, and direction in a way that doesn't compromise who you truly are. In essence the rewrite makes your life more fulfilling by allowing you to be even more of who you truly are, in each and every moment and in all that you do. It's a way to outline and begin visualizing exactly how you would like you and your life to be, if you were living the most authentic and meaningful life you've imagined. It's also a way to help you discover the ways in which you can realize your imagined life or something better.

To start the process, begin by asking yourself the following question: What one thing can I do in my life, which if I did it consistently, would have the most significant impact on my life today and in the future? Repeat this question for each area of your life, replacing life with career, family, marriage, relationship, free time, spiritual life, finances, health, etc.

Use your answers to rewrite your life story in a manner that provides you with a sense of purpose, meaning, and direction; a life where you feel you would be eternally fulfilled, where you would describe your life as being blissful.

With your new story in hand, begin taking consistent steps to make it become your reality.

The writing forms we've discussed are the ones I've personally found to be the very effective. Many books and online resources exist if you wish to learn more about journaling or writing for personal growth and healing. You'll find two companion reports on the subject at www.WomensWholenessConnection.com entitled, *"Journaling for Happiness and Well-Being"* and *"25 Power Questions for Effortlessly Transforming Your Life"*.

Sharing With Others To Tell Your Story

The forms of sharing we will explore for telling your story all involve personally interacting with one or more individuals. The point is to communicate with someone, in-person, over the phone, or via a live electronic feed such as FaceTime or Skype. Whenever possible, go for an in-person setting as it gives you the benefit of being able to see the other person's body language and they yours.

The benefits of sharing your story, live and in-person, are your partner can 1) be a mirror for you, allowing you to see things you otherwise wouldn't (your blind spots) 2) provide you with valuable feedback about the themes and undercurrents they pick up 3) ask revealing questions that take you deeper and deeper below the surface so that you get to the heart of the matter and ultimately meet your true self, and 4) be a sounding board to help you hear what you are nonconsciously thinking and saying. Sometimes we learn the most by just having someone to listen.

Each of the following sharing interactions can last from a few brief minutes to multiple lengthy sessions. Shoot for at least 30 minutes.

1. **Conversations With Close Friends and Family**

   We typically find it relatively easy to share things about our lives and ourselves when talking with close friends, family members, or other confidants. However, this isn't always the case as illustrated in Cara's story.

   The advantage of friends and family is an established comfort level and familiarity. They often already know a lot of our story. If they are good listeners and sounding boards, as Sam was in Cara's story, they can be very helpful to us, especially if they are also gifted at providing constructive feedback and asking helpful questions. They are also frequently a good source for venting, provided the venting session doesn't turn into a pity-party.

The disadvantages of friends and family are 1) they can be too sympathetic, and 2) they don't always want us to heal and grow because their own insecurities make them feel we will leave them behind as we move on to greener pastures. Remember, friends and family often have just as many hang-ups as we do; therefore, they often aren't really capable of providing much help.

2. Coaching Sessions

Coaches are a great resource. Life, success, and personal empowerment coaches are typically skilled in assisting their clients with various aspects of their personal growth and development, including the discovery of the client's life purpose and mission. They typically share advice, offer guidance, assist in the development of plans and goals, and act in an accountability capacity to improve the client's follow through so they can more effectively accomplish their goals and begin living their desired lives.

A good coach will focus all of their attention on you, the coachee, from day one. They are encouraging and supportive, and assume strength and capability, rather than weakness, helplessness, or dependence. They will listen and intuit, not only to the words you say, but also to the words and energies behind your words. They will ask you a lot of guiding questions to help you achieve greater awareness, discover your *own* solutions, and become a more empowered individual. Ultimately, the coach is there to shine a light on your truth, by being absolutely truthful about where you are strong, where you hold back, where you give up, where you are in denial, where you deny yourself, where you rationalize, etc.

Working with a good coach will provide you with knowledge, understanding, and strategies to effectively and more rapidly improve the quality of your life. Sessions tend to run from 30 to 60 minutes, once every week or two, and utilize a co-active form of communication that assumes possibilities, capability, and choice, while continually shifting the focal point of the conversation to deeper and deeper levels of personal connection. Sessions typically begin with a brief discussion of the coachee's achievements and celebrations, and end with actions the coachee is committed to accomplishing within a specified period. They can be in person or over the phone.

Every coaching situation is unique. No one coach, or type of coach, is perfect for everyone, or every need. However, coaches are one of the most effective ways to quickly improve the state of your life. They are open and objective, and focused entirely on helping you to create the life you desire in as short a time as possible. They will see the best in you and help you draw it out.

3. Counseling Sessions

Counselors typically have degrees in psychology, psychiatry or a related field. For our purposes, they include psychologists, psychiatrists, licensed mental health counselors, behavioral therapists, psychoanalysts, and rehabilitation counselors, although marriage and family counselors, as well as clinical social workers may also be included. These individuals tend to focus on helping their clients and patients manage or overcome various emotional issues and disorders, such as stress, anxiety, panic, depression, PTSD, relationship challenges, abuse (child, physical, sexual, substance), and learning difficulties.

Sessions are typically interactive, held in the counselor's or therapist's office, and focus on resolution of the client's given emotional challenge, such that the client is able to live a healthier and more fulfilling life. They tend to focus on exploration and discovery of the underlying causes for the client's condition, providing methods for managing the condition, and ultimately finding solutions to resolve the condition or allow the client to effectively cope with it. Sessions often utilize talk therapy, although some may use other forms of therapy such as hypnosis. Sessions with qualified practitioners are often covered by medical insurance.

Counseling sessions are often beneficial for those whose life is being dramatically disrupted by an emotional affliction, such as those previously listed. Some counselors may prescribe the use of drugs to help the client manage their condition until it can be brought under control or resolved. Successful sessions lead to the ability to more effectively cope, the ability to make healthier life choices, a marked reduction in symptoms, better stress management, improved self-esteem, freedom from addictions, increased assertiveness, and an improved outlook on life.

As with coaching, counseling is unique to the individual and their situation. If you feel you would benefit from professional counseling, recognize you may need to try several different counselors before finding one that's a good fit for your particular needs.

4. **Support Groups**

Support groups are designed for their members to provide each other with various types of nonprofessional and nonmaterial support regarding a particular shared condition that is especially burdensome to the individuals. The support often includes listening to, accepting, and validating each other's experiences, providing and evaluating relevant information, serving as accountability partners, and providing guidance to help other members through the next stage of their recovery. For temporary conditions, the support is generally geared toward helping the individual to overcome and move beyond the condition or experience.

Many types of support groups exist. They are typically organized and managed by their members, who have personal experience with the group's particular focus, or by a professional whose role is to facilitate the group. Member run organizations include various types of self-help groups. Some common focus areas for these groups include managing addictions, such as alcoholism and eating disorders, coping with painful or life-threatening medical conditions, such as cancer, diabetes, and AIDS, and coping with the aftermath of life-altering events, such as rape, stroke, loss of a limb, or loss of a child.

Groups can be found in many cities and towns, as well as online. For some conditions, online groups may be the only effective choice. Two unique aspects of many of these groups are 1) member anonymity, which can be beneficial for those who are anxious or embarrassed about sharing, and 2) the sense of community and understanding they provide their members. Online groups often provide these qualities in spite of the geographical distances and the lack of face-to-face interaction between their members.

If you have trouble sharing, or don't feel you have anyone with whom you can share, support groups may be a good fit for you. If you have a particularly burdensome condition, they may also help you to better cope with the condition so that you can more effectively apply your energies to creating the life you desire.

5. **Experiential Workshops**

Experiential workshops are designed to help the participants master what they have come to learn while they are in the workshop, so they are ready and confident to apply it when they return to their everyday lives. They are highly interactive and use a variety of experiential and accelerated learning techniques that employ all the senses and emotions.

Participants actively engage their whole being in the learning process. They participate in simulations of real world situations to incorporate the learning into their minds and bodies, which provides immediate and lasting learning. Simulations are typically followed up with short debriefings between two or more participants or the leader of the workshop. The purpose of these debriefings is to solidify the participants learning and provide opportunities for them to learn from one another's experiences as well as those of the leader.

This type of workshop is often very transformational for the attendees. The style and content of the workshop allows the attendees to both learn and heal through the real-time application of the techniques being taught and the sharing of their experiences in a supportive and encouraging environment.

For a concrete example, consider the guiding questions from earlier in this step. Say for example you were at a workshop that was teaching what they are and how to use them. In an experiential workshop the workshop leader would demonstrate their usage with one of their staff, or possibly one of the attendees. The leader would then have all of the attendees partner up and practice using what they have just learned in various real life situations. Once the exercise is complete, partnered participants debrief with each other, discussing their experiences and what they learned. The leader will then usually ask for a few volunteers to share their experiences and lessons with the entire group.

Many workshops of this type exist. Most are held live, but some are held as telecourses. Experiential workshops are much more fun and effective than the common lecture style employed in most conferences and seminars. Personal experience has shown me that those with fewer participants (less than 40) are generally more transformational, although well-orchestrated workshops with hundreds of participants can be highly effective and equally transformational. An added benefit of this style of workshop is the relationships you make. Very often you leave having created new friends that stand the test of time and distance.

Experiential workshops draw out the best of who we are, helping us to see ourselves and our experiences in a whole new light. I highly recommend you give them a try.

Actions To Understand, Share, and Re-Story Your Life

The storytelling methods outlined in this step are extremely safe to use for most individuals. They are meant to help you quickly and effectively retire your demons, heal, and become whole again, so that you experience all of the benefits previously discussed, and more. Put them to use often and you'll quickly find yourself feeling freer, lighter, and more fully engaged with life.

Here are some recommended story telling exercises to help you quickly experience a new level of growth and healing. Have fun with them.

1. **Journal for Discovery and Clarity**
   Purchase a notebook or journal to collect your thoughts and perform the various writing forms previously described. Any notebook will work, but using a nice journal is more appealing to

the senses. Your journals should be treasured, so make them special to you.

Refer to the *Methods of Writing for Telling Your Story* described earlier for a refresher when performing the following writing exercises.

a. Regularly journal to explore your feelings and emotions, especially when you find yourself down, upset, or troubled. With practice you will be able to shift your mood within a matter of minutes.

b. Employ freeform or non-dominant handwriting for at least 10 minutes per day for the next 30 days. Do them both, or alternate their use. After 30 days repeat the exercise as you find useful, preferably once per week. On some days, just write with no particular purpose in mind. On others, pick a topic you want to explore and let it flow. Either way, don't think, just write. When you've finished, review your writing for any insights, being sure to act on what you've learned.

c. Perform the guiding questions exercise described earlier. Do it every day for 30 days, then whenever it could prove beneficial for discovering useful insights or empowering solutions.

    This technique is especially powerful when used in combination with exploring your feelings and emotions. For instance, asking yourself *"What about the situation upset me? Was there a particular trigger?"* can be very beneficial, as can asking yourself *"What about his/her actions specifically upset/triggered me?"*

    Create your own questions relevant to the situation at hand. Ask, answer, and apply what you learn. I once did this regarding a co-worker with whom I was constantly butting heads and getting upset with for reasons that completely eluded me. Long story short, he had the habit of saying no without listening, which to me sounded as if her were saying it's his way or the highway. This triggered old issues I had with my father. It pushed the same buttons, although he and my father couldn't be more different. Once I discovered this trigger I had a conversation with my co-worker, which readily improved our working relationship. As it turned out he wasn't aware of what he was doing or how it was being perceived. In the end I discovered his intentions were entirely different from my triggered perceptions, which led to better overall communication between the two of us.

    d. Re-story your life as previously described. When you've finished, read what you've written to inspire yourself. Additionally, create actionable goals and begin acting on them to turn your new story into your reality. Regularly reread what you've written. Feel free to refine and add details that inspire you. Repeat the full exercise once or twice per year to continue taking your life to new levels.

2. Share with Someone You Trust

It's important to have someone with whom you can talk, share, and explore your feelings, emotions, and experiences. We don't easily heal and grow in a vacuum. Writing is an important part of the process and highly beneficial, but most real transformation and healing occurs because of the interactions we have with others. It sets into motion what we can then explore further through writing and additional sharing.

The section entitled *Methods of Sharing for Telling Your Story* described five highly beneficial possibilities for sharing with a trustworthy individual or group, in a safe and encouraging environment. The following sharing methods are recommended as part of your healing strategy and ongoing journey. Choose the ones that are most applicable to your situation and resources.

    a. Find a trustworthy friend or family member with whom you feel safe. Ask them if they would be willing to be your healing partner. This means you are willing to be there for them as well. Share and explore experiences you've been ashamed and fearful to talk about. Talk about what troubles you and why, as well as what excites you. Ask them to tell you how your story made them feel (especially if you are emotionally challenged like Cara was), to provide you with any insights they may have picked up on, and to point out anything they feel you are denying. Allow them the freedom to dig below the surface of your answers.

Since we live in such a demanding world, where everyone's time seems to be so limited, it is best to have more than one person with whom you can share. Whether it is one person, or many, please don't overwhelm them. Be respectful of their time and capacity to support you.

b. Find a coach and work with them for at least six months. If it's obvious they aren't a good fit, then by all means find someone else. When you are more familiar with the coaching process, you may want to be more selective or have multiple coaches for specific purposes.

Although coaches do charge a fee for their services, they are worth it for the progress you will make. If you don't have a personal friend, family member, or some other form of support group, you should definitely consider a coach. Even if you do, you might still consider a coach. They can help you gain the confidence and communication skills you need to attract trustworthy people into your life. They are also a wellspring of advice and resources for you to draw from to rapidly improve the quality of your life.

c. If you have a debilitating and burdensome condition, especially one that is potentially life threatening, it's recommended you find an appropriate counselor or support group with whom you can work to manage or resolve your condition.

Whether we want to admit it or not, professional help and therapeutic measures are sometimes required to regain control of our life. The demons we experience sometimes affect our minds and bodies so intensely that medicinal treatments are temporarily necessary to reestablish more normal functioning, such as with hormonal imbalances that negatively affect our emotions and turn our lives into chaos.

If you're currently in this category, please don't feel ashamed. Get the treatment you need so you can heal and move on with your life. All sorts of treatments exist, including ones that are totally natural, with few to no side effects. You could be pleasantly surprised to find that many of your troubles stem from nothing more than food intolerance. Eliminate the offending food and voila, you're experiencing normal functioning once again.

d. Attend experiential workshops at least once or twice a year, more if you can manage it. Pick ones that fit your specific needs. When you attend, fully participate. Give it your undivided attention. If you play full on you will derive benefits beyond anything you can imagine.

Workshops range from a couple of hours to several days in length. Prices vary from under $100 to several thousand. Begin at whatever level will get you started and experiencing the benefits. Once you've begun you'll readily determine how best to proceed. Coaches are a wonderful resource for discovering what's available and applicable to your needs. If you don't have anyone to ask, go online and spend some time researching what's available.

3. **Create a Support Network**
To facilitate your healing, you want to create a multifaceted support system, which combines journaling with several forms of personal sharing. Pick three to five forms that are most appropriate to your situation. Start small and buildup. In time you'll create a very effective support network as appropriate to your life and goals.

Examples:
Three Forms:
- A close friend
- A support group (e.g., for grief or abuse)
- Journaling

Five Forms:
- A close friend or co-worker

- An accountability partner
- A personal coach (e.g., life, health, business, success...)
- Periodic experiential workshops
- Journaling

Part Two

BECOMING YOUR BEST SELF

~~~~~

Every journey has a secret destination of
which the traveler is unaware.
– Martin Buber

Step 7 – Be Who You Were Born To Be: You Are Much More Than A Victim or A Survivor

Cheri's Story

Cheri was a highly respected surgeon who had graduated with honors from Harvard Medical School. All her life she had been pushed, prodded, and told she would become a world famous surgeon and that was that. No one even bothered to consider whether Cheri was actually interested in being a surgeon. It was just assumed from the start she would indeed be a surgeon. Therefore, Cheri's youth was devoted to grooming her to that end. Any time she expressed other interests they were dismissed as irrelevant or denigrated to the point of making them seem to be foolhardy ideas at best. As a result Cheri capitulated very early on, because any form of resistance or denial was always met with a rash of disapproving insults followed by a doubling down of medically related studies and ghastly dissections.

Several years after starting her practice Cheri began to experience a constant nagging from within. She felt a strong pull to be living a life that was markedly different from the life associated with being a surgeon (i.e., long hours, always on call, high stress, life and death decisions, medical conferences, hospital fund raising events, seemingly obligatory status symbols of wealth, etc.). Her heart and soul tugged at her, constantly whispering to her about her childhood and youthful desires to be a writer. What she wanted more than anything was to write poetry, short stories, and novels that dripped with flowery and evocative language that stirred the imagination and touched the soul.

Day after day Cheri felt this tug, but the rational part of her mind kept telling her it was just a fanciful dream, saying, *"You've made it. Look at all you've endured to be where you are. Who in their right mind walks away from such a prestigious, high-paying, and important job to go sit on the beach and in coffee shops to write poetry, especially after having sacrificed their entire youth in pursuit of such a goal? You are a surgeon for God's sake. You save lives. What you do is important. Writing poetry is for flakes. Besides, how do you expect to make a living writing poetry? Have you lost your mind? If you really must, why not just write poetry and stories for fun? You can always write in your free time and still be a famous surgeon."*

In time it was all Cheri could do to drag herself into the hospital. Fearing she might cause irreparable harm to one of her patients, because of the unyielding cries from her inner guide, Cheri decided to take a short leave and get away from it all to give herself some time to reflect on what had become a never-ending pull to walk away from her life as a surgeon. Days later Cheri found herself unwinding on a beach in Hawaii having an amazingly refreshing conversation with an elderly woman with a sage like countenance. After some discussion of her feelings and current predicament, this sagely woman advised Cheri to allow herself to go with the flow of her spirit, to open up to her own natural rhythms and see where they led.

Within days Cheri felt a peace and calm unlike any she had ever experienced. Her thoughts became surprisingly clear. Deep and unfulfilled interests and passions from her youth began to surface. Ingenious ideas and solutions began weaving their way into her thoughts. To further explore these newly surfacing insights and feelings, Cheri began journaling and meditating in hopes of reconnecting with her innermost self and her most deeply rooted desires. She also began spending a great deal of time with her sagely island friend, exploring perspectives on life that only someone of more advanced years and experience can provide.

After a few weeks of island life, Cheri returned to the mainland and her position as a surgeon with a newfound lease on life, as well as a plan for walking away from her surgeon's life to become the writer she had always wanted to be. Her time away had given her the opportunity to really connect with who she felt herself to be at her core, as well as to discover how she could realistically go about living the life she so desperately desired. Granted she was scared, and this new life she sought definitely came with certain risks, hardships, and sacrifices in comparison to her current life, but hey, she thought, isn't it true that all walks of life come with their own inherent risks, hardships, and sacrifices, with the most profound hardship and sacrifice being to give up on your true nature and dreams in order to live your life as a square peg in a round hole.

Shortly after returning from her Hawaiian retreat, Cheri left her life as a surgeon to begin her new life as a writer. To tide her over during the transition of living without any meaningful source of income Cheri chose to live very minimally. Additionally, she chose to take a much less taxing job as a waitress, which was more a means to explore her more care free and wilder side than it was to earn an income. By all accounts Cheri's standard of living radically deteriorated during this transition period, but from her perspective it couldn't have been more freeing.

Within a couple of short years Cheri succeeded in completely recreating herself and her life. In that brief period she became the published author of numerous poems and short stories, as well as a best-selling author for the inspirational and autobiographical account of her life transition from discontented surgeon to ecstatic writer.

Today Cheri is also a celebrated speaker and workshop leader. She spends most of her time teaching other discontented souls how they too can find the courage to make the transition from ordinary to extraordinary – to live an authentic life as their truest self, utilizing their inborn gifts and talents to fulfill their heart's innermost desires, while simultaneously contributing to the betterment of the world.

You Deserve To Be All of Whom You Were Born To Be

Each of us is born whole and complete with a unique set of gifts, aptitudes, and dispositions of being. When we live our life in alignment with these inborn traits we find we are remarkably fulfilled. When we don't, life seems to be filled with frustrations, pain, and chaos. We also tend to experience a near constant tug from within to be someone different or be doing something different than we currently are.

This is the law of nature. We will never feel comfortable in our own skin so long as we are going against our inherent nature and living an inauthentic life. Just as a wolf cub raised with sheep will eventually awaken to its true nature, we also awaken to our true nature – or at least hear the discontented stirrings of that nature.

Cheri's story is a perfect illustration of this natural law. In her youth she was coerced in to becoming a surgeon, but her true self knew she was meant to be a writer and a teacher. In time Cheri's true self succeeded in getting enough of her attention that she made the effort to evaluate her life's path, ultimately choosing to venture down a completely new and fulfilling path that allows her to live in near perfect alignment with her passions, gifts, and inner most desires.

Most of us don't heed the messages from our innermost self with as much respect and consideration as Cheri. In fact, most of the time we outright ignore these messages, discounting them as childish dreams, a mid-life crisis, or the regrets of an unlived life. In a vain attempt to quiet the chatter we often employ a variety of self-numbing substances and activities (such as food, drugs, alcohol, TV, shopping, or gambling) so we can continue to soldier on with the day-to-day routines of our current life. This is true whether our day-to-day routine entails a less than satisfactory relationship, a less than satisfactory job, or any other less than satisfactory circumstance we choose to continue with because we are fearful of the unknown path our innermost self is urging us to explore.

Realize you are neither crazy nor alone. Fear of the unknown is natural. It is common to us all. Additionally, it has been conditioned and programmed into us to fear following a path that strays from those that are deemed to be normal and respectable according to the conventions of our cultural, familial, political, and religious mores. This is even more applicable when it comes to women, and doubly so for the vast majority of those who have been significantly mistreated or traumatized, as we more than any have lost touch with our true selves.

Regardless of how you currently see yourself or what it is you currently do, realize those messages, stirrings, and yearnings you experience are occurring for a reason. They are there to guide you. Their purpose is to help you discover your true path, the path that will allow you to live a purposeful and fulfilling life in alignment with the person you were born to be – the person who is the most authentic expression of your innermost being, the one who speaks to you through the voices of your heart and soul.

If you are routinely experiencing any type of nagging feelings, yearnings, or desires to live a different life, make the time to begin exploring these messages. Utilize some of the techniques outlined in the action sections of Steps 2 through 6 to more deeply explore what your innermost self is trying to tell you.

A word of caution. You want be sure the yearnings and desires you are experiencing are actually yours, that is, they are not being projected upon you by others, and they are not your blind attempt at convincing yourself to live up to some form of familial or societal expectation. Additionally, you want to make sure your yearnings aren't just a fantasy, that is, a dream like desire to live a life that looks remarkably better on the surface than your current life (such as sometimes happens when we envy someone else's life – e.g., celebrityitis).

Once you've determined that your yearnings and desires are indeed *your* heartfelt yearnings and desires, you will then want to instill a solid belief that you are worthy of living a life that will fulfill these desires. And finally, you will want to become mindfully aware of when and why these feelings, stirrings, and desires manifest so you can be very clear about the aspects of your life that are likely to require some degree of change for you to experience their fulfillment.

Practice being open to these messages. Use some of the journaling techniques previously covered to visualize what your life might look like if you were to choose the alternative path your heart desires. Trust that the messages you are receiving are vitally important and should be respected. Play with the ideas that surface. By doing so you will be honoring and loving your true self. Above all else, believe you deserve to be the person you were born to be, living a life of wholeness that utilizes your unique gifts and talents in a way that fulfills your innermost yearnings and desires.

Realize too that when we live in alignment with who we were born to be, not only are we happier and more content, but we also tend to be more giving. In effect, we do things that not only fulfill us, but also serve the greater good (where the greater good is anything beyond ourselves).

You Are A Remarkable And Unique Being

Regardless of what you may have been led to believe, you are a remarkable being. You are remarkable by virtue of the fact that you are here, alive and well. Think of the odds of you having even been born. One tiny little egg and millions upon millions of tiny little sperm, of which only one survived long enough to fertilize the egg that gestated and grew to be the tiny little person you were when you were born into this world. How much more remarkable can it get.

If you're still pooh-poohing how remarkable you are, think about this. The odds of you being born are so astronomically small that the chances of you having been born are essentially zero. Scientists have calculated the probability of you existing as you, in today's era, to be about 1 in 400 trillion *(Ali Binazir Blog, June 15, 2011)*. Other estimates put the probability at such a miniscule number that it completely boggles the mind (think 1 divided by 10 followed by hundreds of zeros). Whatever the actual number, it is infinitesimally small, but you made it, you're here.

To put this into perspective, compare the odds of you being here to the odds of being struck by lightning and those of winning a $340 million lottery jackpot *(ImprovisationNews.com Aug 16, 2011)*. The odds for being struck by lightning are 1 in 576,000. The odds of you winning that $340 million jackpot are about 1 in 175,000,000. Your chances of having been born in today's world of over six billion people are significantly less than 1 in 400,000,000,000,000. Face it, that's remarkable.

However, you are not only remarkable, you are also unique. There is no one else on the planet just like you. There never has been, and there never will be. Even if you could clone yourself, you'd still be unique. So what does this mean in regards to your being the person you were born to be? In its simplest terms it means you have a unique position to fill in this world, a position that can be filled by no one else but you. And discovering what that position is begins with listening to the messages you receive from within, especially those that occur as a deep-seated pull or heartfelt yearning.

You Can Have Healthy, Intimate, And Loving Relationships Regardless Of Your Past Experiences

Relationships, relationships, relationships. Where to begin? First, I know of no one who doesn't want to have healthy, intimate, and loving relationships, regardless of their past experiences. You might say it is encoded in our DNA. I also know that many of us feel we are incomplete (unwhole) when we lack these types of relationships. These feelings are so common we have come to accept them as truths. We feel we are incomplete if we aren't in a significant relationship with a life partner or some other person of significance. This is due in part to how we have been conditioned to believe we need someone, or something, to complete us. Think about it, it's in our idioms (I'll have to ask my better/other half, in reference to a spouse), our wedding vows (we now join these two together as one), our advertising campaigns (Coca Cola's Open Happiness campaigns), and so on.

Second, part of being human and living a human life means being in a relationship with others. Relationships are a way of life. Throughout our lives we are involved in all sorts of relationships. We have relationships with our parents, siblings, teachers, mentors, peers, friends, boyfriends, girlfriends, spouses, children, coworkers, bosses, religious leaders, and numerous others. We even have relationships with people we barely know, such as acquaintances and strangers we meet on the street or in a store. These just happen to be brief in nature.

Third, healthy and loving relationships are vitally important to our well-being. Think about the difference in how well a baby thrives based on nothing more than the amount of loving touch it receives from a caregiver. We all need love and affection to thrive. However, as we all know our relationships are often fraught with pain, disappointment, and even cruelty. And for those who have been significantly mistreated, relationships can be a huge source of conflict, not only between themselves and others, but also within themselves. This internal conflict is most often the result of our not being in alignment with our true self. It is a very common effect of having been abused, neglected, or traumatized. Add the typical conditioning and programming we all experience to the mistreatment and you end up with a person who has no idea who they really are, what will fulfill them, or how to be in a relationship, with someone else or themself.

Fourth, to be the most authentic and whole version of ourselves, which is what we are really after, we must have healthy, intimate, and loving relationships with ourselves. This is vitally important. It sets the stage for our being who we are meant to be. It also sets the stage for our being able to truly experience healthy, intimate, and loving relationships with others, regardless of our past experiences.

Accepting Your Innate Wholeness

As just mentioned, having healthy, intimate, and loving relationships, begins with you first having a healthy, intimate, and loving relationship with yourself. And one of the keys to having a healthy, intimate, and loving relationship with yourself begins with you accepting your innate wholeness.

As previously discussed in Step 4, we are all already whole. We were born whole, yet our programming, conditioning, and traumatic life experiences have tricked us into believing we are anything but whole. This belief and the painful feelings it induces are what keep us looking outside of ourselves for something to complete us (a spouse, children, the perfect job, the big house, etc.). Therefore, until we accept our innate wholeness and fall in love with ourselves (our true selves), no external addition will improve how we feel for long. They may temporarily make us feel more whole, but only temporarily, because true wholeness comes from within.

Therefore, to live the life you desire, complete with healthy, intimate, and loving relationships, it is imperative for you accept you are already whole. When you can accept that wholeness is your fundamental state of being you will immediately begin to heal. This acceptance will allow the disregarded and long-ignored aspects of your being to surface from their long-forgotten hiding places within your mind, body, and soul.

Recognize your feelings of being unwhole, including feelings of extreme loneliness, being totally alone in the world, and of being invisible, are a direct consequence of your having walled off, disregarded, and long-ignored various aspects of your true self.

To clarify what I mean I'll share a personal experience that helped me to accept this truth and ultimately begin having the type of relationships I had only ever dreamed of, not only intimate relationships with men, but also harmonious and loving relationships with family members I had previously deemed impossible.

For much of my life I felt I was doomed to live a life of loneliness and invisibility, that I was destined to be alone, even when I was with people I cared about and whom I believed cared about me. It seemed like every relationship I had was fated to be painful and unfulfilling. Somehow I would end up being mistreated, physically, psychologically, or spiritually. To add one injustice to another, I had the ever-increasing feeling that parts of me were not only missing, but irretrievably lost. Sometimes I wondered if maybe I hadn't been dealt a full deck at birth. I frequently thought, *"How can I be whole? How can I heal the wounds inflicted from my most horrific experiences? I know there has to be a way. But how, when so much of me feels lost to the ravages of my tormentors and time itself? And what if I was born with missing pieces, what then?"*

As I've shared in various amounts of detail in early portions of this book, life through my early 20's was devastatingly brutal to my self-worth. As a result of numerous forms of abuse, neglect, and a whole host of traumas, that included two forms of sexual abuse, I had walled-off and learned to disregard and ignore many aspects of my true self. A small sampling includes 1) walling-off my feelings and emotions to the point where I had to relearn how to recognize, describe, and express what I was feeling, 2) completely blocking out the sexual abuse I had experienced as a young child, 3) disregarding some of my innate gifts and talents because they were repeatedly described as frivolous, or I was told I wasn't any good at many of the things I in fact was good at, and 4) denying aspects of my femininity because of excessive teasing and taunts from peers and family members, in addition to deep-seated fears resulting from sexual abuse.

In an attempt to heal myself and ultimately feel whole I spent many years journaling, studying various self-help and personal growth materials, and being deeply introspective. I also employed many of the tools and techniques I've outlined in this book, including periodically sharing some of my deepest secrets and feelings with a trusted friend or confidant.

Little by little I succeeding in healing myself to one degree or another, recovering various parts of my being that I had inadvertently locked away for safekeeping. But it seemed that no amount of conviction or effort would allow me to feel like a whole woman, comfortable with my femininity and sexually intimate relationships, regardless of how much I desired it. The turning point came when I happened upon a very wise man who shared with me that I was already whole, that I always had been and always would be, and the only reason I felt unwhole was because I had disowned and hidden parts of myself away for safekeeping in order to cope with the experiences of my childhood.

This was a totally new concept for me, as I am sure it likely is for you. But think about it. How can we *not* feel unwhole when we disown, disregard, ignore, and lock away some of the most vital aspects of our very being? And how can we truly feel whole, be healed, and be the person we were born to be, until we accept our innate wholeness and reintegrate the vital aspects our being that we have relegated to the dungeons of our mind and body?

I'm urging you to take a bold step and accept your innate wholeness, so you can begin the deepest and most powerful healing you will ever experience. The upside is enormous. Before you know it you will have the healthy, intimate, and loving relationships you desire.

Learning To Love Your Body

A part of being whole, being who you were born to be, and ultimately having healthy relationships, is being comfortable in and loving your body. If you are like myself and many other women, and even many men for that matter, your conditioning, programming, and life experiences have turned you against your body, so much so that you can't even see yourself, much less see how beautiful you are.

To prove this to yourself I'd like you to perform a little experiment, which will require a full-length mirror. Hopefully you have one in your home. If not, take a trip to a local department store's dressing room. Once you've positioned yourself in front of the mirror, you'll want to strip down to your birthday suit (if you are in a department store you can leave your bra and panties on). Now take a look at yourself. Really look at yourself. What do you see? I'll bet it's not you that you see. Likely all you see are so-called bodily flaws and imperfections, such as fat thighs, knobby knees, a large nose, crooked teeth, moles, scars, and other such physical characteristics, which are not you, for you are not your body. And you are most definitely not these so-called imperfections. But hey, if you saw body parts you felt good about, congratulations, you're doing better than most and are well on your way to feeling comfortable in your body.

So, while we are not our body, and our body does not make us who we are, it is crucial for us to be comfortable in our body, if not actually love our body, in order to live the whole and fulfilling life we desire. If you need additional incentive for learning to become comfortable in your body, learning to really love it, think about the side benefit many people have experienced when they became comfortable in their body. They easily dropped excess weight or put on weight if they were too thin; and many of their various aches, pains, and dis-eases eased or disappeared. What a great benefit, the more comfortable we are in our body, the more readily it regulates itself back to its naturally homeostatic state.

But how do we learn to love our body when we have so long felt uncomfortable in it, and in many cases hated it? For starters, just appreciate it and all that it does for you. And just as in Step 2 where you practiced loving and honoring yourself, telling yourself *"I Love You"*, do the same with your body. Love and honor your body. Tell your body how much you love it and how much you appreciate what it does for you. Regularly give it the attention it rightfully deserves, through nutritionally sound foods and drinks, exercise, play, breath work, touch, and intimacy. Remember, your body is a temple; it is your vessel in this life. Treat it with the loving kindness and reverence you would a great work of art or a holy place of worship. Loving your body will change your life for the better.

Reclaiming Your Sexuality

Our sexuality is a big part of who we are. It affects us on many different levels, with two of the most obvious being our sexual desires and our sexual attractions. Additionally, it tends to impact how we feel about ourselves and how easily we fit into various groups or identities (e.g., cultural, spiritual, ethnic, political, etc.).

When we have lost touch with who we are, for whatever reason, but especially as a result of any significant abuse (be it physical, sexual, psychological, neglect, or discrimination), a physical disfigurement, or an impairing physical injury, our sexuality can become severely damaged. When our sexuality becomes damaged we shut down much of our vital energies and life force, becoming a shell of the person we were born to be. This in turn impacts all areas of our life, but most especially our relationships, which includes our relationship with ourselves.

Because of how dramatically this loss of vital energies affects the quality of our life it is vital that we do everything in our power to reclaim our sexuality in all of its radiant glory.

As there are a fair number of distinct issues that people deal with regarding their sexuality, and the particular issues often change with respect to age and life events, we won't explore anything beyond the basics for learning to be comfortable in and with your body. There are two reasons for this, 1) I'm not an expert with the various issues people deal with regarding their sexuality, although I believe they all stem from a crises of self-worth, and 2) this topic is easily a book on its own.

With that being said I urge you to explore your sexuality in a safe and healthy manner, getting to know it and love it. If need be, find a specialist or support group who deals with your particular concern (e.g., trauma from sexual abuse, psychological issues stemming from a non-traditional sexual orientation, psychological issues stemming from disfigurement or sexual infirmities such as those sustained from an injury, loss of self-confidence, or diminished desire that comes with age, child birth, and other natural changes to the body).

Remember, much of your vital life force is tied up in your sexuality, most importantly in how you feel about your sexuality. It therefore behooves you to reclaim your sexuality regardless of your age, your sexual orientation, your specific relationships, your physical appearance, or your physical ability to engage in certain sexual acts.

Don't let your conditioning, programming, experiences, or the whims of societal mores steal away this most precious and vital part of your being. It is part of who you are, the real you, so be proud of your sexuality. Love it just as it is, because it is perfect just as it is. When you can love your sexuality in its entirety, regardless of natural proclivities or physical impairments, you will experience a dramatic increase in vital energy and a marked increase in your total well-being.

Reclaim Your True Self – Putting It All Together

"The greatest thing in the world is to know how to belong to oneself." ~ Michel de Montaigne.

Sometimes a thing has to be destroyed; the walls must be torn down before we can see what has been hiding there all along. This process of destruction is often necessary for us to reconnect with our true self and live a meaningful and fulfilling life as the person we were born to be. But what you might be asking are we to destroy? That is a perfectly reasonable question for you to ask. For starters we must dismantle our belief system so that we may break free of our limiting labels and false identities, because only then can we truly belong to ourselves.

Whether we want to believe it or not, our demons are continually blinding us to what is possible for our lives. They have and continue to prevent us from being the remarkable and unique beings we are – beings that are born whole, complete with a host of gifts, natural talents, and deep-seated virtues that drive us to feel and act in ways that encourage us reach our full potential and feel fulfilled. Our demons, coupled with the conventions of society, have distorted our perceptions. Their constant influence makes us believe we are victims who must struggle to survive in a world that largely wants us to become homogenized – to fit neatly into a small number of cookie cutter molds.

How can this be? There are nearly seven billion people on this planet, with no two being identical. Yet society wants to classify us into surprisingly few categories, as evidenced by the various labels we are given and ultimately identify ourselves with. While labeling is to a degree necessary for an organized society to function, it is also dangerous, because labels in and of themselves are imperfect distinctions that limit our belief in ourselves and box us into an unfulfilling life (remember the square peg in the round hole – it just doesn't fit – and if you whittle away at its edges to make it fit, then it's no longer a square peg; it has been forced to be something it was not meant to be).

Labels can help us to find a place of belonging, but they can also create barriers. None of us has or ever will fit neatly under any one particular label or identity, no matter how much we may desire to belong. We are complex creatures that are by our very nature a confluence of the various generalities applied to us (e.g., woman, mother, daughter, sexual abuse victim, teacher, choir singer, disabled), as well as the many colorful aspects of our underlying personality and innermost self. To illustrate, take a look at Figure 4. While rightly a simplistic view, it adequately illustrates that our true self resides deep within the intersection of all of the various labels and identities we take on, coupled with the unique aspects of our fundamental being (personality, genetic makeup, inborn gifts & traits).

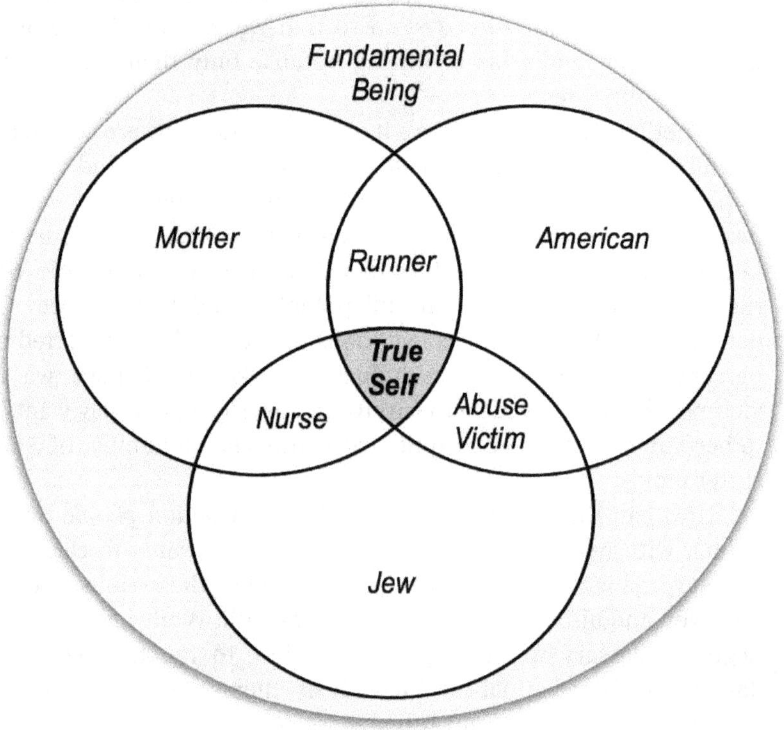

Figure 4: Venn Diagram of Personal Labels and Identities

Our inner guide tells us who we really are. She is constantly guiding us, telling us which directions are right for us. So instead of fighting her, why not tune in. As Tama Kieves puts in her book, *This Time I Dance, "Life turns deliciously quirky when you stop resisting yourself and, instead, honor the intuition that tugs at you like a puppy on a leash in the park."*

Just as a bird can't cling to the nest and also soar to new horizons, neither can you. You must be willing to let go of the old labels you have been living with, as well as the person you have chosen to be up to this point. Open up. Look inside. Really look. Can you see yourself? – Your true self? Maybe not just yet, but it will come if believe you are worthy and allow it. You can soar with the best, because you are one of the best. So start believing and start soaring. Show the world the beautiful being that is aching to make its presence known.

Reclaiming your true self is a process, so in the words of Rainer Maria Rilke *"Be patient toward all that is unsolved in your heart, and try to love the questions themselves."*

Understanding The True Meaning (Purpose) of Life

The questions *"What is the meaning of life?"* and *"What is the purpose of life?"* are age-old questions that have been asked for almost as long as human beings have been asking questions. And to my knowledge there has never been a completely agreed upon answer for either question. With that in mind I'd like to posit the answer I feel is the *true meaning* or, if you will, the *fundamental purpose* of life. And even if it isn't the *fundamental purpose*, I believe you will find it incredibly useful to you on your journey, not only for becoming whole again, but for navigating the ever increasing complexities of life, especially those resulting from our various political, cultural, and spiritual philosophies.

Are you ready for it? Drum roll, please. *The fundamental purpose of life is self-mastery,* nothing more and nothing less. Wow! What a simple answer. But what exactly is self-mastery? The dictionary defines it as the power to control one's impulses, actions, and emotions, which to a degree is a perfectly reasonable definition. However, I believe there's a more complete definition, since self-mastery, which is literally being the best you possible, is a process that incorporates self-awareness, self-discovery, and self-trust, all of which we've been exploring throughout the nine steps of this book.

Looking at each component individually will provide a more complete understanding of what I mean by self-mastery, and therefore the fundamental purpose of life.

1. **Self-Awareness**: The act of being mindful of how you are showing up in the world, as well as how it is your true self desires for you to show up. Remember the messages of your inner guide?

2. **Self-Discovery**: The process of discovering your truest, most authentic self (the person you are at the deepest level of your being) while striving to reach your full potential (self-actualization).

3. **Self-Trust**: The ability to trust and follow the wisdom of your inner guide – courageously exploring the paths it beckons you to follow.

So there you have it. The purpose of life is self-mastery. But how will you know when you have achieved self-mastery? And how does self-mastery apply to what you do with your life?

First, self-mastery is an ongoing process that continues throughout life. It occurs in stages, just like the various skills you set out to master. Take playing the violin. Mastery occurs in stages. First you learn very basic chords and bowing techniques. Next you learn to play very simple songs. Then you progress to more complex chords, bowing techniques, and songs. The process repeats itself over and over again. With the completion of each pass you are able to play increasingly complex pieces with greater ease. Yet no matter how long you play the instrument you will always find there is something new to master. This is exactly how self-mastery works. With each level of mastery you'll find you are navigating your life with more ease and joy, regardless of the challenges you encounter.

Second, when you are living your life as the truest and most authentic version of yourself you will be doing exactly what you are meant to be doing at this particular point in time. So it's not so much what you do, but rather that what you do is aligned with who you are at your core. This is self-mastery as it applies to what you do with your life. So if you feel called to be an artist, then being the best expression of an artist as you can possibly be at the time is self-mastery. The same is true if you feel called to be a chef, a teacher, a politician, a scientist, an ordained minister, or any other vocation.

It's not what you do. It's the emergence of the best expression of you through what you do. As already discussed, there's always a more masterful expression of you waiting to emerge. Sometimes the only way that expression will appear is through a completely different vocation from the one you're currently engaged in, even if you've been at it for most of your life. That is, there is no one true vocation that is right for you. There is only one true purpose – to show up as the highest and best expression of your true self, through whatever means makes that possible.

To provide perspective, I'll share another personal experience. Coming out of college I became an engineer for NASA's Jet Propulsion Laboratory (the proverbial rocket scientist), designing, building, and operating various unmanned spacecraft whose purpose are to robotically explore our solar system. After doing this work for around 10 years I began to feel I was meant to be doing something different with my life, although I had no idea what that something was or why I was experiencing the urge to move on. Following the leads of my inner guide I eventually discovered the path I was being led to follow and why.

Over the course of several years I repeated the self-mastery steps of self-awareness, self-discovery, and self-trust a number of times, not really knowing what I was doing. In time I learned to trust the messages from my inner guide. With each level of mastery I was hearing and understanding more and more of the yearnings of my heart and soul. I was also rediscovering many of the innate gifts, interests, and passions I had known as a child. This gradual awakening led me to explore a variety of different paths I might follow whereby I would experience the peace and fulfillment I desired. It also led me to realize the work I was doing was out of alignment with my true self, that is the work I was doing would never allow me to be the best expression of my true self, even though I didn't dislike what I was doing and was quite good at it.

After several years of seeking a solution to my growing discontent I discovered the only way I could be the best and most authentic expression of myself was to follow an entirely new path. Believe me this was scary. I was walking away from something I'd spent half a lifetime doing to begin anew. But the time had come for me to courageously follow the guidance of my soul and be the person I was being called to be from within.

To date that path has materialized with me becoming an author, speaker, and personal empowerment coach, where I assist unfulfilled individuals in discovering their true identity, passions, and personal gifts, so they can experience the wholeness of their birthright and live a soul-fulfilling life doing what they love. But that's today. Since there are more levels of self-mastery to come, I fully expect my expression and the path it takes to continue evolving as I climb the self-mastery ladder.

It's important to accept that self-mastery is an ongoing process. Trust it. Trust yourself. Believe in these words from Ralph Waldo Emerson, *"Self-trust is the first secret of success, the belief that if you are here the authorities of the universe put you here, and for cause, or with some task strictly appointed you in your constitution, and so long as you work at that you are well and successful."*

Being The Person You Were Born to Be vs. The Person You Think You Are

In my opinion, the greatest tragedy in life is how the majority of us go through life, or much of it, pretending to be someone other than who we really are. From birth we are bombarded from all directions to be all sorts of things, but rarely are we encouraged or guided to become the unique individual we are. Parents, grandparents, teachers, siblings, and peers all have their ideas about who we are and what we should do with our life. Additionally, our religious institutions, cultural identities, and even the media all herald something about who we should or shouldn't be, what we should or shouldn't want, and how we should or shouldn't conduct our life. Such is the nature of humanity and the cultures in which we are born.

Yet it is in being the person we are at our core that brings the most meaning, satisfaction, and fulfillment. Being anything else always brings pain, frustration, and discontent. Always. The only difference between one person's level of discontentment and another's, or even your own at different points in your life, is the degree to which you are living your life as the fullest and most authentic expression of your innermost self.

Think about it, would anyone who was living the fullest and most authentic expression of themselves knowingly behave in a self-destructive manner, or worse yet commit suicide? I don't believe so. Every person I've ever known, myself included, only engages in self-destructive behaviors as a result of their discontentment, which for some leads to an ever-increasing sense of hopelessness that anything can ever be done to resolve their pain.

From this we can easily surmise that virtually all self-worth issues are directly related to the degree with which we are living our lives as the truest expression of the person we were born to be. The more out of alignment we are, the lower our self-worth. The lower our self-worth the more self-destructive we become, especially when we lose hope or feel completely powerless to break free of the overbearing rule of an oppressor (be it a tyrannical leader, a well-meaning parent, or our inner demons).

The movie *"Dead Poets Society"* provides a poignant example. In this movie, John Keating, the English teacher at an elite, all male, prep school, uses what the establishment considers to be unorthodox teaching methods. He encourages his students to think for themselves, to see things from different perspectives, and to focus on the idea of Carpe Diem, that is to seize the day.

Neil Perry, one of the students attending the academy, wants to become an actor rather than the doctor his father insists he will be. He wants desperately to participate in a local theatre production of *A Midsummer Night's Dream,* but knows his very controlling father, who has his life completely planned out for him and sees anything not related to his becoming a doctor as superfluous, a failure, and a reflection on him personally, will not permit it.

Neil asks his teacher, Mr. Keating, for advice. Mr. Keating advises him to talk to his father and make him understand how he feels. Neil is afraid to talk to his father believing he won't listen, so he goes against Mr. Keating's advice and participates in the play. Neil is quite good and lands the lead role of Puck.

On opening night his father shows up at the end of the play absolutely furious. When the play ends, Mr. Perry takes Neil home where he yells there'll be no more theatre or Welton Academy; tomorrow he is enrolling him in military school to prepare him for Harvard and a career in medicine – end of discussion.

Neil is devastated. He feels there's no way he can make his father understand his feelings. Unable to cope with the future his father has laid out for him he commits suicide. Afterward, his father feels awful, realizing his calamitous mistake (i.e., how he had pushed his son to be someone he wasn't in order to make up for his own perceived failings and insecurities).

Was any of it worth it? Not that I can see, and in the end nor could Neil's father. But as we all know this is a common story, although not every story ends in suicide. Time and time again individuals struggle and suffer for large percentages of their lives, if not all of their lives, solely because they live an inauthentic life, pretending or tying to be the person someone else said they were or should be, or the person they have come to think they are, as opposed to the person they really are.

Just because we are drawn away from our true self in our youth, does not mean we aren't ultimately responsible for the person we choose to be as an adult. I know this may seem hard to comprehend given our conditioning, programming, and experiences, but I assure you it is true. As an adult, you hold the reigns of control. No one other than your true self has the right to dictate who you become or what it is you do with your life. Therefore, if you aren't already living an authentic life, being the person you were born to be, doing something you love, you must understand you have the ability to change it anytime you choose. That means you can change who you are being, what you are doing, who you spend time with, how you treat yourself and others, and anything else that affects your well-being. Whether you choose to be whole are not is entirely up to you. The same goes for when you make the choice to take action and make it your reality.

Please realize this doesn't mean you should act irresponsibly in order to fulfill your hearts desires, especially if you have children or other family members under your care. What it means is you act in accordance with your deepest, most heartfelt desires in a manner conducive to you being your true self and fulfilling your innermost needs and desires, without causing undue mental or physical harm to those for whom you are responsible. Where there is a will there is a way. Be open and creative. Get your family involved in a mutually beneficial way. It's guaranteed if you want it badly enough you'll find an acceptable solution.

Also realize that each of us is continually being influenced and pressured to go against our true self. Marching to the beat of our own drummer has a tendency to make others uncomfortable, especially if they are out of touch with their true self. This is the nature of our culture, our tribes if you will. Their purpose is to keep us in line, to have us fit in, which unfortunately means living within a narrowly defined set of acceptable and often outdated roles, values, and mores that are largely designed to keep the tribe safe.

As children we learned the stories of our culture (our mythology). These stories trap most of us into living an inauthentic life that leaves us yearning for what is frequently described by the masses as a fantasy life. And since the life we so desperately yearn for is labeled as nothing more than a fantasy we go out of our way to numb ourselves so that we can continue living the culturally acceptable story life.

The reality is we always have the choice to create a new story for ourselves; we can step outside the box in which we have placed ourselves, or better yet we can throw the box away altogether. If you feel the call to live a more fulfilling life, one that's aligned with your true nature, then there's no better time than the present to get started. Begin tearing down the walls keeping you bound to an unfulfilling life. Venture outside your comfort zone. Try on the roles and ways of being that have been calling to you from within. Explore new territories. Take a few risks. You can start small or go all the way. The choice is entirely yours. And remember, if you feel fear, it's more likely you're actually feeling excitement. So go ahead. Answer those heartfelt calls. If you blunder, it's ok. Blunders are how we grow, how we achieve self-mastery. Know if it feels right in your heart and soul, then it's highly probable you're on the right track, because it's a rare occurrence for our true self to lead us astray.

So dream big, live big, and above all else, live your life as the being you were you born to be, doing something that fulfills your soul. It's time to let your heart sing. Just go for it. There's never going to be a better time than now.

Happy are those who dream dreams and are willing to pay the price to make them come true. ~ Anonymous.

Creating Alignment Between Your Thoughts, Your Beliefs, and Your True Self

Did you ever dream you'd be here, on the verge of living a soul-fulfilling life based on the truest sense of who you are? Did you ever dream you'd be capable of being whole again? And what about the possibility of having healthy, intimate, and loving relationships?

You've come a long way. It's really quite an accomplishment. So please congratulate yourself for having come this far. You've definitely achieved a level of self-mastery by the very fact that you've made to this point. But you're not out of the woods yet. To continue making any significant level of progress it's going to take commitment. It's also going to require you to take the work you did in Steps 3 and 4 to a whole new level, which means you must make sure your thoughts and beliefs are in alignment with your true self.

I'm sure you're thinking to yourself, create alignment between my thoughts and beliefs and my true self? What does this even mean?

It's really quite simple. It means you do everything in your power to ensure your thoughts and beliefs directly support you living your life as your truest and most authentic self; that your thoughts and beliefs are in agreement with the messages coming from your inner guide (your heart, soul, and intuition – your higher self).

Up to this point you've mainly focused on self-awareness, with only a small a bit of attention being given to self-discovery and self-trust. From this point forward you're going be putting a lot of attention on the self-discovery and self-trust pieces of the equation, but you're not going to stop the self-awareness piece because it's still an integral player in your becoming whole again.

One of the main aspects of self-discovery is getting to know who *you* are really are. To help you get to know the real you, you'll be using the mindful awareness practice you began in Step 3. It's time to really tune in on the messages emanating from your higher self. You're also going to be making a conscious note as to whether your thoughts and beliefs are aligned with those messages. If they are, great; if they aren't, then it's time to do some intentional thought replacement to help you more fully express your true nature.

Last but not least is self-trust. It's imperative you trust the process and yourself. I know you've had some challenges with this in the past. That's ok. You can do it. Take a leap of faith here. If need be, trust the wisdom of those who have gone before you. Have heart and be courageous. It's the only way you're going to live an authentic, soul-fulfilling life as the whole and magnificent being you are.

Living In The Present Moment

Living in the present moment is an essential component for living your life as the unique being you were born to be. It helps you get in touch with the real you. In the present there is no past or future. In the present there are no problems. In the present you just are.

What living in the present means is to be completely present to the moment that is. That is, you aren't mentally off somewhere in the past or future, but rather in the here and now. It also means you are totally in your body, not off somewhere else, such as another part of the room you are physically in, another building, a field somewhere, or in conversation with someone in your mind, but fully in your body.

One of the great benefits of being completely present to the current moment, and of being fully in our body, is the profound sense of peace we experience. For each moment we spend fully present to the moment that is, and fully in our body, is a moment we spend in complete harmony with ourselves, and the world around us. It's also a moment in which we are totally in tune with our truest self.

Living in the present moment is a highly beneficial practice that 1) calms the mind, 2) reduces stress, tension, and pain, 3) generates a sense of peace and tranquility, 4) opens the channels to your intuition and higher self, and 5) helps you heal. It's a great way to instantly increase your sense of well-being and strengthen the connection to your innermost self.

Living in the moment is a practice, which takes practice. One of the easiest ways to learn to be in the present moment is to focus on your breathing. You don't have to do anything else. Just focus on your breathing. Inhale then exhale, again and again and again. If you are entirely focused on your breathing you will be in the present moment. You can perform this practice anywhere you happen to be, regardless of what you are doing (sitting, lying down, walking, running, driving, talking, watching TV, etc.).

Make living in the present moment a part of your daily routine. Spend a few minutes each day focused on your breathing, pulling yourself back into your body, tuning completely into the moment that is. As time goes on, you'll learn to be in the present moment without having to consciously focus on your breathing. The more you are in the moment, the more you'll be in touch with your true self, and the more harmonious your life will be.

Actions To Facilitate Living In Alignment With Your True Self

1. Affirm Your True Self

Repeat the following declarations with intense feeling and emotion, at least five times each morning and evening for a period of at least 30 days.

- I am whole. I was born whole.
- I am healthy, happy, and whole.
- There is nothing missing. I am complete just as I am.
- Wholeness comes from within. I need nothing to complete me.
- I feel whole when I love myself. I LOVE MYSELF! I LOVE MY BODY.
- I listen to and trust my higher self.
- I am an attractive, powerful, and loving woman.
- I am confident, charismatic, and courageous.
- I am a generous giver and an excellent receiver, in love and in life.
- I have many healthy, intimate, and loving relationships.
- I am a powerful creator.
- I live life in the present moment, here and now.
- I live life with passion and purpose.
- I live in peace and joy.
- I LOVE MY LIFE.

2. **Acknowledge Your Sexuality; Love Your Body**
Look at yourself in the mirror. See the beautiful and attractive woman you are. See the real you. Show compassion and love for the vibrant, sensual, and sexual woman you are. Tell the woman you see how much you love her. Tell her how ravishingly beautiful her body is. Now take time to touch and caress that beautiful and sensual body. Use a massage oil with a fragrant or healing scent. Explore your body. Get to know it well. Learn where and how it likes to be touched.

Don't worry if you don't believe what you are telling yourself or your body. Just keep telling yourself and your body how beautiful, vibrant, and sensual you are. Tell yourself and your body you will never again so inhumanely neglect and mistreat them. Tell yourself and your body you promise, from this day forward, to take care of all their needs. Then do something specific to show your good faith in taking care of their needs, such as eating a healthful meal, going for a walk, getting a massage, or taking a nap if you routinely push yourself beyond your physical limits.

Repeat the verbal part of this exercise daily in front of a mirror. Repeat the remainder of the exercise at least once a week until you are very comfortable with your body. In no time at all you'll begin loving your body exactly as it is and be thoroughly comfortable with your sexuality.

When you feel ready, do this exercise with a trusting partner, preferably an intimate partner.

3. **Visualize Being In a Healthy, Loving, and Intimate Relationship**

Find a quiet place to spend a few minutes contemplating what a healthy, loving, and intimate relationship looks like. Think about the kind of relationships you desire, with a life partner, your children, your parents, your siblings, and so on. Describe them in as much detail as you possibly can. Make them feel real. Capture them in your journal so you can refer to them when you feel off track in any of your current relationships.

Think about what actions you can take right now to improve your current relationships. Describe in your journal what you can do to make one or more of your current relationships more loving and harmonious. Visualize the relationship as you'd like it to be, but don't expect to change the other person. Here we are only talking about actions you take in regard to how you are being (i.e., how you show up or present yourself) or how you are interacting with the other person.

Repeat this exercise often. Early on it's a good idea to do it several times per week.

4. **Describe Your True Self**

Have a conversation with your true self. Get to know her! Ask her to describe herself to you. Ask her what her inborn gifts are, what her talents and skills are, what her loves are, what her passions are, what she'd love to be doing with her life, what her dislikes are, what she definitely doesn't like or want to do, and so on. Listen intently to what comes from within. Use your journal to capture the questions you ask, as well as the answers you receive.

It is often more effective to use your non-dominant hand to capture the answers from your true self. For some reason it more easily puts in touch with that small voice we so often ignore. This may be because the use of our non-dominant hand gives us access to less dominant parts of the brain while it is effectively distracting the dominant part that wants to see this as a silly exercise.

Don't worry about how slow or messy your non-dominant hand is. Just allow the answers to surface, capturing them as best you can. You can always go back and rewrite them later to make them more legible.

Spend at least 30 minutes on this exercise, repeating it at least twice per week, more if you possibly can. You'll be surprised at what you learn.

5. **Practice Alignment (between your thoughts and beliefs, and your true self)**

Continue capturing your thoughts and beliefs as you did in the actions sections of Steps 3 and 4.

Now begin routinely comparing your thoughts and beliefs with what you are learning about your true self (e.g., from the previous action). Notice where there is disagreement and where there is alignment. Ask yourself if your thoughts and beliefs are congruent with, or contradictory to, what you know about your most authentic self, the self that originates in your heart and soul.

Wherever there is disagreement or contradiction, try to understand why. Then, using the process described in Step 4 for performing intentional thought replacement, begin instilling new thoughts and beliefs that will better serve you in becoming the fullest and best expression of your true self.

Remember, we are as we think and believe, so to live as the fullest and best expression of our true self, we must ensure our thoughts and beliefs are congruent with that most authentic part of our being.

6. **Practice Being in the Present Moment**

Spend a few minutes each day focusing on your breathing until you are totally in the moment. Try to become aware of nothing but your breath. When thoughts enter your mind, let them go.

Periodically tune in to where you are. Notice whether you are in your body or someplace you hadn't realized you were. Do this a few times per day. Ask yourself, where am I? Am I in my body?

If not, ask yourself where you are. If you aren't in your body, focus on becoming fully present and centered in your body.

An additional practice you can employ to facilitate being in touch with your true self and being fully in your body, is to add a mantra to your breathing exercise. One of the ones I like is to use is, *"peace"* on the in breathe, and *"love"* on the out breath. Practice making your inhalations and exhalations slow, long, and deep into your belly.

I think....you still have no idea.
The effect you can have.
-Suzanne Collins

Step 8 – Discover Your Value To The World: You Have Much To Offer

Lori's Story

Lori is one of those especially gifted people, who for most of her life had absolutely no clue of the gifts and talents she possessed. From her mid-teens through her late thirties she seemed to just drift, briefly landing wherever the tides of the season took her. Each new metaphorical harbor introduced a new Lori, a Lori very unlike the previous one; a Lori that changed her character, her form of employment, and her manner of expression as readily as the wind changes direction.

During this period of her life, it wasn't uncommon for Lori to change her job, her personality, and even her country of residence up to a half-dozen times per year. For a while she'd be a waitress by day and a pop singer by night. Then she'd be a tour guide, describing the wonders of the ancient cities of Italy and France, while living it up with her latest boyfriend. Next she'd become a ski instructor, while dabbling with painting character portraits and telling fireside stories for the season. At one point she even decided it was time to get serious and make something of herself; so she began attending nursing school to become an in-home nurse, while working nights and weekends as a part-time nanny to support herself. Regardless of what she pursued, within less than a year of each new beginning she would once again find herself aimlessly adrift, wondering why it was she couldn't settle into any one thing or be content with any one guy.

If you were to ask Lori what made her such a drifter, she'd honestly tell you she really didn't know. From her standpoint there'd never been anything particularly unpleasant or dissatisfying about what she'd chosen to do. She almost always got along with her co-workers, she seemed to make friends easily enough, and she found the vast majority of her forays to be uncharacteristically easy, considering she had little to no prior experience with most of them when choosing to make them her livelihood du jour. Yet within a few short months of each new beginning, she'd find herself feeling the same deep-seated emptiness that had haunted her for as long as she could remember. She'd begin hearing the characteristic whispers that said this wasn't where she was meant to be. There was something important she was meant to be doing with her life, something that was meaningful and valuable to the greater good of humanity.

If you were to ask those who know Lori why they thought she was such a drifter they'd almost always say she seems to have lost her way; she has no idea who she is, what she wants, or how remarkably talented she is. Many have said she could easily become a famous portraiture artist, poet, singer, storyteller, or even an adventure travel and tour guide, of the likes of Artemisia Gentileschi, Emily Dickenson, Celine Dion, Clarissa Pinkola Estes, or Megan McCormick, and that's only the possibilities for her more adventurous and artistic side. Some have said she could equally be a huge success in a number of other less artistic fields if she only had the wherewithal to focus her energies.

The source of Lori's unrest, and her ever-changing personality, lifestyle, and livelihood, stemmed from her years of being subjected to the restrictions and confinement that came with attending a religiously affiliated boarding school. Lori was an unusually precocious child, and her precociousness, coupled with her penchant for adventure and a marked dislike of what she considered excessive and ridiculous rules, left her feeling as though she were forcibly being pushed to become a cookie cutter version of her teachers or the mothers of the majority of her fellow students, women who were prim, proper, and, to her mind, devoid of a life force.

Throughout her primary school years Lori was repeatedly punished whenever she stepped outside the confining box created by the schools strictly enforced rules, restrictions, and narrowness of thinking. Anytime she showed an interest or aptitude for anything that didn't fit within the narrow guidelines of the school, she found her talents and interests being suppressed. Rather than celebrating and encouraging them she was instead ridiculed and punished, being forever branded as a troublesome student that wouldn't follow rules. Over time Lori became disconnected from herself and her interests since she wasn't allowed to explore them. To appease her tormenting guardians she learned to play the role of near model student, but in her mind she continually dreamed of the day she would escape her restrictive environment to find a place she belonged.

After nearly two decades of drifting, feeling just as unsettled as she did as a child, Lori sought help from an old acquaintance, a woman she very much admired for how together she was and how effectively she utilized her various talents to do something significant. This acquaintance mentored Lori in a way that helped her develop and focus her talents and interests. She also introduced Lori to a life coach. While working with the coach Lori learned how to be introspective. By listening within and completing a variety of discovery oriented processes Lori soon realized what was most important to her. She also learned she could combine what was most important to her with her deepest pains, passions, and life experiences to create a lucrative livelihood, that would not only fulfill her, but would also provide tremendous value to innumerable others who felt as lost and unfulfilled as she had for most of her life.

Shortly after beginning the sessions with her mentor and coach, Lori started feeling really good about herself and her life. She settled into a vocation that involves her working with groups of adults (typically aged 20-40), who, like herself, had been stripped of their sense of self. As she loved travel and adventure, Lori engaged with others of a like mind to make available a variety of life camps designed to serve the needs of these lost souls. Using adventure activities, art, singing, storytelling, poetry, and other artistic expressions, she teaches people how to reconnect with their true self through the exploration of their interests, talents, and passions. Today, Lori utilizes virtually all of her interests and talents in a productive and fulfilling manner.

The Answers Lie Within

We all possess a number of priceless gifts buried within the fabric of our being. We also have the capacity to access these gifts and apply them in the most extraordinary ways. These gifts emanate from the intangible parts of us we so often ignore (the messages, inclinations, and desires originating from our heart, soul, intuition, and higher self – our true self). They manifest themselves in our various mental and physical abilities, with no two persons' gifts manifesting themselves in exactly the same way (although they may be quite similar).

No matter your age or what you have experienced in life, you have access to these great riches – your personal gifts, if you will but listen within and act upon your emerging interests, passions, and talents in a manner that is congruent with the desires of your heart and soul. By doing so you will be living your life as the fullest and best expression of the person you were born to be, just as Lori and several of the other women introduced in this book are now doing.

Each of us is highly gifted in our own way. We all have the same raw materials within us as any of the widely known geniuses throughout history (e.g., Leonardo Da Vinci, Albert Einstein, Michelangelo, Marie Curie, and Saint Hildegard). The only difference between these geniuses and the rest of us is the manner in which our gift expresses itself. And for many of us that gift has yet to be expressed at all, as we have yet to listen within so that we may discover our unique gifts and the form in which they may best be expressed.

I know for a fact that many of you are thinking *"yeah right, me, a genius, what hallucinogen are you on?"* I assure you I am not hallucinating, nor am I making this up. We are all geniuses in our own way. And for you to believe me you're going to have to put aside some of the old concepts you have about who you are and what is possible for your life. For starters you need to relinquish your old labels, most especially the ones telling you you're too dumb, learning challenged, not smart enough, not old enough, too old, a victim of circumstances, or anything else that limits you, because these are nothing more than stories you were told or have been telling yourself, and have sadly accepted as your truth. Yet nothing could be further from the truth. You are none of these or the many other labels you've reluctantly accepted and have thereby allowed to limit the possibilities for your life.

Muster up the heart and courage to step outside your restrictive box for a moment. Pretend what I'm saying is true. Throughout the ages, people the world over have proven the truth of what I'm saying time and time again.

To provide a concrete example, I'll focus on a few well-known individuals who have been labeled dyslexic (i.e., highly learning challenged) and had a rough start in life, yet they went on to discover and apply their genius in some very remarkable ways, some of which still affect or touch our lives today. Most of these people were told they'd never learn to read or write, were poor students, and in all likelihood would never amount to much. Yet they became highly respected doctors, lawyers, politicians, entrepreneurs, inventors, scientists, musicians, writers, artists, and actors, among other notable professions.

A few of these notable people include Leonardo Da Vinci, Tommy Hilfiger, Walt Disney, Whoopi Goldberg, Cher, Keira Knightly, Albert Einstein, Thomas Edison, John Lennon, Dr. Harvey Cushing (neurosurgeon), George Washington, Erin Brockovich, Richard Branson, Henry Ford, Eleanor Roosevelt, Steven Spielberg, Hans Christian Andersen, and Agatha Christie. The list goes on and on. There are so many I could easily fill a page or more with only those that are well-known historical figures or current day celebrities.

People who have been labeled dyslexic are but one example. Pick any label you desire; do a search and you will find the same results. There are countless numbers of people, regardless of their labels or the challenge they've faced, who've had the courage to march to their own drum; to listen within, recognize their genius, and employ that genius to the greatest possible advantage, not just for themselves, but ultimately for the benefit of the masses.

You have this same capacity for greatness. Isn't it time you quit labeling yourself and take a stand for what's really possible for you in this life?

Realizing your precious gifts, your genius, is possible. It starts with you reconnecting with your true self. Step 7 delved into this topic in considerable detail. However, as it is my wish that you are given every opportunity to live your life as the fullest and most authentic expression of the remarkable being you are, this step will delve into how you can begin to recognize your unique gifts and genius, so that you may more fully express the best of yourself in all that you do.

When you know what you gifts are and find the means to consistently apply them in a meaningful way you will experience fulfillment. You'll also feel your vocation provides some measure of value to the world. Potentially it will leave a significant legacy for future generations. Regardless of how your genius manifests, it is by the very nature that it is expressed in your daily life that you find the meaning and fulfillment you are looking for.

So rather than living a life of regrets and unfulfilled dreams, take a stand for you. Don't go to your grave saying you wish you'd have had the courage to try such and such. You are not defined by your labels, your circumstances, or what you do, unless you choose to be. Be open to the possibilities. Look inside. Listen for that small voice from within that knows what is best for you. It's time to live a life of no regrets. Be all of who you are meant to be, not just a shadow of your potential. The only part of you resisting this change is your conditioned mind, and as you learned in Step 4 you can retrain your mind to be your greatest ally.

The world is waiting for your genius. Make a vow right now that you will put your doubts aside and continue on this exciting journey you've begun. Realize the employment of your gifts is a significant piece of the wholeness puzzle. The more you are able to employ this unique part of yourself, the more quickly you'll climb the rungs of self-mastery, whereby you'll more fully live a soul-fulfilling life as the amazing being you are.

Listen To The Messages Of Your Heart And Soul

"We search for happiness everywhere, but we are like Tolstoy's fabled beggar who spent his life sitting on a pot of gold, under him the whole time. Your treasure – your perfection – is within you already. But to claim it, you must leave the buy commotion of the mind and abandon the desires of the ego and enter into the silence of the heart. ~ Elizabeth Gilbert.

As previously touched upon, the answers we are looking for come from within. However, as we've also touched upon, we spend so much of our time in search of distractions and escape from the near constant commotion of our mind that we miss what is right under our nose – our true self, our passions, our gifts, our talents, our genius, and our right livelihood (which for most of us will change several times throughout our lifetime).

Rather than going within to the quiet resting place of the heart, we search outside of ourselves for a way to quell our fears of change, of life, and of death. We search for meaning and purpose, for a feeling of security and happiness, for a way to make sense of the vagaries of life, but mostly, be it our intention or not, we seek to escape the whirlwind of thoughts and feelings going on inside of us. Hence the reason so many turn to drugs, alcohol, work, partying, TV, online gaming, gambling, romance novels, and affairs. They are searching in the wrong place.

Our habitual striving for entertainment, achievement, to fit in, and to live up to the expectations of others keeps us constantly focused outwardly, which keeps us turned away from what we seek most, the wholeness and fulfillment that only comes from being in tune with that which comes from within – that which we only get to know by tuning into the quiet, subtle messages of the heart and soul.

It's time to let go of your expectations and tune in to the truth that comes from within. Whether you are a very young adult wondering what to do with your life, in your middle years experiencing a so-called mid-life crisis, or a senior looking to regain a sense of self and purpose, the process is the same. You listen within. You trust the messages of your heart and soul. You look to your pain, your life's dreams, your interests, your passions and loves, your strengths, and your innate gifts and talents. It is from these you will find what it is you truly seek; a way of being and living that is congruent with your truest self – a method of being whereby you experience meaning and fulfillment.

If you are experiencing any type of ongoing discontentment or mental unrest, it's time to tune in to your heart and soul. In time this will quiet your mind and guide you to the answers you seek. From this inner place you will discover the direction that is right for you.

It's time to embark on one of the most adventurous journeys you've ever taken – the journey to discover the mysteries hidden within your very being – the mysteries that make you the remarkable person you are – the mysteries that will completely change your life.

To get you started I'll guide you through a discovery process that will help you to recognize your unique gifts. In Step 9 we'll explore some of the ways you can congruently employ them to transform your life into one that's better than anything you've ever imagined.

Discover Your Unique Gifts (Your Personal Genius)

Discovering your unique gifts, your genius if you will, is a process, and it's a relatively simple process at that. For the most part it relies on your observations and honest answers to a number of questions that are designed to draw out what is most meaningful and fulfilling to you.

Think of these questions as the means by which you will be creating new and exciting possibilities for your life. Also, think of them as a means for expanding your awareness, and ultimately the means by which you will proceed to alter your reality. For what is the purpose of a question if not to create possibilities that didn't previously exist. In the words of Gary Douglas, *"Choice creates awareness... question creates possibilities... where awareness and possibility intersect... a new reality is born"*

If you are tired of living an unfulfilling life, filled with frustrations, disappointment, and unfulfilled dreams, then it's time for you to begin your journey of self-exploration, so you may discover the most amazing treasure ever, the gift that is you, in all its many facets. What you are about to uncover is a diamond in the rough, a diamond you will continue to shape and polish for the rest of your life. Go forth from this moment as if every day of your life is an adventure in finding out just how amazing you are.

As you proceed to answer the following questions notice how your answers make your body feel. You might notice a sensation of feeling heavier or lighter? Or you might notice a sensation of feeling emptier or more complete? You will know your answers are truthful if they make you feel physically lighter and more complete as a being. The lighter and more complete you feel, the closer you are to what your true self finds to be most meaningful and fulfilling. Don't worry if you're feeling a little fearful, it's really just excitement about the amazing possibilities you're about to discover.

Be prepared to be enlightened, because you're about to realize a great number of things aren't exactly as you had thought them to be.

Once you have answered all of the questions, go back through your answers to find the most significant patterns (the top five to seven repeating items). The items that show up again and again point to what is most important to you. They'll also provide a good indication of your unique gifts. They might also show you how you could employ your gifts to provide definitive value to the world.

It's important to remember to tune in and notice how you feel when you answer the questions. This isn't about what you think is right or what you think you should do. It's about hearing and feeling what makes your heart sing and your soul dance. It's about reconnecting with your true self.

Before you start, take a few moments to center and ground yourself. Take a few deep breaths, bringing your awareness into your body, really focusing on connecting with your heart. Think about the feelings of peace and love. When you feel tuned in, take your journal and begin answering the following sets of questions.

Your Dreams Are A Guide

"Dream and give yourself permission to envision a You that you choose to be." ~ Joy Page.

We all have dreams. From the time we are very young children we dream about who we will be when we grow up and what we will do with our lives. Our dreams inspire us. They push us to try new things, to stretch beyond our current abilities. Our dreams are the fuel that ignites our lives, no matter our age.

Walt Disney stated in Sleeping Beauty, *"A dream is a wish your heart makes."* I say, how can we deny our hearts? To deny our hearts is to deny our truth. To deny our truth is to deny our life.

Ask yourself the following questions:

- What are the dreams you had for your life as a child?
- What are the dreams you had for your life as a teenager?
- What are the dreams you had for your life as a young adult?
- What are the dreams you have for your life now?
- Are there any commonalities between your dreams at the various points in your life? What are these commonalities?
- How often or completely have you actually lived your dreams?
- What would it take for your to live your dreams now?

Common themes running through your dreams provide clues to your passions and deep-seated interests, as well as your potential strengths and innate talents. Compare these themes to what you discover after you've answered the questions in the following subsections.

How You Spend Your Time and Energy Is A Guide

How you are spending your time and energy says a lot about what is most important to you. There are a variety of ways to look at how you are spending your time and energy. These include what you do with your time (including how you expend mental and physical energy), how you fill your space, how you spend your money, what you think about (especially what you find inspiring), what you talk about (both to yourself and others), and when and where you are most organized and disciplined in your life.

To give you a better picture of what you're looking for let's explore more deeply what is meant by how you spend your time. When thinking about how you spend your time, look at how you actually fill your days. For a minimum of a week, keep track of exactly what you do each day, including how long you devote to a particular activity (e.g., reading, writing, cooking, watching TV, toting your kids around, socializing, etc.). At the end of the week, add up how much time you devoted to each activity. Most often, the items you are spending the most time on will be the ones that are most important to you.

Make sure you keep track during a week that is typical of your regular life, otherwise you'll skew the results. Be honest with yourself. Don't fudge the results to make them seem better or different than they really are.

To illustrate I'll take a page out of my own life from a few years back. Outside of my job, I determined I was spending the majority of my time reading, writing, watching TV, attending personal development conferences and networking events, and drawing or painting.

Before doing this exercise I would have listed the top five things I spent my time on, that is the things I thought or wanted to think were most important to me, as learning, personal growth, health and fitness, personal relationships, and artistic endeavors. What I discovered from the realities of how I was spending my time was that learning and personal growth were given extremely high priority, leisure (mostly in the form of TV watching) was given a significant priority despite it not being in the original top five, personal relationships and artistic endeavors got an honorable mention, and health and fitness (once a high priority) had all but dropped off the radar.

As you can see from my results, the reality is not always as it appears. Accept what you find. Awareness as we've already learned is the first step in creating the changes we desire.

The purpose of the exercise is to recognize your patterns. They'll tell you what is most important to you at the present time. Once you've answered all the questions throughout this entire section your overall patterns will emerge.

After you've discovered your patterns, you can then determine how important and fulfilling a particular activity really is. In some cases you'll find the activity itself isn't all that important and meaningful, but rather the underlying need it is fulfilling is what is important. For instance, TV watching wasn't particularly fulfilling for me. It was however a convenient method for fulfilling two key needs: 1) to feel connected, or more accurately to be distracted from being alone (I was alone a lot during this period), and 2) to take a break from the intensity of my job and other activities, which at the time were very mentally draining. A little more scrutiny showed that my increased viewing time also coincided with the period where I was still healing from a severe knee injury. Prior to the injury I tended to pursue physical activity when I needed a mental break. So what was important to me was giving myself a well-needed mental break so I could recharge my batteries.

Let's now look at what is meant by how you fill your space. As with your activities you want to look for the significant patterns – the things you find the most of throughout your living space. These items will say a lot about is most important to you. Pay particular attention to the things you have prominently displayed and commonly leave out in the open. If it's hidden away it's probably not particularly important at this time of your life.

I'll again illustrate using a personal example. If you were to come into my home you would see lots and lots of books and other learning materials. You'd also see that everything is well organized. From this you might surmise that learning is very important to me, and truth be told I value learning and personal growth almost as much as I value breathing. If you categorized the books I own and took the time to discover which are most readily accessible, you'd have a pretty solid idea of the types of things I'm interested in learning and which are most important to me. And based on what I previously shared about how I was spending my time you'd see a picture emerging that says a lot about what I find most meaningful and fulfilling.

Using the above examples as a guide, answer the following questions:

- How do you spend your free time? On what activities?
  - *Keep track over an extended period (minimally a week, but a month or more will provide more accurate results). If you're spending your free time on work (i.e., your job), ask yourself what about your work is important to you?*

- How are you expending your energy?
  - *This may sound a lot like how you are spending your time, but it is in fact different. We expend a lot of energy that is not necessarily accounted for by what we do with our time. An example is being upset about how your husband and your children don't pick up their dirty clothes. Obviously there is something important to you that is being violated. These expenditures of energy will tell you a lot about what is important to you if you look deeply enough.*

- What do you most frequently think about?
  - *What topics do you find yourself thinking about most often? Is it finding a mate, taking a dream trip, losing weight? Whatever it is, don't forget to dig a little deeper to really get to what is important. For instance, taking a dream trip could be to feed your adventurous side that needs a regular fix. On the other hand, it could merely mean you desire some well-deserved down time to quietly recharge your batteries. It could even mean you want to explore your wilder side, a side that is severely repressed by your day-to-day routine.*

- What do you most often talk about (with others and yourself)
  - *Our topics of conversation are very telling about what is important to us. As always, go below the surface to*

get to what is really important. Keep digging until you find what is meaningful to you or fulfilling a need?

- What items fill your personal space (in your home, your office, your car)?
  - *Pay extra attention to the times that are most visible. Remember, anything hidden away is likely not particularly important to you, even though it may once have been very important. This is common. Think of how a toy becomes unimportant to a child as he grows and matures. The same thing happens to us as adults.*

- On what do you spend your discretionary income?
  - *Are you spending the majority of your discretionary income on your child's education, weekend ski trips, art supplies? Each of these says something specific depending on the given individual (e.g., your child's education is very important to you; leisure, adventure, fitness, and/or socializing are important to you; and exploring your creative side is important to you).*

- Where are you most organized?
  - *Is your yard immaculate, but your house a mess? That says something. It could mean you love being outdoors, communing with nature, and bringing the blank canvas of your yard to life. On the other hand, it could mean you care more about external appearances and perceptions, so you keep your yard tidy even though the rest of your life is in a shambles. This latter meaning might require further digging to determine what in fact is really important to you, because it probably really isn't what your neighbors might think.*

- Where are you most disciplined?
  - *This is much like the previous question. Look to where you are very self-controlled and regimented. For instance, you're never late for a meeting or you never miss a scheduled workout. Look below what you find to make sure you've hit upon what is indeed important to you. For instance, look to why you are never late? Dig*

> *until you determine what it is that is truly important to you.*

- What or who inspires you? What about them inspires you?
    - *Think of the things, events, and people that when you see, watch, or hear them you feel a rush of love come over you, find tears streaming down your face, or feel an exciting energy spreading throughout your body. Think also of those things that compel you to take positive action, as in the case of something you won't stand for (i.e., child abuse).*

Your answers to these questions will reveal a lot about is most important to you. However, you will often need to dig below the surface to determine what it is that is really important to you, as illustrated in the examples given with how you are spending your energy and where it is you are most disciplined. You'll get the most reliable results when you keep digging until nothing else comes up. Then dig just a little bit more.

Pay close attention to the items that get your emotional juices flowing (either positively or negatively). They are very telling about what is really important to you, especially when you've taken the time to dig below the surface.

Once you've answered these questions you should definitely see some patterns emerging. But there's more, so let's keep going.

What You Love and Are Good At Is A Guide

The things you are both good at and love to do are very good indicators for what is really important to you. These things say a lot about what you find both meaningful and fulfilling.

Please understand that just because you are extremely good at something doesn't mean you necessarily find it important or fulfilling. You can be one of the very best at something, but if you don't enjoy doing it, it doesn't count.

For example, let's say you're a fabulous cook but you take no pleasure from cooking. In this case cooking wouldn't be considered to be important to you, even if it's an activity you regularly engage in. It could be you only do it in order to feed your family nutritious meals. If you look more deeply you'll probably discover that it's something about health or family that's important to you.

On the other hand, let's say you're an average cook but you absolutely love cooking. You spend hours of your free time searching for new recipes, watching cooking programs, and preparing your new discoveries to share with your friends and family. In this case, cooking is very important to you, but it might also be the adventure of creating something new, or the time you spend socializing with the friends and family you've chosen to share your gastric masterpieces.

Ask yourself the following questions to discover what you are both good at and love doing:

- What are you really good at?
  - *These will typically be the things you are better at than most of the people you know.*

- What do others say you're really good at?
  - *Ask yourself where people often compliment you, tell you well done, or seem to envy your talent?*

- Do you really enjoy, or, better yet, love doing what you're good at?
  - *Ask this question for each item you listed yourself as being exceptionally good at.*

Repeat these questions until you've discovered everything you can possibly think of that you are both good at and love doing. As always, dig below the surface to make sure you've hit upon what it is about these things you find most meaningful and fulfilling.

Your Pain Is A Guide

Of all the areas we have explored, our pain is often the most telling in regard to our unrecognized gifts. The pain we experience in our life says a lot more than we give it credit for. It's very often the strongest indicator for what is really important to us. It tells us where we feel strongly about something. It tells us where we (and others) are being violated. It tells us about the things we won't tolerate. And anywhere we have overcome something extremely painful it tells us something very profound indeed. It is here that our pain tells us not only what is immensely important to us, but also where we can provide definitive value to the world.

Whether we choose to believe it or not, there is a purpose for our pain and the roads we travel throughout our life. Our many experiences, both the good and the bad, all go into the equation that makes us who we are. They are, for better or worse, a necessary part of the self-mastery process. And since we can't undo what has already occurred we might as well use it to our advantage.

Numerous cultures, religions, and spiritual traditions believe we – our soul – live many lives in the human form on a path toward ascension. In each of the human lives we are born with a set of lessons we must learn. If a lesson isn't learned in a particular lifetime then it will carry forward into the next one, and so on, until we have finally learned all the lessons we came here to learn, at which point we ascend. Whether there is truth to this or not, it is evident by the way life unfolds, that we each have unique lessons we are here to learn on our path to self-mastery, or as Maslow puts it in his hierarchy of human needs, self-actualization (which is the level at which we are the highest and best expression of ourselves, having realized our full potential, in addition to having found meaning and fulfillment). See Figure 5 for a complete picture of Maslow's hierarchy of human needs.

So no matter how we look at it, the pain in our life serves a purpose from which we derive value. It helps us to find our strengths and grow as an individual, which is required for self-actualization. It's also the means by which many find their direction in life (often referred to as a life calling or purpose); that is, they turn the definitive value their pain provided them into a gift they in turn give to the world.

As Greg Montana puts it, *"your pain is your credential"*; it gives you the experience and authority to give something of value to the world. Wherever you've experienced a deep and abiding pain that you've overcome, you have the credentials, the expertise, and the authority you need to use your experience to provide a product or service that will help others to overcome the pain they are suffering from similar ordeals. Hence why our pain is one of the most significant indicators of the gifts and value we have to offer to the world.

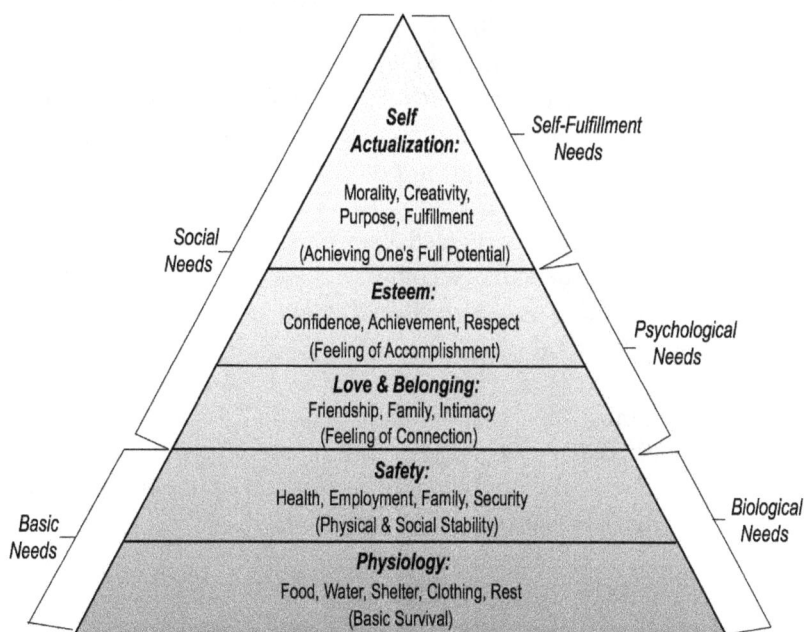

Figure 5: Maslow's Hierarchy of Needs

Ask yourself the following questions in for both the past and present to discover the unique gifts you have to offer as a result of your pain:

- Where do you carry a deep-seated pain as a result of some form of trauma, abuse, or neglect? What is the pain? How does it manifest? What do you feel would ease the pain?
  - *These pains provide a window to your hidden gifts. Look closely.*

- What do you feel is most missing from your life?
  - *Think about where you feel a void or emptiness? I once felt as if I had a gaping hole in my heart that could never be filled.*

- What makes you feel so angry you desire to hurt someone or break something? What do you feel is being violated when you become this angry?

   o *Anger often results from a trigger that's associated with unresolved pain from past experiences that we have yet to fully heal. This is why it is important to look at what is being violated. It's also a clue to things you won't tolerate and are therefore committed to changing in some fashion (e.g., stopping child abuse).*

- What have you struggled with and overcome that you can now help others to overcome?
  - *Anything you've mastered to one degree or another is a possibility.*

- What most concerns you about your life? About the world?
  - *These areas are likely tied to something you care deeply about and would like to do something about if you only had the courage or the resources.*

- What do really want in life?
  - *If you aren't sure what you really want, start with what you don't want and work backwards.*

- If you were to write a book what would it be about? What would you want your readers to know when they've finished?

- What do you want most for the world?

- What is the most meaningful change you would like to see in the world?

You have much to give. Let your pain be your guide. You'll be surprised at where it leads you.

With all of my many gifts and talents, I can honestly say it has almost always been my pain that has been the key determinant for the paths I've chosen to following throughout my life. And the path I'm on now is no different. This book, as well as my coaching programs, talks, and workshops, were all born out of my deepest and most profound pains – the pains that closed off some of the most remarkable aspects of my being for decades on end, in addition to the pain of silently watching others suffer similar or worse fates.

Regardless of the source of your pain or how it has affected your life it is a gift. If you acknowledge this gift it will miraculously transform your life. If you use it to empower and inspire others they will heal and grow with you, as the world automatically becomes a better place.

Feedback From Trusted Sources Is A Guide

While feedback from outside sources is not always useful, in this case it can be extremely valuable. This is because we are most often blind to our gifts, strengths, and talents, in addition to what is really important to us. Also, we tend to see things not as they really are, but either as we desire them to be or much worse than they actually are. Because of these tendencies it can be extremely beneficial to obtain outside perspectives.

Now that you've answered the above questions about yourself, you'll want to find three or more individuals whom you feel you can trust to answer some of these same questions based on how they see you. These individuals can be friends, family members, mentors, coaches, co-workers, etc. – basically anyone who knows you relatively well. Be sure you feel comfortable asking them to perform this exercise. You need to be able to trust they'll provide an honest assessment.

Ask your volunteers to answer the following questions about you. Let them know you desire their objective observations rather than their opinions:

- What are your dreams?
- How do you spend your free time?
- How do you fill your space?
- Where do you expend most of your energy?
- On what do you spend your discretionary income?
- Where are you most organized?
- Where are you most disciplined?
- Where are you most dependable?
- What do you most often talk about?
- What are you really good at – better than most?
- What do you love to do?
- What seems to bother you the most? (e.g., What makes you extremely upset?)

- What really excites you?
- What are your strengths, gifts, and talents?

Compare their feedback to your answers. Anything that lines up with your responses will confirm what you discovered on your own. For anything that surprises you or seems inaccurate, consider whether it might in fact be valid – i.e., it could be one of your blind spots.

If you just can't see their point of view I recommend having a conversation with the person, asking them to explain their response. Approach them with a sense of curiosity rather than defensiveness. If you still can't see what they see, feel free to disregard their input. If you have a revelation then by all means add it to your list. You might also want to consider if their view is a variation of one of your findings.

"Recognize that "we don't always see things as they are, we see them as we are." ~ Anais Nin. Sometimes we have to challenge our point of view to see a truth – to let go the view that isn't serving us. Are you willing to challenge your point of view, to change it if need be, to become a fuller, more complete expression of the person you really are?

∴

A Word of Advice:

Most of us are unable to see a good many of our genuine qualities without the assistance of an outside party. It is therefore recommended you work with someone who is adept at guiding others to see what they cannot otherwise see. Coaches, mentors, and counselors are generally very adept in this capacity.

Remember this quote? *"It's hard to see the whole picture when you are in the frame."* This is exactly why a coach, mentor, or other skilled person is so invaluable. They help us to see what we ordinarily can't, which accelerates our healing and self-mastery.

Coaches and mentors are generally more effective than close friends and family members. They are impartial yet caring. They don't become emotionally upset or feel left behind when we begin to heal, grow as a person, or venture off to explore new directions for our life.

Working with the right coaches and mentors helps us to see our blind spots, alternative perspectives, and solutions we wouldn't ordinarily see. This dramatically reduces the time and money it takes us to achieve our desired goals. For many, myself included, it equates to a reduction of several years' time and many thousands of dollars.

If nothing else, working with a good coach or mentor has a way of keeping us moving forward when life would otherwise derail us. This is another of the reasons they can save us considerable time and money. I know I've always made significantly more progress during the periods when I've worked with a coach than when I didn't. Yes, there is an upfront cost, but it more than pays for itself with the results you'll experience – namely a much higher quality of life, including more peace, happiness, and fulfillment.

Life is short. To get the most out of it, it pays to have an experienced guide. Think of the journey you are embarking on as you would a trip through the remote jungles of South America. You'd never venture on such a journey without an experienced guide to lead the way. You'd probably also never take the trip without first working with a seasoned coach to get you mentally and physically prepared for the environments you'll be exploring. Your inner world is much like the jungle. To find the magnificent treasures buried within it helps to have a seasoned guide to lead the way.

Actions For Discovering Your Most Precious Gifts

1. **Review Your Findings from the Discover Your Unique Gifts (Your Genius) Exercise**
    Regularly review your findings from the exercise you completed in the *Discover Your Unique Gifts* section. Compare your answers to what you discovered about yourself in Step 7, Action 4. Note where there is congruency. See congruency as added confirmation that your results are correct. Begin thinking about how you can apply your gifts to live a meaningful and fulfilling life that provides value beyond just yourself.

    If you have yet to perform these exercises, complete them as soon as possible.

    What is important to you will change with time. It is therefore recommend you repeat this exercise at least once per year, preferably every six months. Each time you repeat it you'll notice some items remain unchanged, while others have shifted up or down in priority. A few may have dropped off the list altogether, or they may have emerged in an entirely new form. This is normal. It's a byproduct of your healing, personal growth, and overall self-mastery.

Major life changes, such as a birth, death, child leaving home, retirement, new job, or physical relocation, tend to cause significant shifts to what is most important to us. Anytime you experience a big change in your life it is recommended you repeat this exercise. You'll more effectively navigate the transition if you know what's really important to you and why.

2. Questions To Regularly Ask Yourself

The following questions are very revealing when asked regularly. They open you to possibilities you would never otherwise envision. They'll help you get to know your true self, and live a richer, more fulfilling life.

When asking these questions, be as open as you possibly can. You want the answers to come from your innermost self, not your ever ready to answer inner critic. Give yourself some space to hear what surfaces. Record your findings in your journal. Be curious. Be open to greater possibilities. Ask additional probing questions to dig even deeper. Act on your answers.

- Who are you being today? Who would you like to be today?
- How much of the gift you are will you allow yourself to acknowledge? To be?
- What grand and glorious adventure can you have today?
- What can you celebrate today? About yourself? About your life?
- What if your life was a celebration? How would you then choose to live it?
- What if everything you think is wrong about yourself is actually greatness you have yet to perceive? To acknowledge? To apply?
- What reality would you like to create for your life?
- What is right about your circumstances that you're not getting? Not accepting? (Ask this question in relationship to something that feels off or wrong.)

- What is right about yourself that you're not getting? Not accepting?
- What have you made greater than yourself that is preventing you from living the life you desire?
- If you were an energy that allowed you to manifest the life you desire, what energy would you be (e.g., happiness, peace, love, inspiration, confidence, success)?
- How does your life get any better than this moment?
- What can you choose to do today that's just for you? Just because you're you and you're alive?
- What is/was right about today?
- What other questions could you ask that would allow you to more fully be your true self right here, right now?

Periodically compare your answers to appreciate the progress you're making. You'll notice your answers are continually becoming more expansive and affirming.

3. Take Time To Just Be

Periodically give yourself time to just be. Do whatever allows you to relax and tune in to your innermost self. The point is to let your mind go quiet so you can hear what wants to surface.

There are a variety of techniques you can use, such as meditation, but you can just as easily go for a walk or a hike, take a stroll on the beach, or sit quietly in your favorite natural habitat (such as a park, by a river or stream, on the edge of a lake, or in your backyard garden).

Give yourself at least an hour to completely decompress and just be. Whenever possible, give yourself a full day or more.

When you feel tuned in, perform some of the writing exercises suggested in Step 6. They'll help you further reflect upon how you can most effectively utilize your gifts, and what is most important to you, to create the life you desire.

From this quiet place you'll discover a whole new wealth of possibilities.

4. Watch and Read Inspiring Stories

Periodically read, listen to, and watch inspiring stories, biographies, lectures, and speeches. They'll illuminate possibilities for your life if you will but allow yourself to believe.

Just as the characters in the books and movies, or those delivering the speech or lecture, have often overcome great obstacles to lead remarkably fulfilling and exceptional lives, so can you.

Here are a few I've found to be extraordinarily inspiring:

- The Last Lecture (Randy Pausch Lecture & Book)
- The Ultimate Gift (Jim Stovall – Book & Movie)
- Way of the Peaceful Warrior (Dan Millman – Book & Movie)
- Mono Lisa Smile (Movie)
- Dead Poet's Society (Movie)
- Good Will Hunting (Movie)
- Finding Forester (Movie)
- Unstoppable & Unstoppable Women (Cynthia Kersey Books)
- Chicken Soup for the Soul (Books - Take your pick)
- Martin Luther King Jr.'s *"I Have A Dream"* Speech
- Steve Job's Stanford Commencement Speech

There are literally thousands to choose from. Choose the ones that speak to you.

5. **Affirm Your Gifts and Your Value to the World**
Repeat the following declarations, with intense feeling and emotion, at least five times each morning and evening for a period of at least 30 days.

- I am a unique and remarkable being.
- I am exceptionally gifted and talented.
- I have much to offer to the world.
- I use what is most important to me, along with my gifts, talents, and pains, to make a real difference in the world.
- I believe the purpose of my life is self-mastery.
- I LOVE MY LIFE.

Life is not a private affair.
A story and its lessons are only useful if shared.
-Dan Millman (from Way of the Peaceful Warrior)

Step 9 – Help Others To Fast Forward Your Own Healing: Let Your Pain and Passions Lead The Way

Tara's Story

Until her mid-forties, Tara continually found herself alternating between relative happiness and deep depression. When happy, she felt she could conquer the world, as if anything were possible. When depressed, she felt as if a hidden tide of pain and misery had swallowed her whole, sucking her deep into the depths of a subterranean cavern filled with nothing but loneliness and despair.

Tara's depressed periods always left her bewildered. She just couldn't understand why she would suddenly feel so immensely unhappy and forlorn. To her eye she'd done everything was supposed to do to make a person happy. She'd been a good girl – she followed the rules, taken care of family members, received a university education, built a career, married a nice guy, created a nice home, and had two beautiful children. She'd even done some travelling and volunteer work. Yet she still frequently became depressed, always longing for some unknown something to fulfill her.

After a few years of this cycle Tara decided there had to something she was overlooking. Knowing she had repressed a significant portion of her early youth, she wondered if maybe there wasn't a link between her depression and the events she had worked so hard to bury. With this idea as a starting place, Tara began reflecting deeply on her life. She also began keeping a diary of what was going in her life to see if she could detect what was triggering her more intense mood changes.

Over the course of many months Tara became aware of three very telling patterns. First, she realized she was continually repeating several of the traumatic and abusive aspects of her childhood in her current relationships, although in more subtle ways. Second, she realized she had a tendency to internalize the pain and problems of her friends, family, and co-workers, as if they were her own. In public she'd lightly shrug it off, but internally she'd feel overwhelmed and put upon. Third, she realized she often felt broken and empty, as if portions of her being were completely missing.

These discoveries helped Tara begin the healing process. The more healing she experienced, the less frequently and radically her mood would shift. To accelerate her progress, Tara decided it would be beneficial to work with a professional counselor. After a few months of limited progress with a psychologist, Tara began to doubt the process. She was tired of rehashing the past and being asked to consider drugs to combat her depression. What she really wanted was to know her essential self and feel whole; to her this meant discovering who she really is, and learning to reintegrate and embody the parts of herself she had long suppressed.

With this goal in mind, Tara sought other means for working through her feelings, mood swings, and tendencies to play superwoman. After some trial and error Tara found two fabulous mentors whose focus was authentic communication with oneself and with others.

In some of her mentors' small, group workshops Tara opened up in ways she'd never dreamed possible. Through her sharing, the sharing of other the participants, and the feedback from her mentors, Tara at long last understood the source of her pain and misery, which allowed her to quickly heal. After only a couple of months of participating in these group events, Tara had put an end to her debilitating cycles of depression.

Today Tara is genuinely happy and fulfilled in her everyday life. Following what she believes to be her calling, Tara is now working with several youth and women's groups that provide support for victims of excessive trauma and abuse. To give back in a more profound way, she actively facilitates a variety of transformational programs designed to expedite the healing process while simultaneously awakening the participants to their most essential self. She believes that helping others to heal and be free to authentically express themselves is the best way to make a real difference in the world.

Before Tara experienced her own healing she would never have believed she had so much to offer, or that she could be so fulfilled doing something born of the pain she had suffered for so long. Today Tara believes everything we experience in life is a gift with a singular purpose – to advance us on our unique path to self-actualization, where we will find meaning and fulfillment through our distinct contribution to the world.

You Can Live A Loving, Fulfilling, and Whole Life

You *can* live an incredibly loving and fulfilling life; one in which you are completely whole and free from the demons who have haunted you for much of your life. This life is just as realizable for you as it has been for me, the women described throughout this book, and countless others the world over. All it really takes is a decision to make it your reality, a solid belief that it can be your reality, a willingness to make peace with your past, and a devotion to the processes of self-mastery (self-awareness, self-discovery, and self-trust).

I hope by now you believe it is possible for you to live a loving, fulfilling, and whole life. I also hope you've made the decision that nothing is going stop you from having this life as soon as possible.

While I can't guarantee how long it will take you to experience this life for yourself, I can guarantee you it's possible, and it takes much less time than you could ever imagine. For some it happens very quickly; for others it takes a awhile. How long it will take you depends very much on how quickly and thoroughly you are able to let go of your old paradigms (your taken-for-granted, limiting beliefs and assumptions), the depths of the layers you must master, and the consistency with which you dedicate yourself to living your life as the highest and fullest expression of your most authentic self.

Regardless of the time it takes you, you must believe it is worth the effort. With each step forward you will be experiencing a whole new you – a you that you will love, a you that will love her life, a you that will make a marked difference in world by the very fact you have stepped into the role you were born to live; the role where you live your life as the fullest and best expression of the person you were born to be – a person who came here with a unique set of gifts the world is waiting to experience.

Breakthroughs most often occur when we least expect them. The majority it would seem are born out of extreme adversity, a near or actual breakdown, or a near death experience. More rarely does it seem they are born out of the still quietness of the mind or some fortuitous event. Regardless of the circumstances that ignite the breakthrough, the underlying driver is almost always the same; the pain of continuing as is has become much greater than the fear of doing something bold to forever resolve the pain.

But this doesn't have to be the case. You don't have to wait for the unexpected to occur, or for the pain to become so extreme you will no longer tolerate it. You can experience breakthroughs much more predictably. In fact, you can create them on a regular basis by deliberately engaging in the self-mastery process. Through the deliberate application of self-mastery you are choosing to take full responsibility for your life and everything you experience. By taking full responsibility you will experience repeated breakthroughs. Best of all you'll experience the loving, fulfilling, and whole life you desire. Stay focused on being your best and most authentic self and in no time at all you'll find you are living a life that is more fantastic than any you've ever dreamed possible.

If for any reason you are still balking, remember that *you* and *only you* are responsible for the state of your life. *You* are attracting everything that occurs in your life. So, starting now, *be a conscious creator*. Tap into the wellspring within, the wellspring connecting you to the universal source of infinite love and abundance. It's always available to you. All you need do is 1) identify what you want, 2) give it your attention, energy and focus, and 3) allow it to manifest as your reality (three step manifestation formula from M. Losier's book, *"Law of Attraction"*).

Align Your Life With What Is Most Important To Your True Self

The most expedient path to live a loving, fulfilling, and whole life is to align your everyday life with what is most important to your *true* self. In truth you are already doing this. However, if you aren't experiencing the results you'd like, it means you aren't yet fully aligned with the fulfillment you desire; i.e., what is most important to you.

I really want you to understand this because it's key to you living the life you desire. Alignment has two basic components: 1) the energy we put out, which is basically our thoughts and beliefs regarding the desire and our ability to manifest it, and 2) the actions we take with respect to the desire.

Do you remember the energy (*vibe*) discussion we had in Step 2? It's basic tenet is like attracts like. To experience (attract) what you desire, you must resonate at the energy level of your desire. If you desire love, you must resonate love. If you desire wealth, you must resonate the feeling of wealth.

More concretely, you must think, believe, and act as if your desire is already part of your life. Minimally you must believe it is already on its way. If you desire to have a loving mate, start acting as if you already have a loving mate. Make space for him (or her). Visualize your life as if he were already part of it. Begin doing some of the things you'd do together. In doing so you will be resonating at an appropriate frequency to attract him into your life.

Contrast this with how most of us tend to go about it. We sulk about what we don't have. We put out the energy that it's never going to happen. In turn we get a less appealing form of our desire. Either way we are getting what we have aligned ourselves with.

To further illustrate, let's look back to what you learned in Step 8. Think about how much time you're actually spending on the things you discovered to be most important to you. Let's say your analysis revealed nine things. The more important items are higher on the list. They get more of your attention. The less important items are lower on the list; they are easily forfeited to anything higher on the list.

However, this is only part of the story, because there is a whole range of expressions for how we fulfill what is important to us. At one end of the spectrum we experience a healthy fulfillment of our desire. This occurs when we resonate at a higher, fuller, more complete expression of our most authentic self. At the other end of the spectrum we experience an unhealthy fulfillment of our desire. This occurs when we resonate at a lower, less complete expression of our most authentic self. At the higher end of the spectrum we are happy and fulfilled. At the lower end we are unhappy, discontented, and unfulfilled, despite often experiencing some measure of gratification.

Think of it this way. Let's say TV watching showed up as number three of nine on your most important list, which you find disconcerting. Let's also say after digging a little deeper you discovered what's really important to you is leisure time; you desire to step away from the intensity of your day to revitalize your innate energy, spirit, and creative juices.

TV watching is but one expression of leisure time. And in this example it doesn't appear to be your most fulfilling expression. Those disconcerting feelings you are experiencing means that TV watching is distracting you from being your best self and having the life you desire. To experience a higher expression of leisure, and therefore a higher, fuller expression of yourself, you would be better served if you replaced your TV watching habit with an activity that more effectively revitalizes your energy, spirit, and creative juices. Some possibilities to consider are meditation, walking your dog in the neighborhood park, and taking a nice long bubble bath. If you're the more adventurous type, a day of kayaking or a nice long hike in the glory of nature might be just the ticket you're looking for.

To live the whole and fulfilling life we desire almost always requires some adjustments. Most of the adjustments are related to how we are focusing our energies; that is, we must adjust our thoughts and our actions so they align with our desires. The more positively and fully we focus our attention and energies on our most important desires, the more fully aligned we become with our true self, and the more quickly and easily we begin experiencing the wholeness, love, and fulfillment we seek.

Understanding these truths helps us to comprehend the choices we have made in the past, and ultimately to make better choices in the future. When we align our choices with what is absolutely most important to our true self, we automatically live more peaceful, loving, and fulfilling lives. Additionally, we don't question why we are doing something or whether we should do it, because we know in our heart and soul that it is the right choice for us at this particular time.

It's only when we make choices that are out of alignment with our true self that we feel frustrated and dissatisfied. Living in alignment with the best expression of our true self and what is most important to us automatically brings us more joy, meaning, and fulfillment. It also makes us more effective and productive. And the old stresses, tensions, and guilt we previously experienced just fade away.

I can emphatically attest to these truths. I've proven it to myself time and time again. When I'm aligned with the best expression of myself that I know how be in the given moment, following the urges of my heart and soul, and putting my gifts and talents to use in a meaningful way, I experience more joy, love, and fulfillment than I had ever imagined possible. And when I'm out of alignment, I once again find myself becoming stressed and discontented.

Once you've begun living in alignment with the higher expressions of your true self, you will notice a marked difference in the quality of your life. In time you'll learn to quickly recognize when you are out of alignment, which will immediately shift you back into a higher energetic expression (in your thoughts, beliefs, and actions). If you find yourself feeling dissatisfied in any way, consider how you can shift your energy, attention, or behavior. Change your energy, your attention, or your behavior and you'll change your life.

Apply Your Gifts and Strengths

Meaningful expression of our gifts, talents, passions, and loves is to my knowledge a necessity for living a loving, fulfilling, and whole life. When we are meaningfully expressing our gifts, in a way that provides value beyond ourselves, we are in effect living in alignment with the highest and best expression of our true self.

By now you should have a relatively good idea of your gifts, talents, strengths, passions, and loves. You should also be pretty confident you know what's really important to you. And if you gave thoughtful attention to the actions in Steps 7 and 8, you should be swimming with possibilities about how you can meaningfully apply your gifts and strengths to create the fulfilling life you desire – where you get to live every day as the highest and best expression of your truest self.

Remember Gary Douglas's words "... *where awareness and possibility intersect... a new reality is born."* This is what awaits you, a new reality; a reality that is much more rewarding than any you've ever imagined.

I know you may be feeling just a bit overwhelmed from everything you have discovered thus far. You've got so much to think about. There are so many new possibilities for your life. In fact, you're probably wondering exactly where and how to get started. That's largely what this step is all about. By the time we've finished you'll have identified a number of ways you can immediately begin applying those magnificent gifts of yours.

Before moving on I want to address any feelings of overwhelm you might be experiencing. First, you don't have to take on everything all at once so don't even try. We don't want you giving up before you've even started. More importantly, realize there are no impenetrable barriers barring those you create in your mind.

In my opinion, the best place to start is with what absolutely speaks to you the most at this very moment. Do anything you can to commence applying your gift, talent, passion, or love in a manner you find both meaningful and fulfilling. It doesn't have to be big, and it doesn't need to take more than a few minutes of your time. What's important is that you just get started, being sure to keep an open mind to what is emerging.

If you are unsure what most speaks to you, give yourself some quiet time with your inner guide. Ask her where to begin. Ask her these three questions: *What do I really want? What speaks to me the most? What activities do I so thoroughly enjoy that I lose track of time?* Believe the answers will come. Believe you will absolutely make the best choice for yourself at this point in time. And remember, blunders and missteps are ok. They're how we learn and grow. They are an inherent part of the self-mastery process and this journey we call life. If for some reason you don't feel confident about what shows up, repeat the process every day for 5 to 10 days. Then get started with whatever shows up most frequently.

Have courage and faith in yourself, your true self. Go forth with a sense of purpose and vigor unlike any you've ever known. The most amazing life you could ever imagine is waiting for you just around the corner. So let your gifts shine like the brilliant jewels they are.

Make A Contribution

One of the most significant ways we can experience a sense of love, wholeness, and fulfillment is through the contributions we make to another's life or the betterment of the world. Contributions from the heart make us rich in the truest sense of the word.

If you are looking for a way to do something meaningful with your gifts, consider how you could make a contribution that provides some form of value to the world. It doesn't have to be big, and you don't necessarily even have to see the results. All you need is for it to feel right in your heart.

There are countless ways you can make a contribution. They can be as simple as picking up trash on the side of the road, or helping an elderly woman carry her groceries into her home. At the other end of the spectrum, they can be as grandiose as contributing the funds to erect a new wing of a hospital that helps to save the lives of thousands of children stricken with life threating illnesses, or volunteering your time and energy to help rebuild the homes and lives of those affected by war or natural disaster.

However you decide to make a contribution is entirely up to you. The important thing to remember is the more it aligns with your gifts and what is most important to your true self, the more meaning and fulfillment you can expect to experience. This is because it will be coming from your heart.

Anytime you do something from the heart, which is an expression of your true self, it will automatically be meaningful and fulfilling. Contrast this with the things you do out of a feeling of obligation, or because you *think* it's the right thing to do, and you'll immediately sense the difference.

If you're unsure how you can make a contribution that provides value beyond yourself, which is also meaningful and fulfilling to you, ponder what would've made a significant difference to the quality of your life had someone contributed their time, energy, or other resources to support you when you needed it. Remember, it doesn't have to be anything big or elaborate. For example, maybe you needed help with your homework, a friend to talk with when you were down (or excited), or even just a heartfelt hug every now and then. You could now make these gifts available to someone you know who really needs them.

The possibilities for you to make a contribution are endless. With a little thought, or dare I say a question to your innermost self, you'll discover innumerable ways you can make a contribution that is sure to improve the quality of your own life as well as the lives of others.

If you're still scratching your head, take a cue from Lori and Tara's stories. Begin by applying the gifts born of your own pain. Use them to help another person who's struggling with relatable pain and experiences. In the process you'll further heal yourself. In time you'll discover how you can best contribute your gifts to make an even more significant difference.

The World Is Waiting For You and Your Gifts

In the off chance you haven't quite caught on, I'm going to be perfectly blunt. You have much to offer the world in the form of your gifts, and the world *IS* waiting desperately for you to share those gifts.

Before you start begging to differ, I'm asking that you bear with me for a moment. Give me the benefit of the doubt while you consider the following.

All personal gifts have a purpose. If they didn't, then why would we have them? And what is their purpose if not to be shared with the world? And what of the lessons we learn as a result of our many adversities and experiences? Are they not gifts in and of themselves? And if they are gifts, are they not also to be shared?

Personal gifts come in all shapes and sizes. Some are innate. They manifest themselves as physical or mental abilities, such as those we commonly recognize in a star athlete, a musical prodigy, a scientist who discovers a breakthrough cure for a disabling disease, and so on. Others are born out of great pain and adversity. Used advantageously, pain combined with our innermost desires for something better has a way of giving us the heart, strength, and capacity to overcome the greatest of odds. In the process we uncover hidden gifts and passions. Applying those gifts and passions with purpose, we in turn provide value for the greater good.

As an example of this latter type of gift, think of the mother who founded Mothers Against Drunk Driving (MADD) after a drunk driver killed her daughter. How many children have been saved from senseless death, and how many families have been supported after their child was killed or injured by a drunk or drugged driver, as a result of her applying the gifts born of her own tragedy? Had this mother not applied her gifts, it's very likely that thousands more children would have been injured or killed at the hands of a drunk or drugged driver. This is but one example of thousands where people have applied their gifts in a way the world was just waiting for someone to stand up and do something.

If you're still struggling to see yourself in this capacity, think of yourself as the Phoenix who rises from the ashes. You are reborn anew; complete with the wisdom and knowledge of your previous self. Additionally, you now recognize all of the gifts you'd previously hidden away in the debris of your life (like Lori in Step 8), as well the many new ones you've gained as a result having successfully overcome your many adversities (like Tara).

Believe that all of your many gifts have some inherent value to someone other than yourself. It's only a matter of you recognizing their value and thereafter making them available to the world.

Listen to your heart. Hear its whispers. Your value is staring you straight in the face. Open yourself to the possibilities that have been patiently waiting for you to step up and shine, like the brilliant jewel you are. If need be, find a mentor or coach to light the way. They can help you see what has been sitting right under your nose all along.

Allow Yourself To Be Vulnerable and Courageous – It Will Transform Lives, Most Especially Your Own

Once upon a time not so long ago I was terrified to tell my story. Out of fear and shame I kept a tight lid on some of the very things that would set me free. From a young age I had been programmed to believe we are to remain silent about our personal (and family) skeletons, pain, and hardships. Even most of the positive experiences were off limits. But something within kept nagging at me; some part of me knew I needed to speak up and share if I was ever to heal and become whole again.

Little did I know at the time how much the act of sharing helps us to heal, not only ourselves but also others. Reflecting back to the times in which I had allowed myself to be courageous and vulnerable enough to share, I realized I had repeatedly experienced this miraculous phenomenon over and over again. Today, I know for a fact that sharing is one of the most effective methods available for healing and becoming whole again. I also know just how scary it can be to open up and be that vulnerable. But when done with the right people, in a caring and supportive environment, it can be one of the most profoundly healing and liberating experiences of our life, not only for us, but also for those we share with.

Case in point. In January 2011 I found myself on stage in front of about 40 other individuals, sharing things I had never dreamed possible. What transpired for me on that cold, snowy day in Denver, Colorado, was the most profound healing I have ever experienced. Demons that had plagued me for decades were vanquished within a matter of minutes. To date I remain fully liberated from their demeaning control.

But I'm not the only one who benefited from my sharing that day. Many others in the room experienced their own healing, or began the healing process, because I had been courageous and vulnerable enough to stand up and share some of my deepest pains.

Through the course of my sharing, other group members sharing, and our facilitators sharing and feedback, many of us markedly altered our perceptions and realities for the better. My own life magically transformed, almost instantaneously, all because I allowed myself to open up and be vulnerable. Through this process I was able to face my demons head on, seeing them for what they really are. Once I had faced them, they were no longer a threat, which meant that the many parts of myself that had been hidden away for safekeeping could once again take their rightful place in my life.

Most amazingly to me was the dramatic shift I experienced from that moment forward. Everything in my life seemed to improve almost instantaneously, yet the only thing that had actually changed was my perception; that is, how I saw myself, my experiences, and my place in the world. In those few moments on stage I was the Phoenix. Rising from the ashes (in reality tears) I was reborn anew, having liberated virtually all of my true self while retaining the complete knowledge and wisdom of my previous self; quite the opposite of a karmic rebirth where we are reborn without any conscious knowledge of our past self.

In my newly reborn state, I literally glowed with all the possibility that life has to offer. Not only did I feel reborn, but I also began receiving non-stop comments about my amazing transformation and how wonderful it was to see.

However, as liberated and thrilled as I was with my metamorphosis, I was even more ecstatic about the awakening of what I now consider my true calling. For the first time in my life I readily experienced my own inherent value; the value I had been completely blind to despite it always having been there, and my having been blindly sharing it for the better part of my life.

Within a few short months of that snowy January day, I knew exactly how I could consciously share my gifts, and in the process live an incredibly meaningful and fulfilling life. This book is but one of the ways I have chosen to share these gifts.

Whenever you experience yourself shrinking or holding back from life, consider these words from American author, Anais Nin: *"Life shrinks or expands in proportion to one's courage."* Then muster up your courage, allow yourself to be vulnerable, and take a bold step forward. The only way to experience the life you really desire is to let yourself out of your self-imposed cage. So unlock the door, throw away the key, and take a step. Then take another step, followed by another, and another, and another. Before you know it you will have mastered the art of courage, and in the process you will have markedly transformed your life, likely having helped many others along the way.

Help Others Heal To Heal Yourself

I've heard it said if we don't share our gifts and experiences, some might even call it our wisdom, that we are being selfish. Over the course of my journey I've employed a wide variety of tools and techniques to facilitate my personal growth and healing. Of all of them, I believe the one that has had the most profound effect, bringing about the most rapid and significant levels of healing and growth, has been sharing – most especially when I've courageously shared my deepest and most profound feelings, wounds, and traumas with the intent of helping someone else to heal by showing them their own inherent strength, gifts, and worth.

Whether we realize it or not, we are all mirrors and teachers for one another. By awakening others to their truth, we almost always awaken ourselves to our own truth, which in turn heals us and leads us to another level of self-mastery.

A key reason for this is that what we share with others is not only what they need to hear and experience, but also what we ourselves most need to hear and experience. For example, you share with someone who has a poor self-image how remarkably beautiful they are. By sharing your observation with them you are shining a light on the beauty they cannot see within themselves, while simultaneously reflecting back to yourself your own inherent beauty, a beauty you may have previously dismissed or barely have come to accept.

As mirrors for one another, we help each other to see our true selves, our best selves, the selves we so often ignore or feel ashamed of because of the internal and external bullying we have lived with for much of our lives. With this in mind, you should internalize this truth: through the sharing of your gifts, which includes your wisdom and vulnerability, you are creating an opening for both you and those you share with to more fully heal and be more of the whole and amazing beings you are. Any angst you might feel before or during your share is completely worth it because you are providing an invaluable service that has the potential to keep on giving.

Life is in effect a school. It is the ultimate teacher. As you are a part of life, you have a unique role to play in your brief time here on planet Earth. Part of that role includes the sharing of your story and your wisdom so that others may benefit. But realize the wisdom I am speaking of comes mostly from within, from your heart, soul, body, and nonconscious mind. Additionally, virtually all of your indirect experiences come from within. Therefore, it is essential, as we have already discussed many times, to stay attuned to what is coming from within, from your innermost self, as this will help you to know when and what to share so that you may make the greatest contribution.

It's important to understand that the value of your knowledge and wisdom comes not from what you know, but from what you do with what you know. Just knowing something will never nourish your soul. Knowledge in and of itself will never bring you peace, happiness, or fulfillment. It is only by sharing your knowledge with feeling, emotion, and energy, in a way that positively benefits the greater world, that it truly makes a positive difference to your life. So don't just know something; act on what you know. Share what you know at the highest vibrational level of feeling, energy, and emotion you can possibly muster. I guarantee it'll make a huge difference to the quality of your life.

Live Your Dreams – Starting Today

You're in the home stretch. But there's one last piece to the wholeness puzzle I feel is vitally important to bring into the picture before we wrap up. That piece has to do with you living your dreams, and not just someday, but today.

I know you may not believe me at this very moment, but rest assured you can live your dreams today, and each and every day hereafter. And very shortly, I hope to prove it in such a way that you will begin taking at least one small action toward living your dreams, starting this very day.

Dreams Are The Fuel Of Life

"The future belongs to those who believe in the beauty of their dreams." ~ Eleanor Roosevelt.

Dreams are the fuel of life. They give us a reason to live boldly, to take risks, and above all to take on the seemingly immovable obstacles that would otherwise keep us trapped in a life that barely meets our most basic needs (as shown in the bottom tiers of Maslow's Basic Hierarchy of Needs – Figure 5).

However, to make our dreams a reality, they require something to put them into motion, something to lubricate the runway so we move past the obstacles that continually show up to block us from starting or completing our most rewarding journeys. The lubricant I'm referring to is our thoughts and beliefs, coupled with a bit of magic I'm going to call passion.

But there's a catch to this lubricant. It requires our most diligent attention, much like the lubricants in our car. If we don't take care to continually replace our thoughts and beliefs with positive and supportive ones, they become stale and gummed up with all sorts of negativity and limitations, causing not only our dreams, but also our bodies and our lives, to slow down, stall out, or even worse to come to a grinding halt (just as our car does if we don't replace the oil on a regular basis).

Stale and outdated mental lubricants cause us to quit believing in our dreams, and ultimately ourselves. Or, maybe it's the other way around; we quit believing in ourselves, and therefore our dreams. Either way, the result is the same. Our dreams are relegated to nothing more than fantasies; something that's impossible for us to achieve. This will always be the result when we relinquish our power to our demons; that is, when we let the negative and limiting soundtracks of our inner critic and her committee of fans and supporters run the show we call our life.

I know we've discussed ad nauseam about how important our thoughts and beliefs are to the quality of our lives, but it's worth reiterating their importance, especially here. If you truly desire to live your dreams it is vitally important for you take extra special care to nurture those dreams with the highest quality thoughts and beliefs possible. Therefore, to give your dreams the best possible chance of becoming your reality you will want to continually apply what you learned in Steps 3 and 4.

Be Your Own Hero

"If you take responsibility for yourself you will develop a hunger to accomplish your dreams." ~ Les Brown.

It seems that only a few of us are fortunate enough to begin living our dreams from a very early age. The rest of us, for whatever reason, have put our dreams on hold. If you're one of those who have relegated their dreams to the backseat of life, it's time for you to dust those dreams off and bring them back into the forefront of your life where they belong. Depending on your perceived level of worthiness you might find this requires a good bit of courage, because to live your dreams you must believe in them as well as yourself.

At this very moment I'm sure you've got all sorts of "buts" (demon voices!) cropping up, providing you with all sorts of excuses why you can't possibly focus on your dreams right now. To help you begin overriding those limiting soundtracks, and hopefully begin taking the actions you need to make your dreams your reality, I'd like you to think about this: If you aren't actively taking steps to fulfill your dreams you are by default fulfilling someone else's. Don't believe me? OK. Think about this. Every time you say no to your own dreams and desires you are either directly or indirectly fulfilling someone else's dreams and desires.

Need a concrete example? OK. I'll use our TV watching example again, since so many people have a tendency to use TV watching as a means to distract themselves when they are procrastinating out of fear or overwhelm, or have altogether given up on their dreams. When you watch TV as a means of avoiding taking the actions that would help bring your dreams to life you are unwittingly fulfilling many other people's dreams at the expense of your own.

Look at it this way. The actors, producers, studios, and networks want you watching, because without you, and millions of others like you, their dreams go unfulfilled. Without a sustained viewership the program won't air, the actors are out of a gig, and the station has empty airtime. If too few programs are being watched the production houses and broadcast stations go under. So, as you sit there idly watching hour after hour, you are fulfilling the dreams of countless others while your own life and dreams are surreptitiously passing you by.

Don't get me wrong. I'm not saying you should never watch TV, or that those whose dreams are made possible by your viewing are unimportant. What I'm saying is don't give up on your own dreams. Take concerted and consistent action towards making them your reality. You deserve it.

So where does this hero thing come in? What exactly does it mean to be your own hero? And how do you become your own hero?

Being your own hero is somewhat of a prerequisite to living your dreams. Think about it. Who else, but you, can make your dreams your reality? No one. The only person who can make your dreams come true is you.

Being your own hero means living your life in alignment with what you hold most dear – in essence living your life as the highest and best expression of your true self. It means having the courage, fortitude, determination, and perseverance to make your dreams your reality, which at times will require you to make some significant sacrifices.

Becoming your own hero is what these 9 Steps have been all about. In short it means having the willingness to plumb the depths of your being, exploring all aspects of your life, until you have discovered what is most important to you in each area of your life, and then acting upon your discoveries so that you are living in alignment with what is most essential to you as a self-actualized being.

Actualizing your inner hero is therefore nothing more than the process of self-mastery, which was covered in the preceding steps.

Live A Standout Life That Makes A Difference

"Every great dream begins with a dreamer. Always remember, you have within you the strength, the patience, and the passion to reach for the stars to change the world." ~ Harriet Tubman.

One of the most amazing side effects of you living your dreams is the positive effect it can have on the lives of others. When you change your world for the better, you will most assuredly change the world in an advantages manner for countless others, whether you are aware of it or not.

235

Take for example the fortuitous effects resulting from you having improved your attitude; that is, the beneficial side effects of you vibrating at a higher, more positive energy level. When you are happier and more optimistic, those around you tend to become more pleasant and cooperative. People become drawn to you. Opportunities begin popping up as if by magic. You experience more abundance. Darkness turns into light, spreading way beyond your personal being.

While arguably a simple example, it shows just how easy it is to live a standout life that makes a real difference. Doing nothing more than living in alignment with your true self is really all it takes. So, get started today. Live your life in alignment with your true self, with the things that are absolutely most important to you. Take the necessary steps to make your dreams your reality. In the process you'll make a tremendous difference.

If you're not yet convinced it's that simple, or you aren't sure what living in alignment with your true self would like, a simple place to begin is with your irritations. Irritations are a signal you are out of alignment in some way. Focus on turning them into inspiration. When you are inspired your energy will shift, you'll recognize an abundance of opportunities, and you will take action. Repeated cycles of inspiration and action will lead to the fulfillment of your dreams. Through the fulfillment of your dreams you will automatically being making a positive difference to countless others.

When in doubt, always remember this truth: The most rewarding lives, which impart the greatest good, are almost always born of the simplest of actions.

Be the person you were born to be. Act on what is in your heart. And live your dreams. As a result you will live an extraordinary life that is far more rewarding than any you may ever have imagined. Additionally, you will have paved the way for many others to do the same.

One of my favorite sentiments, that sums this up nicely, was expressed by Bill Clinton in his speech to the 2004 Democratic National Convention, where he stated *"America just works better when more people have a chance to live their dreams."* And it's not just America; it's the whole world. When we are living our innermost, heartfelt dreams everything just works better: our lives, our relationships, our communities, and the world at large.

Get Started Today

"So many of our dreams at first seem impossible, then they seem improbable, and then, when we summon the will, they soon become inevitable." ~ Christopher Reeve.

Christopher Reeve makes a good point, a point that hinges on the need to just get started. If you haven't yet gotten started on making your dreams a reality, I beg you to ask yourself, *"What am I waiting for?"* *"Why am I not taking the necessary actions to make my dreams my reality?"* And please, be honest in your assessment. No one's going to know your answers except you unless you choose to share them.

Now that you've had some time to explore what's been stopping you, determine how many of your reasons and justifications fell into these categories: I don't feel equipped to live my dreams (e.g., you lack expertise, time, resources). I'm afraid of the unknown. I'm not sure where to start (i.e., it feels too big to take on). Likely it was the majority if not all of them.

Regardless of your presupposed reasons, there isn't a single one of them that is in actuality a showstopper (unless perhaps you are in a coma, at which point you wouldn't be reading this book). The truth is we never have dreams for which we are not equipped to fulfill in some capacity. I say in some capacity because there are a few physical technicalities that do give rise to the odd exceptions.

For instance, as a rule you can't change your height, so if you are particularly short and dream of being a pro volleyball player you might encounter some difficulties. Or, if you're 6 feet tall and dream of being a thoroughbred-racing jockey, it's not going to happen because you'll weigh too much (the limit is 108-118 lbs. fully clothed and geared up). That being said, it doesn't mean you can't fulfill you dream in some related capacity. Using the volleyball example, you could start and play in a league for those of shorter stature (e.g., under 5'5"). Or, you could become a volleyball trainer (in a semi-pro/pro league, or in a high-school or college where you help prepare gifted athletes desiring to go pro).

Barring these types of physical constraints, there is virtually nothing preventing us living our dreams, except for the limitations we place on ourselves through our thoughts and beliefs.

So this time I'm asking you, *"What are you waiting for?"* *"Why aren't you taking the necessary actions to make your dreams your reality?"* And please don't say it's because you are afraid of the unknown (however you disguise it), or that you don't know where to start. These are absolutely the lamest excuses of all, especially in today's world where so much information and personal expertise is readily available to help you dispel your fears and get you started, most of which can be found right at your fingertips. Google ring a bell?

If you are like the majority who don't take action to improve their lives and live their dreams, it is for one reason only – you are not yet uncomfortable enough with your present circumstances. Rather than braving the unknown, you choose to live with the status quo. While the status quo is undeniably easier to navigate (you already know what to expect, at least most of the time), it's never going to give you the life you desire.

If for some reason the status quo is the life you desire, you can feel free to stop reading right now. However, if you really and truly want to make your dreams your reality, then stay with me for just a few minutes more.

Living your dreams requires inspiration. Without inspiration you either won't begin at all, or you won't continue taking the necessary actions to see them through. As inspiration is so instrumental I'd like you to consider the following questions and statements. Take some time with them. Let them sink in. Ask your inner guide what she feels.

Questions and Statements To Inspire You Into Action:

- What am I telling myself about my worthiness when I deny my dreams?
- What would it take for me to begin living my dreams right now?
- What message am I giving to my children if I continue to put off/deny my dreams?
- The impossible only seems impossible when I believe it's impossible.
- A little bit today is way better than waiting for someday.

If you need further inspiration to help you get started or keep you fueled, begin regularly listening to inspiring speeches, reading inspiring stories and biographies, or watching inspiring movies. A simple Google search will provide a wide variety for you to choose from. For a more personal treatment you can attend classes, seminars, and workshops related to your dream; get in involved with a group that puts your dream into action; work with a coach or mentor who has expertise in the area of your dream; or be a coach or mentor for a someone else in need of direction (a child perhaps?).

Recognize that no matter where you are or what is going on in your life, you can get started today. Begin by taking baby steps. Visualize your dream as your reality. Break it down in to manageable chunks. Create a plan. Set some goals. Above all, just get started. You won't regret it. In fact, it's just the opposite. If you don't get started you will have regrets. You'll go to your grave disappointed and angry with yourself. On your deathbed you'll be thinking, *"If only I had taken a risk." "If only I had gotten started."*

Recognize too that living your dreams will require sacrifices. Just as Olympic athletes have to sacrifice many things during the periods they are training and competing, so too will you have to sacrifice certain things to realize your dreams. Some of these sacrifices will be small and short term, while others will be much larger and more permanent. They'll range from giving up self-defeating habits to leaving your job or maybe even your country. Whenever you feel challenged to take action, ask yourself, is it better to live my dreams now or to live a life of regret? Either way, the choice is yours.

Think about it this way, regrets weigh heavy on our hearts and minds, while sacrifices made to realize our dreams are quickly seen to be worth the small price we paid. A realized dream makes our heart sing, our energy soar, and our confidence explode. Regrets are just the opposite. They make us feel heavy and weighed down, as if we are carrying around hundreds of pounds of extra weight with no relief in sight. Don't let the life you imagine pass you by solely because you chose to play it safe and do what was expected. The last thing you want is to get to the end of your life and find out you never really lived.

As you can see, regret is no way to live, so why even take the chance? Get started now. Take one small action today that puts you on the path to living your dreams. It can be as simple as making a list, or visualizing yourself as if you are living your dream life today (not someday, TODAY!). When you've completed your first step, make sure you know what your next step will be and when you plan to execute it. It's really that simple. If you do this on a regular (near-daily) basis, you will in effect be living your dreams today. I say in effect because a dream is more an experience, or a journey, than it is an actual destination. That is, there is never a specific arrival point, because when you feel you have arrived there will always something more you desire. That's the beauty of self-mastery. We are always becoming more -- fulfilling more of our potential, which means we will always have new desires.

Whenever you feel stuck or overwhelmed, think upon these wise words, which are attributed to the ancient Chinese philosopher Lao-Tzu, *"A journey of a thousand miles begins with a single step."* Once you get started you'll wonder why you ever thought it was going to be so difficult. You'll also find that it is much, much easier than you ever dreamed possible to keep yourself moving in the direction of your dreams, and that it is ever so rewarding as Anais Nin states in this famous quote: *"Dreams pass into the reality of action. From the actions stems the dream again; and this interdependence produces the highest form of living."*

Tap Into Your Invisible Support System

You are a powerful and magical being. From the moment you arrived here on planet earth, if not before, you have been co-creating your life, including your myriad of circumstances, with the aid of the universal consciousness – that goes by whatever name you choose to give it. This is real power; a power you can tap into to begin consciously, rather than nonconsciously, creating the life you desire.

Whether you yet believe this or not, the reality is you *have* been choosing your circumstances. Per the natural law of vibration, commonly referred to as the Law of Attraction, you attract to you (manifest) the things, circumstances, and conditions whose energy patterns correspond most closely with the vibrational energy of your most predominant thoughts, feelings, beliefs and actions.

This is vitally important to understand when it comes to living in alignment with your true self and manifesting your dreams, because it means you have way more control than you've ever believed you have. It also means you have a huge support system that is already acting on your behalf to make your dreams come true.

To take advantage of your own immense power, and this universal support system, you need simply concentrate your attention, focus, and actions on your desires. Stated another way, when you want and believe in something strongly enough, and you take persistent, directed actions toward its realization, the entire universe will conspire to help you realize your specific desire or something better.

Where before you couldn't see the path forward, and you had no idea where the resources would come from, they now begin appearing as if by magic. It's a matter of *like attracts like*, which follows the same basic principle as stated by the Buddha when he said: *"When the student is ready, the teacher appears."* So begin thinking of all the reasons why your dreams can become your reality, and start taking some intentional steps to get the ball rolling. When you do, you'll draw to you the teachers and resources you need, as well as untold opportunities to not only live your dreams, but to take them to levels greater than you have yet to imagine.

∴

Living a loving, fulfilling, and whole life, where your dreams are your realities, and you are sharing your gifts with the world, is in essence quite simple. At its core it is nothing more than the energy vibrations you emit. Stated in more common terms, it is your steadfast belief in yourself and your dreams coupled with an ongoing succession of simple and relevant actions.

So wherever you are on your life's journey, get started today. Believe in yourself, your true self. Allow her to emerge and lead the way. Believe in your dreams. KNOW *you* are worthy of them. Allow them to manifest as your reality.

Begin looking at your life as the grand adventure it is. Muster up your courage and take a big, bold step out of your comfort zone (your self-imposed cage). Quit needing to know the next step. Quit worrying about humiliation and rejection. Quit fearing the things you can't control. It's time for you to show up and live your life in a way that enlivens you and makes your dreams come true. So go ahead. Take a giant step out into that big, blue ocean of possibility. Ride the waves. Have fun with them. Enjoy the challenging ones, which may appear as detours, as well as the calmer ones, taking care to always keep your thoughts trained on your success! Before you know it, you will find yourself living a life that is more rewarding than any you had previously dreamed possible.

And for those times when you find yourself doubting your innate gifts, your dreams, or your inner wisdom, **Stop** – right where you are. Realize you have once again allowed your demons (limiting thoughts, beliefs, feelings, and reactions) to gain control. **Reset.** Take a few big, deep breaths while extending yourself a moment of compassion. Take responsibility for your life and your responses to it. **Start.** Focus on what you want and what you can do right now. Immediately follow up with an action that moves you forward.

Through these actions you are choosing to accept your truth, to live in a state of mindful awareness, and above all to trust in yourself (your true self) – which sets you free.

Actions To Fast Forward Your Healing and The Manifestation Of Your Dreams

1. **Declare Your Greatness to Yourself and the Universe**
    Repeat the following declarations, with intense feeling and emotion, each and every day.
    - I am ENOUGH.
    - I am worthy of my dreams.
    - I live my life as the fullest and best expression of my TRUE SELF.
    - I am a master magician. I CREATE my life.
    - I create the future I desire. My VISION is my future.
    - I am my own HERO(ine).
    - I inspire myself, and others, to greatness.
    - I LOVE MY LIFE.

2. **Practice Being Vulnerable and Courageous**
    Being vulnerable and courageous requires practice, but it's worth it because of its many healing benefits. Start by finding someone with whom you feel safe enough to open up to. This could be a friend, a family member, a co-worker, a coach or mentor, or even a group, such as a support group or the participants at a seminar or workshop. Then be bold and share something you've been

holding within, something that once released will help you and those you are sharing with to heal and grow.

3. **Get Out There and Share Your Gifts**

As already discussed, there are countless ways for you to share your gifts, and the world is desperately waiting for you to do so. Here are a few actions to get you started:

   a. Make a list of your personal gifts, talents, passions, and loves
   b. For each, make a list of all the possible ways in which you could share it, STARTING TODAY
   c. Pick the one, or two, that resonates the most – preferably one you feel will make a real difference (even if it's only to a single person)
   d. Get out there and begin sharing as often as you can

Examples:
   - Bi-weekly tutoring for your neighbor's child
   - Weekly volunteering at a Girls Club as a mentor and role model
   - Weekly tutoring in an adult literacy program
   - Weekly visits to a lonely senior citizen – to just be a friend
   - Weekly delivery of home cooked meals to a local senior citizen

You get the idea. Pick something relevant to your gifts and passions. If desired or fitting make it something that directly supports your continued healing as you are making it available to the world.

4. **Put Your Dreams Into Motion**

Making your dreams your reality requires action. Here are a few simple steps you can take to put them on the fast track to fulfillment:

   a. *Ask yourself, "What do I really want?" What are my dreams?"* You can use the list you created in Step 8 if you desire.

b. *Prioritize your dreams.* It is highly unlikely you can work on all of them at the same time, so choose the one or two that are most important to you at this point in time.

c. *Make a list of the action steps you can take to make your dream(s) your reality.* You don't need to know all of the steps; you just need to have enough to get you started. The rest will reveal itself as you go along.

d. *Visualize your dream(s) as your current reality.* Do this daily, preferably as you awake and just before going to bed. (Make sure you add as much emotion and sensory detail as you possibly can. See it, feel it, hear it, taste it, smell it.)

e. *Take action.* Work step by step through the actions you listed in 4c.

f. *ALLOW IT TO UNFOLD.* Don't get hung up if it things look a little different than you've been imagining them –they're going to look different than you've imagined, but they're also most likely going to turn out far better than you've imagined.

5. **Extinguish Limiting Beliefs**

This is a three-part action, whose purpose is to remove limiting blocks, so that you may more quickly and easily manifest a lot more of what you DO want, and a whole lot less of what you DON'T want.

- Part 1 (write on a 3x5 card or piece of paper):
  - Write down a limiting belief you have about yourself or your ability to live your dreams
  - Write down all of the things this belief stops you from doing, being, having, or attracting
  - Write down all that would come to you more easily if you didn't have this belief, but instead had an opposite or more supporting belief

- Part 2 (set the card aside)
  - Meditate on your dream as your reality; a reality that doesn't include this limiting belief, a reality where everything it has prevented is now easily showing up (spend at least 3 minutes)

- o Now let it go. Sit in quiet meditation, breathing softly – knowing in your heart your dreams are becoming your reality (spend at least 1-2 minutes)

- Part 3 (burn the card)
  - o Burn the card. Literally. Burn it until nothing is left but ashes. As the card is burning repeat to yourself, I allow my dreams to unfold. My VISION or something better IS my LIFE.
  - o Toss the ashes to the wind, knowing in your heart that you have everything you need within you to manifest your dreams and live your life as the fullest and best expression of your true self.
  - o Say to yourself I am a master magician. I CREATE my life. My VISION or something better IS my LIFE.

Repeat this exercise as necessary for any and all of your limiting beliefs.

Afterword: Allowing The Magic Of Your Wholeness To Heal The World

Whatever you'd like to change about your life, or even the world, the starting place is always with you. It starts with you reclaiming your WHOLENESS, which means living your life as the highest and best expression of your true self.

As a WHOLE being you live free of the emotional bondage created by your demons. As a WHOLE being you have the wherewithal to hold your own with anyone or anything you encounter (real or imaginary). As a WHOLE being you have the ability to realize your tremendous value as a person. As a WHOLE being you live in connection with your heart and the oneness of all creation. As a WHOLE being you possess great power, the power to change the world. As a WHOLE being there is nothing you cannot do.

As a result of your WHOLENESS you'll find that your presence is more radiant. You emit a special beauty that emanates from within; a beauty that beneficially affects the well-being of countless others, many of whom are well beyond your given proximity. This beauty draws to you the people and resources necessary for you to manifest your dreams. Through the manifestation of your dreams, you will become more and more self-actualized. The more self-actualized you become the more you will automatically help to heal the human condition – a healing that is desperately needed if we are to prevent our own demise.

You have come far on this journey, but you are at now at a crossroads. Where you choose to go from here is entirely up to you.

Before you walk away and fall completely back into the rhythms of your present life, please consider the following options, including the sacred duty entrusted to each us inhabitants of planet Earth.

First, you can continue on with your life, as it currently is, doing absolutely nothing with what you have learned (although I'm not entirely sure that's really possible since going back to a lower level of being is not only impossible, but futile). Second, you can apply what you've learned on a small scale, affecting nothing more than your most immediate circumstances and personal dreams (which is perfectly acceptable in the beginning – you have to walk before you can run). Or third, you can apply what you've learned on a grand scale, beneficially affecting not only your own life but as many other lives as you possibly can, through the sharing of your gifts, talents, passions, and loves (which will happen to some degree whether you have this intention of not – so why not make it your intention).

As to the sacred duty I mentioned, it is my opinion that as inhabitants of this planet we have a moral obligation to leave things in no worse condition than we found them, and where feasible to leave them in better condition. As a member of the human species, we, more than any other species, have the power to annihilate or to heal. As a result of your own healing and WHOLENESS you have the ability to affect great change. As you begin to put your own house in order, make a pledge to step out and help others do the same. The more of us who live our lives as the WHOLE and unique beings we were born to be, the greater the healing momentum our species and the planet as a whole will experience.

Change is all around us, and it is occurring ever more quickly. Despite the turmoil we see playing out, there is more peace and cooperation now than ever before. More and more people are awakening to the truth of LOVE and WHOLENESS. We can take advantage of this tide, or we can turn a blind eye. Which will you choose? For the sake of us all, and the overall health of our planet, I hope you choose to ride this rising tide and spread the gift of WHOLENESS.

Once upon a time Albert Einstein keenly reflected, *"I don't know what weapons World War III will be fought with. But World War IV will be fought with sticks and stones."* Living in WHOLENESS creates inner peace. Inner peace creates outer peace. When enough of us are experiencing inner peace we will have tipped the scales toward peace in the outer world. Peace starts within. It starts with WHOLENESS. It starts with YOU living your life as the highest and best expression of your true self.

∴

The overarching message of this book is LOVE: love of self, love of life, love of all creation. Love emanates from within, from our hearts and souls. It expresses itself most readily when we live our lives as the WHOLE beings we really are – the divine beings we are at our core. It finds more ways to express itself the more effectively we align our lives with the nature of our truest and most authentic selves.

Life is a grand adventure. Cherish the moments. Carve out space for silence – a regular time and place to connect with the love and wisdom of your heart and soul. Connect too with the universal consciousness – that great mystery which is the source of all. Trust what comes from within. Open yourself to the mystery of what lies ahead. Set your intentions. Go forth with a sense of wonder. Embody your light. Let it shine, for it is far brighter than you've ever imagined. Venture further and further off the beaten path of your preconditioned inner and outer worlds. Spread love and goodness. And share your gifts.

In a nutshell: Stop hiding who you are and start showing up in life. Unapologetically be the person you were born to be. Approach all you do with the confidence of someone who knows the infinite power they possess. Allow your light to shine so brightly it leads others out their own darkness.

∴

It is my fondest wish that this book has ignited an unyielding belief within you that you can live a loving, fulfilling, and whole life, whereby you live your dreams while making a significant contribution through the sharing of your gifts. If you have been so moved, use that desire to inspire you into action. Take a stand for yourself; your true self. Do whatever it takes to retire your demons and live your life as the WHOLE and AMAZING being you are. Rebel against whatever stands in your way, without causing harm to yourself or anyone else. Above all, remain loyal to your true self. If you are ever in doubt, take a few moments to listen within; trust your heart – it will steer you true.

In parting I'd like to leave you with this poem about being:

"Dare to Be!
When a new day begins, dare to smile gratefully.
When there is darkness, dare to be the first to shine a light.
When there is injustice, dare to be the first to condemn it.
When something seems difficult, dare to do it anyway.

Women Overcoming Demons

When life seems to beat you down, dare to fight back.
When there seems to be no hope, dare to find some.
When you're feeling tired, dare to keep going.
When times are tough, dare to be tougher.
When love hurts you, dare to love again.
When someone is hurting, dare to help them heal.
When another is lost, dare to help them find the way.
When a friend falls, dare to be the first to extend a hand.
When you cross paths with another, dare to make them smile.
When you feel great, dare to help someone else feel great too.
When the day has ended, dare to feel as you've done your best.
Dare to be the best you can –
At all times, Dare to be!"
~ Steve Maraboli

Appendix:
Commitment Certificate

WOMEN OVERCOMING DEMONS
9 STEPS FOR BECOMING WHOLE AGAIN

This certifies that I

_____

have committed on this day

_____

to

BECOME WHOLE AGAIN

I Promise Myself and A Power Higher Than Myself
In Front of These Witnesses
That From This Day Forward
I Will Do Everything In My Power To Become Whole Again
and Live My Life as the Fullest Expression of My True Self

_____
Witness 1

_____
Witness 2

Selected Bibliography

You can get lost in all the books out there. So, if you're looking for some additional resources to inspire you and help you on your journey back to wholeness I've included some of the ones I found to be incredibly enlightening, influential, and inspiring.

Aaron, Raymond. *Double Your Income Doing What You Love*. New Jersey: Wiley & Sons, 2008

Allen, James. *As a Man Thinketh*. New York: Tribeca Books, 2012

Arntz, William, Chase, Betty, and Vincent, Mark. *What The Bleep Do We Know!?* Florida: Health Communications. 2005

Attwood, Chris/Attwood, Janet. *The Passion Test: The Effortless Path to Discovering Your Destiny*. New York: Hudson Street Press, 2007

Ban Breathnach, Sarah. *Something More: Excavating Your Authentic Self*. New York: Warner Books, 1998

Campbell, Joseph. *Pathways to Bliss: Mythology and Personal Transformation*. Novato: New World Library, 2004

Campbell, Joseph. *The Hero With A Thousand Faces*. Novato: New World Library, 2008

Canfield, Jack. *The Success Principles: How to Get from Where You Are to Where You Want to Be*. New York: HarperCollins, 2005

Chopra, Deepak. *The Essential Spontaneous Fulfillment of Desire*. New York: Harmony Books, 2003

Chopra, Deepak. *The Path to Love: Spiritual Strategies for Healing*. New York: Three Rivers Press, 1998

Chopra, Deepak. *The Ultimate Happiness Prescription: 7 Keys to Joy and Enlightenment.* New York: Harmony Books, 2009

Chopra, Deepak. *The Seven Spiritual Laws of Success: A Practical Guide to the Fulfillment of Your Dreams.* San Rafael: New World Library / Amber-Allen Publishing, 1994

Coehl, Paulo. *The Alchemist.* New York: HarperCollins, 1998

Cushnir, Raphael. *Setting Your Heart On Fire: Seven Invitations to Liberate Your Life.* New York: Broadway Books, 2003

Demartini, John. *Count Your Blessings.* Carlsbad: Hay House, 2006

Demartini, John. *The Breakthrough Experience.* Carlsbad: Hay House, 2002

Demartini, John. *The Gratitude Effect.* Toronto: Burman Books, 2009

Dreher Diane. *Your Personal Renaissance: 12 Steps to Finding Your Life's True Calling.* Cambridge: Da Capo Press, 2008

Dyer, Wayne. *Change Your Thoughts – Change Your Life: Living the Wisdom of the Tao.* Carlsbad: Hay House, 2007

Eker, T. Harv. *Secrets of the Millionaire Mind: Mastering the Inner Game of Wealth.* New York: HarperCollins, 2005

The Bhagavad Gita. Translated by Eknath Eswaran. Tomales: Nilgiri Press, 2009

Frankl, Victor E. *Man's Search For Meaning.* Boston: Beacon Press, 2006

Gilbert, Elizabeth. *Eat, Pray, Love: One Woman's Search For Everything Across Italy, India, and Indonesia.* New York: Penguin Group, 2007

Grabhorn, Lynn. *Excuse Me, Your Life Is Waiting: The Astonishing Power of Feelings*. Charlottesville: Hampton Roads Publishing Co., 2000

Hendricks, Gay. *Five Wishes: How Answering One Simple Question Can Make You're Your Dreams Come True*. Novato, New World Library, 2007

Hill, Napoleon. *Think and Grow Rich*. Melrose: No Dream Too Big, 2006

Jeffers, Susan. *Feel The Fear And Do It Anyway*. New York: Ballantine Books, 1988

Kieves, Tama J. *This Time I Dance: Trusting The Journey of Creating The Work You Love*. Denver: Awakening Artistry Press, 2002

Kehoe, John. *Mind Power Into The 21st Century*. Vancouver: Zoetic Inc., 2010

Kehoe, John. *Quantum Warrior: The Future of the Mind*. Vancouver: Zoetic Inc., 2011

Keller, Jeff. *Attitude Is Everything: Change Your Attitude And Change Your Life!* Tampa: INTI Publishing, 2007

Kersey, Cynthia. *Unstoppable: 45 Powerful Stories of Perseverance and Triumph From People Just Like You*. Naperville: Sourcebooks, Inc., 1998

Lobenstein, Margaret. *The Renaissance Soul: Life Design for People with Too Many Passions to Pick Just One*. New York: Harmony, 2006

Losier, Michael. *The Law of Attraction*. New York, Hachette, 2003

Maxwell, John. *Failing Forward: Turning Mistakes Into Stepping Stones For Success*. Nashville: Thomas Nelson, Inc., 2000

Millman, Dan. *Living on Purpose: Straight Answers to Life's Tough Questions*. Novato: New World Library, 2000

Millman, Dan. *The Laws of Spirit: A Tale of Transformation*. Novato: HJ Kramer/New World Library, 2001

Millman, Dan. *The Way of the Peaceful Warrior*. Novato: HJ Kramer/New World Library, 2000

Mooers Montana, Greg. *Unlock Your Heart Virtue: Become the Authentic Leader of Your Life*. Heart Virtue, 2009

Moore, Thomas. *Care of the Soul: A Guide for Cultivating Depth and Sacredness in Everyday Life*. New York: HarperCollins, 1992

Mountain Dreamer, Oriah. *The Call: Discovering Why You Are Here*. New York: HarperCollins, 2003

Mountain Dreamer, Oriah. *The Dance: Moving to the Deep Rhythms of Your Life*. New York: HarperCollins, 2001

Mountain Dreamer, Oriah. *The Invitation*. New York: HarperCollins, 1993

O'Donohue, John. Anam Cara: A Book of Celtic Wisdom. New York: HarperCollins, 1997

O'Donohue, John. *Eternal Echoes: Exploring Our Yearning To Belong*. New York: HarperCollins, 1999

Orloff, Judith. *Emotional Freedom: Liberate Yourself from Negative Feelings and Transform Your Life*. New York: Harmony Books, 2009

OSHO. *Joy: The Happiness That Comes From Within*. New York: St. Martins, 2004

Pauley, Thomas/Pauley, Penelope. *I'm Rich Beyond My Wildest Dreams: How To Get Everything You Want In Life.* New York: Penguin Books, 1999

Pausch, Randy/Zaslow, Jeffrey. *The Last Lecture.* New York: Hyperion, 2008

Pearsal, Paul. *The Pleasure Prescription. To Love, to Work, to Play - - Life in the Balance.* Alameda: Hunter House Publishers, 1996

Psaris, Jett/Lyons, Marlena S. *Undefended Love.* Oakland: New Harbinger Publications, 2000

Qubein, Nido. *Seven Choices For Success and Significance: How to Live Life From the Inside-Out.* Naperville: Simples Truths, 2011

Redfield, James. *The Celestine Prophecy.* New York: Grand Central Publishing, 1993

Redfield, James. *The Tenth Insight: Holding the Vision.* New York: Grand Central Publishing, 1998

Richo, David. *How To Be An Adult: A Handbook on Psychological and Spiritual Integration.* Mahwah: Paulist Press, 1991

Richo, David. *How To Be An Adult in Relationships: The Five Keys To Mindful Loving.* Boston: Shambhala Publications, 2002

Richo, David. *Shadow Dance: Liberating the Power and Creativity of Your Dark Side.* Boston: Shambhala Publications, 1999

Richo, David. *The Power of Coincidence: How Life Shows Us What We Need To Know.* Boston: Shambhala Publications, 2007

Richo, David. *When Love Meets Fear: How to Become Defense-Less and Resource-Full.* Mahway: Paulist Press, 1997

Richo, David. *When The Past Is Present: Healing the Emotional Wounds That Sabotage Our Relationships.* Boston: Shambhala Publications, 2008

Rohn, Jim. *The Five Major Pieces to the Life Puzzle*. Southlake: Dickenson Press, 1991

Ruiz, Don Miguel. *The Four Agreements*. San Rafael: Amber-Allen, 1997

Ruiz, Don Miguel. *The Mastery of Love*. San Rafael: Amber-Allen, 1999

Ruiz, Don Miguel. *Voice of Knowledge*. San Rafael: Amber-Allen, 2004

Sher, Barbara. *Refuse to Choose!: Use All of Your Interests, Passions, and Hobbies to Create the Life and Career of Your Dreams*. New York: Rodale, 2007

Singer, Michael A. *The Untethered Soul: The Journey Beyond Yourself*. Oakland: New Harbinger Publications/ Noetic Books, 2007

Spadaro, Patricia. *Honor Yourself: The Inner Art of Giving and Receiving*. Bozeman: Three Wings Press, 2009

Stovall, Jim. *The Ultimate Gift*. Mechanicsburg: Executive Books, 2006

Stovall, Jim. *The Ultimate Life*. Colorado Springs: David C. Cook, 2007

Widener, Chris. *The Angel Inside*. New York, Doubleday, 2007

Acknowledgements

Many people, both past and present, living and long departed, have influenced my bringing this book to life. Some of you I only know through your works or the works written about you, yet you have often been my most influential mentors and teachers. I wish to thank you all, wherever you are, living or spirit, for your courage to share your stories and your words of wisdom. I humbly acknowledge your contributions to the making of this book, as well as to my healing and growth. Thank you for your insights and encouragement. Thank you for inspiring me to reach for the stars, to follow my heart and dreams, and ultimately to share my gifts with the world.

To my friends, family, co-workers, and acquaintances, of which there are far too many to name, I wish to express my deepest and most heart-felt appreciation for your love and support, your guidance and insights, and your challenges. Each of you has in some way touched me; in no small part you have pushed me to overcome the obstacles thrown my way. Thank you all for being a part of my life.

To my personal coaches, both past and present, I wish to formally thank Ronda Wada, Jim Alvino, Eric Easterwood, Barb Robison, and Margit Macchia. Thank you ever so much for your guidance, and your never-ending belief in me, and my chosen path. Thank you for shining a light on my blind spots. Thank you for your patience and your feedback. To you I express my most profound appreciation.

To Greg Mooers Montana and the participants of the January 2011 AuthenTrain Workshop, I express my most profound gratitude. You deeply touched my heart. Our time together helped me to reintegrate the parts of myself I had thought irretrievably lost. Thank you all for your courage, your spirit, and your love.

To my editor, Maria Boeding, thank you for your patience and positive feedback as I brought this book to completion.

And finally, to my many mentors, heroes, and muses, thank you for your courage, creativity, and tenacity as you forged your unique path; a path that has broken down barriers and created more opportunity for those who follow. You have been an inspiration to so many. May your life's work and stories continue to inspire and shed light on the possibilities that exist for us all, for generations to come.

About The Author

Michelle McCullar is the founder and president of Women's Wholeness Connection™, Inc., a personal growth and transformation organization dedicated to empowering women, so they may experience the wholeness of their birthright and live soul-fulfilling lives doing what they love. She is a distinguished author, speaker, trainer, and personal empowerment coach, as well the creator of the breakthrough system "The HEART Inspired Life". She holds specialized certifications and licensing as a Divine Navigation® Coach and Heart Virtues® Expert. Often referred to as "The Heart Whisperer", Michelle is recognized for her ability to intimately connect her clients with their most authentic selves, as well as her ability for helping them discover their hidden gifts and talents, and the means by which they can apply their gifts and talents for the ultimate in personal meaning and fulfillment.

Holding both Bachelors and Masters degrees from Texas A&M University, Michelle initially began her career as an engineer (the proverbial *"Rocket Scientist"*) for NASA's Jet Propulsion Laboratory (JPL). During her long tenure with JPL she found herself continually yearning for some elusive thing to fill a deep and cavernous hole, a hole she later discovered was the result of living an incomplete and inauthentic life that emanated from the effects of a childhood fraught with excessive trauma, abuse, and negative conditioning. This elusive yearning led to a life-long study of human potential, behavior, and suffering. Initially her studies began as a means for healing herself from the debilitating effects of her childhood induced demons; demons that continually haunted her and in turn were preventing her from leading the whole and fulfilling life she so desperately desired. As her healing progressed she realized she had a passion for helping others to awaken to their own greatness.

Today, after more than 20 years of study and personal discovery, Michelle has made it her mission to apply the wisdom of her experiences to light the way for men and women everywhere to heal and lead the whole, empowered, and fulfilling lives they desire; lives where they are free to authentically express their God-given gifts as they make their unique contributions to the world. She believes her greatest accomplishments to date are having learned to reconnect with her soul, listen to the wisdom of her heart, and find her bliss.

Michelle lives in southern California, where much of her time is devoted to writing, speaking, and holding women's empowerment workshops. She enjoys traveling the world, exploring the great outdoors, and getting to know and understand people from all walks of life and cultures. She is also an avid reader, hiker, photographer, and dry-media artist.

You can learn more about Michelle and her programs at www.WomensWholenessConnection.com and www.facebook.com/WomensWholenessConnection.